My Unexpected Life

A Memoir

By
Mervyn G. Hardinge

TEACH Services, Inc.
New York

PRINTED IN
THE UNITED STATES OF AMERICA
World rights reserved. This book or any portion thereof may not be copied or reproduced in any form or manner whatever, except as provided by law, without the written permission of the publisher, except by a reviewer who may quote brief passages in a review.

The author assumes full responsibility for the accuracy of all facts and quotations as cited in this book.

2005 05 06 07 08 09 10 11 12 · 5 4 3 2 1

Copyright © 2005 Mervyn G. Hardinge
and TEACH Services, Inc.
ISBN 1-57258-281-2
Library of Congress Control Number: 2004105706

Published by

TEACH Services, Inc.
www.TEACHServices.com

"Thou Shalt Guide Me with Thy Counsel." Ps. 73:24 (KJV)

AN EXPRESSION OF GRATITUDE

To my dear friend Ordell Calkins for the hours and days he spent in shaping up the manuscript you hold in your hands.

To my wife, Margaret, for being patient with a husband while he lived in front of his computer, and to my daughter Jeanne (Ekvall) and son Fred for extricating their father from numerous computer glitches that arose in an effort to derail this project.

To the long list of my colleagues who worked with me through the years: please accept this little note of sincere thanks to each and all of you, for the part you played in any success achieved. I look forward to the day when I can shake your hand and give you a hug in the earth made new.

CONTENTS

Expression of Gratitude.......................... iii

Foreword.. xi

Chapter 1   How It All Began..................... 1
   Two Tiger Stories 7
   The Pitcairn Islander............................ 9

Chapter 2   My Small World 15
   Late for School 19
   The Disobedient Engineer 21
   The Milkman 23
   Juicy Balls 25
   The Prick in the Boot............................ 26
   The Boat we Built 28
   Blow Guns and Darts 31
   The Beetle Tree................................. 34
   The Orchid and the Snake........................ 39
   The Disobedient Elephant 42
   The Elephant Takes Revenge 44
   Les and the Baby Monkey 45
   The Fish Tale 47
   My Double Barrel............................... 49
   The Leopard of Jahlulk Bari 51

Chapter 3 My Stay in England	54
My Musical Skills	*55*
A Simple Woman	*61*
A Lowly Custodian	*63*
A Battered Looking Insurance Salesman	*64*
An Unbelievable Experience!	*65*
The Blockade of the Wealthy	*68*
A Great Experience	*70*
A Cat and a Dog	*74*
A Slip of the Tongue	*74*
Mr. Casson, the First Elder	*75*
Chapter 4 Preparing for Medicine	**80**
Obtaining a License	*83*
The Loaded Revolver	*85*
The Folding Bed	*87*
Dr. Pride and Dr. Pomp	*89*
Not a Joke	*92*
The Fly in the Stethoscope	*94*
Sincerity is not Enough	*94*
The Stubborn Patient	*98*
Our First Refrigerator	*107*
Mr. Peptic Ulcer	*109*
The Muffled Bell	*110*
Chapter 5 Teaching Anatomy	**113**
Improving on God's Design	*114*
The Failing Student	*117*
The Humorist	*119*
Toe Nails	*120*

The Flail Arm *122*
A Close Call *123*
My Brother and the Moose *132*
The Cop who Compromised *134*

Chapter 6   My Harvard Experience 137
Three Discouraged Physicians *137*
What Constitutes Flavor? *139*
A Blunder of Blunders *140*
Doctor Malcolm Fair *142*
Mister, It's my Dog not Yours *156*

Chapter 7   At Berkeley and at Stanford 162
Fred's First Tooth Lost! *168*

Chapter 8   Ten Tranquil Years 180
An Incredible Offer! *180*
God Knew Beforehand *182*
Two Flat Tires *184*
Consolidation of the Medical School *186*
The Stubborn Lawnmower *188*
The Pump of the Oil Truck *189*
The Skunk and the Rose Bush *190*
Blackbirds *191*
A Run for my Life *194*
Just in Time *196*
The Five-day Plan for Stopping Smoking *197*
The Head Technician *199*
Toxins in Common Mushrooms? *202*
The Action of Amphetamine and Tranquilizers *203*
A Priceless Gift *204*

Slim and Trim 205
The Coat I Saved 207
The Dentist Who Nibbled 208
Too Much Margarine 209
I'm Not an Animal 211
A Kid's Life or Corn? 212

Chapter 9   My Sabbatical Year 216
My Last Delivery 217
The Empeggi Project 219
A Sad Story 222
The Milling of Corn 223

Chapter 10   A School of Public Health 225
Harvard's Board of Overseers 238

Chapter 11   At the World Headquarters of the Seventh-day Adventists. 240
The Karachi Airport 242
The Angel of the Lord 243
The Great Designer 247
Health Evangelism 252

Chapter 12   Retirement at Last! 254
The Kind-hearted Patrolman 255
Mosquitoes! 257
The Woodcutter 259
The Miracle Cement Mixer 261

Chapter 13   In Sickness and in Health 263

Final Comment 269

Postscript 270

Appendix 1 271

Appendix 2 275

Photo Gallery 277

FOREWORD

As you face life the future is unknown. You make your plans but at best they are only conjecture. Then the best way is to:

"Commit your ways unto the Lord, and lean not to your own understanding. In all your ways acknowledge Him, and He will direct your paths." Proverbs 3: 5, 6.

But wait, dear reader, do you really know what these two verses are saying? God is making a promise that if you will relinquish your free will to Him, that is, give it back to God who gave it, He will make the decisions for you and for your life! Free will, apart from the plan of salvation, is the greatest gift that God has given you. And now it's gone. It's no longer yours. You have given it away. You have become a slave; you do what you are asked to do. God calls the shots, and you obey!

But your slavery is not forced on you; you have chosen it that way. You can pull out of the bargain anytime you want. You can use your own limited knowledge and wisdom to decide your life's activities; or you can allow God, with His infinite knowledge and unlimited wisdom, to make them for you.

To really truly allow God to guide your life is no easy decision. What do so many of us do? We do what God wants us to do as long as it is what we want to do! I've seen this happen in others, and I've seen it happen in me.

The way God directs in our lives only makes sense in retrospect. We do not nor can we discern the future. There is only One who can see events before they happen.

"God can discern the end of His purposes from the beginning; but because the Lord's ways are not man's

ways, they appear dark, severe, and painful to our natures. But God's ways are ways of mercy, and their end is salvation and blessedness." RH, July 3, 1888.

Examples of God's Guidance

God holds the plans for your life. The path He chooses for us may not be strewn with roses. It certainly wasn't for Joseph. Ridiculed and scoffed at in his home, betrayed by his brothers, sold as a slave, and then taken to Egypt. Faithful in Potiphar's house, falsely accused by a spurned woman, again faithful in the dreadful prison, forgotten by a wold-be helper, Joseph could not and did not understand it. He was no exception—none of us are!

But in retrospect, from the high office as Prime Minister of Egypt, at that time the greatest nation in this world, Joseph could see the hand of God in the bitter events he had experienced. "God has worked it out for the blessing of us all," he told his brothers.

Have you ever told the Lord that you want Him to direct your paths, only to pull out of the bargain when things get tough? It's all too easy to do. It's done all the time. We thank God for answered prayers and for His guidance. Then when things turn sour we say we made a mistake. Isn't that slapping the Lord in the face?

And when God instructs us to do something, should we do a feasibility study before we undertake the task? What if Noah had gone to the Pre-deluge Prognosticators, Inc., for their evaluation? Their conclusions are foregone. No ark could be built large enough to house all the animals and birds. And where would all their food be stored for a year? Who would finance such a venture? Who would construct such a ship since no engineering company existed that had had any experience building such a vessel? And if all the above problems were solved, no body of water existed to float such a structure. Their conclusion is obvious—not feasible.

But Noah started construction and after one hundred and twenty years, under the most scathing ridicule, the ark was finished! And it housed all the creatures God impressed to enter, and God provided the food for them day by day as he did for the children of Israel during their migration to the Promised Land. And the water arrived and the ship floated and the skeptics all perished. And friend, it's always that way. God's directives, when carried out, are always met with success. They have never failed nor will they ever. In life's decisions, lean not to your own understanding, and success is certain.

Goals in Life

God does not expect us to sit back and wait for Him to open the door and usher us around. Occasionally He directs us audibly, but usually through His written Word and the events of life. It is by faith that we advance and He then opens or hedges up the way. And please remember

No committee, even if it is made up of ten of your worst enemies, can refuse to give you a position or block a promotion that God wants for you.

Again, I think of Joseph. A committee of ten made up of his own "brethren" took an action "to fix him"; but all they really did was to "set him up high."

Christ never intended His followers to strive for position, promotion or pay.

Position: God knows what we should do in life and will place us in the appropriate place or position at the appropriate time.

Promotion: God also knows when we should be advanced. He has informed us that "Promotion cometh from the Lord." And finally—

Pay: It is true that "a workman is worthy of his hire." But remember the parable that Jesus told of the workmen who were hired first thing in the morning. They made a deal with the

Master. The others employed during the day left it up to the Owner to give them a fair shake. And He did. The one group got what they bargained for, the others much more than their wildest expectations! And so it has always been with the Lord and ever will be.

Why not trust Him?

God spoke to me. I obeyed. Result—My Unexpected Life.

Chapter 1

HOW IT ALL BEGAN

On the Way to Change

Every story has a beginning and mine started before I was born! My father, a surveyor, was working for the survey of India. Mother was a home keeper, and together with two children, lived in Calcutta, until 1912 the capital city of India. Dad's work required him to travel during the dry season. He was in a single cabin of an old fashioned train pulled by a steam engine. It was long before oil powered or diesel electric engines were dreamed of. He was blowing one smoke ring through another, enjoying the cigarette he was smoking, when a strange thought entered his head: Why am I smoking?

As the train clicked-clacked along the lines, the thought kept ringing in his ears. The thought was odd, because he loved his tobacco, and although he smoked a pipe, he especially enjoyed cigarettes. He asked himself, "Do I really want to give it up? Why should I? It does cost me money, and it is a filthy habit. But on the other hand it helps me relax, and does give me enjoyment." He pondered these ideas for a while and finally decided to give it up. Looking at his watch, it was five o'clock in the afternoon. He said out loud, "I'll quit at midnight." From then to midnight he smoked incessantly. At the stroke of midnight he opened the window of the compartment (English trains permitted this) and threw his tobacco pouch, pipes, matches, and all the cigarettes he had left, out the window. From that day, he was then twenty-seven years old, to the time of his death at eighty-eight, he never smoked again!

It was a Sunday afternoon, over a year later, that Dad and Mother were trying to decide what drinks they would serve the guests they had invited to dinner, and they were not thinking about orange or pineapple juice! As they were weighing the possibility of this beverage or that, one of them raised the question as to why they drank. Later that afternoon they discussed the matter some more and decided they would give it up. They continued to serve their friends drinks but from that afternoon on, neither of them ever touched an alcoholic beverage again.

Another year or two went by. Calcutta was rocked by a meat scandal. The papers were full of stories as to the type of meat that was available on the market. My parents had had a couple of revolting experiences themselves. Citizens were demanding that the government do something about the situation and right now. One day as they were talking about the problem, mother turned to Dad and asked, "Why don't we become vegetarians? Many Indians are vegetarians and they seem to get along all right." So they decided they would. Mother called the cook and told him of their decision. His prompt reply was, "I refuse to cook that way!" "If you feel that strongly about cooking vegetarian," Mother spoke quietly, "you will be fired." And fired he was!

Now I should explain that my Mother had been raised in colonial style. She had never cooked in her life! Her parents had migrated to India from southern England and had adopted the way of life of the European colonial. In those early days there were none of the appliances to run a household which we in the western world take for granted. No electricity, no gas or electric stoves, no indoor plumbing; no running water except in the yard outside; no vacuum sweepers; in fact there were none of the amenities of every day living that we enjoy today. Servants of different castes would each do his specific work. The cook would cook; the housekeeper would keep house; the gardener, the sweeper, and the laundry man each performed his special task. The cost of all these services was equivalent to what we, in this country, pay for utilities. And by the way, we do all the work as well!

The Search for a Cookbook

Now that the cook was gone, what was Mother to do? Besides, she didn't have a single recipe! How was she to provide vegetarian meals for the family? But Mother gallantly tackled the daunting task that she now faced. So she called in the water-boy, the cook's aide, and told him that he and she would do the cooking. His job had been to fetch the water, light and bring in the charcoal fires, and wash the dirty pots and pans. Dad would always say that he did not know how he survived while Mother was learning to cook. Her immediate task was to find a vegetarian cookbook, but none could be found even though Calcutta was the third largest city in the British Empire. She wrote to all the major bookstores in London but without success.

A year or so later there was a knock one morning at her front door. On opening it she found a European lady outside, whom she invited in. Mother showed no interest in the religious books the lady was selling. Dad and Mother never attended church except for weddings and funerals. As the unwanted visitor was walking towards the gate which opened onto the city sidewalk, Mother was struck with an idea and called after her, "If you had a vegetarian cookbook, I would buy one."

The sales woman returned and assured Mother that while she did not have a vegetarian cookbook with her, she could order one. Mother, without a moment's hesitation, did just that. "I'll be back in a week or ten days with the book," the lady said with a smile.

True to her word the lady returned ten days later with the long awaited cookbook. Mother could hardly contain herself and paid for it on the spot. She remained standing in the doorway leafing through its pages with gloating eyes. The scores of recipes sent a chill of delight down her spine. This was just what she had dreamed of having! Then the lady broke Mother's rapture with the question, "Do you know how to cook vegetarian food?"

"Oh no," was Mother's prompt reply, "Do you?"

"Well, yes, a little. Would you like me to help you prepare some vegetarian dishes?"

"I would indeed; I'd love for you to." There was not the slightest hesitation in Mother's voice. To have someone help her learn to cook seemed out of this world! And so, week after week, the sales lady came, and, standing by the charcoal burners showed my mother how to prepare vegetarian meals. And along the way, with wisdom and heavenly tact, she began to talk about the Bible and soon got mother fired up. At first Dad would have none of it. His interests lay with tennis and football (soccer). When the visitor entered the front door, he would beat it out the back door for one of his favorite games. But it did not take long before Mother's enthusiasm aroused Dad's interest, and the lady began formal Bible studies with both of them.

Gradually she unfolded the truths of the Bible: the three angels' messages, the Scriptural Sabbath, the state of the dead, the second coming of Christ, and Bible baptism. There was no argument on my parents' part; they drank of the living water as would dry parched land. Every truth presented was like a gift of a pearl of great price. The lady was a Bible Worker, a missionary from San Diego, California.

A Bold Move

My folks were ready for baptism when two missionaries arrived in Calcutta to hold evangelistic meetings. They were Pastors Comer from Salem, Oregon and W. R. French from Utah. Mother attended every meeting. Dad did also except when his work interfered. But Dad could not bring himself to request that he be granted the Sabbath off. The Government of India had never granted such a favor. What was he to do? He had a family to support. Should he risk losing a good stable job? Mother refused to be baptized without Dad. At last, Dad decided he would put his trust in the Lord.

He wrote a letter telling of his convictions and requesting that he be excused from work on Saturdays. His immediate supervisor wrote across Dad's letter, "Mr. Hardinge is obviously out of his mind. Recommend dismissal!" But Dad appealed it up the line to the Surveyor General of India. The reply, in time, came back, "Request granted." As Dad's supervisor handed Dad the letter approving his request, he urged him to resign saying, "You'll never be advanced as long as you refuse to work on Saturdays." But Dad did not take his advice. The Lord had worked wonderfully and Dad's faith and courage were strong. My parents were baptized and became early members of the Seventh-day Adventist church in Calcutta.

Early Years as a Surveyor

When my father first joined the Survey of India he was assigned to work, as one might expect, in the less desirable places. It was the policy of the British Government to completely survey all of India (which in those days included Pakistan and Bangladesh) every 50 years. The reason for this policy was that during that long time period vast changes would occur in different areas of the country. Rivers might migrate by eroding one bank and building land on the opposite bank. Floods might devastate fine agricultural land and forest fires could denude large tracts of land. Cities would enlarge and population growth would destroy cultivated areas. The work schedule required all fieldwork to be done during the winter months, or the dry season. When the monsoons arrived in early summer, the surveyors returned to their offices to plot the records they had made in the months before.

One of Dad's first assignments was to work in the Sunda Bunds. The Sunda Bunds make up a large part of the delta formed by the confluence of two large rivers of India, the Ganges and the Brahmaputra, prior to their flowing into the Bay of Bengal. The Sunda Bunds comprise hundreds of square miles of territory made up of thousands of islands, some small, others large. Some form during one season only to be washed away the following season. Others are relatively permanent. The soil is generally rich and is used for agriculture. Many of the "permanent" islands are forested with both small and large trees. The underbrush is heavy and dense.

When Dad started work in this area the population density was small. The forests abounded with wild life, and game of every kind attracted people from all parts of the world. The Sunda Bunds were famous for the numbers of tigers that inhabited these islands. And still today, a century later, the largest number of tigers extant in the world is still found in this territory!

To map this territory was no easy task. The surveyors were each assigned a houseboat. These boats were large enough to carry the surveyor and his cook, a squad of eleven men, one of whom was the tindle or squad leader, and the captain and his helper. The squad of eleven men was to aid the surveyor in his work. They would pull chains (a measure of length, a chain being 66 feet long or 20.1 meters), cut lines through the forested areas, and help in the countless ways such a life would require.

My father also lived on and worked from a houseboat large enough to allow for my mother, my sister and oldest brother, to live with him. It was not an easy life but this was the only way to do his work. No aerial mapping was even dreamed of! My Dad's duties were to supervise and help some sixty surveyors who worked under him.

The Government had rules that were to be strictly followed. One of these was that no employee was to set foot on any island before nine in the morning, and all workers were to be off an island by three in the afternoon. This rule was to minimize predation by tigers. Tigers tend to be active in the early morning, then lie around during the heat of the day, and resume their activity in the late afternoon.

Tigers in general are not man-eaters. Thousands of natives live and work among them day by day without mishap, each living their own lives. On occasion they do attack humans. Various explanations are given for this. Probably the most reasonable is that the tiger has sustained some injury which so diminishes its ability to catch its usual prey that, to satisfy its hunger, it turns to hunting domestic animals and then their human owners. Not uncommonly a man-eater is found to have encountered a porcupine leaving one of its quills imbedded in a paw, or shoulder joint, or even in its jaw. The wound festers and the chronic infection hinders its ability to catch swiftly moving animals.

Two Tiger Stories

Two, sad events, which I will now retell, were told by Dad to us children over and over again, so the details have remained imbedded in our minds. It was a beautiful cloudless morning, the jungle fowl that thrived in the forests were calling, doves and pigeons were cooing in the trees, and water birds of various sorts were flying back and forth. The houseboat of one of the surveyors, Banu Singh by name, was anchored a few hundred feet from the shore of a small island. His men were restless and wished to perform their physiologic needs, to wash and bathe themselves, and prepare for the day's work. It was yet fifteen minutes before nine.

Tigers do not know they should cease their hunting at nine and begin again at three. So in reality, nine in the morning and three in the afternoon are determined more from experience than for any another reason. At the insistence of his men Banu Singh ordered the captain to move the boat to shore. The captain of the boat balked at the request. He did not want to assume responsibility for breaking the government rule. But Singh, wanting to please his men, insisted. Finally, the captain agreed to Singh's demand but only after Singh agreed to assume all responsibility for any problem that might develop. The captain moved the boat towards the shore and ordered the gangplank to be lowered. The surveyor and his men scrambled onto the shore. About six of Singh's men were lined up between the waters edge and the jungle, a distance of some twenty feet. While squatting, with their backs to the jungle, they went to latrine. Suddenly a tiger sprang from the forest and carried off one of the men.

The surveyor, with his men and the crew, picked up sticks and a drum. With shouting and yelling, and the beating of the drum they entered the forest and searched for their fallen comrade. The noise must have frightened the tiger, which, leaving his victim, vanished in the underbrush. Picking up the dead man they rushed back to the boat, and several hours later arrived where my Dad was stationed, and reported the sad event.

Later that year another of Dad's surveyors, Rammillan, had been working for several days on one of the many islands. When three in the afternoon arrived that day he had but one more reading to make. If he could make that reading it would be unnecessary for him to return the following day, and he could start work on an adjacent island. He sent all but one of his men to the boat. They were pulling the final chain (a measure of 66 feet in length) when a tiger sprang on his man catching him by the head.

At that time and when I was in school, lined paper was not available on which to write our lessons. My Dad had a round rod of brass, one inch in diameter and about 24 inches long. With it Dad would line our paper by rolling it down the page and drawing a line at appropriate intervals. Rammillan, the surveyor, had one of these rulers. He grabbed it and attacked the tiger. Now Rammillan was a big man, more than six feet tall and extremely strong. As the tiger was carrying his prey away he ran to his servant's aid and, with all his might, struck the animal between its eyes. The tiger gave a grunt and dropped his victim. It was dazed and staggered as it tried to walk.

Picking up his man and still clutching his ruler, which was now bent like a bow, he half carried and half dragged his dead worker to the boat. Assembling his men, with sticks in their hands and with shouting and yelling they returned to pick up the surveyor's instruments. The tiger had not moved and was lying on the ground close to where it had been struck. Not having a gun they felt it was best to leave the animal alone. Taking the instruments they hurried back to their boat. Late that evening they came to my father to report the sad news.

In Dad's office at home, close to his desk stood a bookcase. On one of its shelves he kept the bent ruler of the surveyor who had braved the wrath of a tiger in a futile attempt to save his servant's life. My brother and I would, from time to time, pick it up and imagine how hard the tiger was hit to bend such a strong ruler. I wish I had it in my office today!

God Knew Best

Several years passed by when, one day, a letter arrived from the headquarters of the Survey of India in which Dad was informed that he was to be transferred to a more responsible position. My folks hoped that he would be sent to the northwest, which would place them closer to Vincent Hill School, a Seventh-day Adventist school, at Mussoorie in the foothills of the Himalayas. This would make it easier for Phyllis and Ivan, my two oldest siblings, to attend a good church operated school. Mother and Dad's prayers ascended that this request might be granted if that was where His providence directed.

But this was not God's will. Rather, like Jonah of old, Dad was transferred eastward not westward, and was to be the officer-in-charge of the Assam Survey Department. His responsibility would be to complete the mapping of the Province, and areas that had never as yet been surveyed. He would live in Shillong, the capital of Assam, and would take up his responsibility there by September 1 (1915). As you might expect, their disappointment was great. But this is how God had directed and they accepted His decision. Their children would be educated in a Catholic school!

Eventually, 12 years later, still working for the Assam Survey Department of which he was now the head, the time had arrived for Dad to retire. The policy of the Government of India was that any worker even approaching retirement age was retired. But unbelievably the Government approached Dad, asking that he stay on as they wished him to finish the work he was doing. As a result, he was given an extension of another five years, reaching the mandatory retirement age of sixty. This resulted in his rising higher in his position than any officer had ever achieved. Others became jealous and the rules were changed so that this would never occur again! The Lord had vindicated His faithful servant, and the prediction of his earlier boss that Dad would be superseded and never advanced in the service, was proved anything but true.

The Pitcairn Islander

Following my father's retirement from the Assam Survey Department, my parents and younger brother traveled via Australia through the Panama Canal to Southampton, England. After spending a year in Australia and New Zealand, they set sail from Auckland. To their joy, the ship on which they were sailing was to stop at Pitcairn Island. Pitcairn Island is famous for the Mutiny on the Bounty, and also for the fact that at that time almost all of the inhabitants of the island were members of the Seventh-day

Adventist Church. The church leaders in Auckland gave my parents a letter of introduction.

About two days out of Auckland the lady (I'll call her Mrs. Blair) who sat across the table in the dining saloon, began to talk about Pitcairn Island. Mrs. Blair was well traveled and the ships she had sailed on had stopped at Pitcairn on several previous occasions. The islanders, she said, were different from any others she had ever encountered in other ports.

There were two characteristics that stood out in her mind. One was that they were absolutely honest. For this reason every captain on every ship she had traveled on that stopped at Pitcairn allowed the islanders to come aboard to sell their wares. The other characteristic was that they would not bargain when selling their wares. They would set what they believed to be a reasonable price, and this was what they would ask and this was the only payment they would accept.

The last time she stopped at Pitcairn, the captain, as usual, had a rope ladder lowered to sea level to which the islanders moored their boats after they paddled out from the shore. Since there was no harbor the ships usually anchored about 3 to 5 miles from the island. One by one the islanders came on board bringing with them their wares. Among the articles they sold were hand woven baskets, seashells, fruit of various kinds, hand carved canes (walking sticks), and embroidered articles.

Mrs. Blair was reclining on a deck chair watching the islanders, men and women, as they came up the rope ladder, climbed over the rail, and came aboard. They then scattered to all parts of the ship, fore and aft, from the engine room to the bridge. As she watched, an islander came over the rail carrying, under his arm, a bundle of hand carved canes. A fellow passenger, seated on a chair not far from her, apparently interested, got up and walked over to where the islander was standing. He slowly checked each cane and then addressed the man. "How much do you want for this cane?" In a quiet voice the islander replied, "Two shillings and six pence, sir."

The passenger offered him less. The owner of the canes shook his head, "No thank you, sir." Periodically Mrs. Blair noticed the passenger approach the man with the canes. Each time the passenger withdrew disgusted. Sometime later the ship's siren blew indicating it was time for the islanders to leave the ship. One by one they went over the rail, down the rope ladder, and into their waiting boats.

The passenger who was interested in the canes came over and stood by the rope ladder. He looked up and down the deck. Finally the islander with the canes rounded a corner of the deck and approached the rope ladder where the interested passenger was waiting his arrival. He looked at the remaining canes and saw to his relief that the one he wanted was still there.

"Now how much do you want for that cane?"

The islander in his quiet voice said once again, "Two shillings and six pence, sir."

The passenger became angry, caught the islander by his neck, shook him, and then kicked him, throwing him to the deck. The canes scattered in every direction. And as she watched, Mrs. Blair continued, the islander slowly stood up, one by one he picked up his canes, and, then putting them under his arm approached the angry passenger, and looking him full in the face, said, "May the Lord forgive you sir, for what you have done." Then turning, he went over the rail, down the rope ladder to his boat below.

Then, as the little boats pulled away from the ship, over the waters came the sound of that favorite hymn, "God be with you till we meet again." Mrs. Blair ended her account with these words, "Those islanders are real Christians."

The ocean was too rough for the passengers to go ashore when the ship approached Pitcairn. However, a Mr. Christian and a small delegation of islanders came on board, greeted my parents warmly, and presented my father with, of all things, a beautifully hand carved walking stick! It stands in a corner of my office as I write.

Although the actors in this little drama have long since left the stage, and the curtain has come down, the lessons taught stand out in bold relief against the backdrop of selfishness and greed so prevalent today. May we, when tested and tried, present that humble and forgiving spirit shown by that Pitcairn Islander as he slowly picked up his sticks, stood to his full height, and forgave his assailant.

To a New Land

Like many colonials, my parents after retirement dreamed of retiring in England, but their stay there lasted only a few months over a year! In 1936, by God's direct leading (described later), my parents, my youngest brother Allan, and I left England and migrated to the United States. Eight years later, following the completion of Allan's education, they settled in Loma Linda, California, where I was teaching in the School of Medicine, Loma Linda University.

The years went by and first Dad, at 88, and later Mother at 87, died. Shortly prior to Mother's death, she came to live with us; her memory had failed fast. What had happened to her possessions such as books, pictures, and her other heirlooms remains a mystery to this day. They were gone!

What a Find!

I was at the time Dean of the School of Public Health, LLU, when one morning Ralph, the general technician for the school, brought a cardboard box to my office. A lady in town (I wish I could recall her name) was cleaning out her books, and those she thought might interest me, she had placed in the box. She had instructed Ralph that if I had no use for them they were to be thrown away. I was very busy at the time so asked Ralph to put them in a clothes closet I had in my office.

When I moved to other quarters in the school the box moved with me. Finally the time came for me to clean out my office for the last time. I picked up "the box," still un-opened. I had discarded half of the books when I saw a title I had never seen before. It read, "A Vegetarian Cookbook." As I took it from the box I wondered who was the publisher. I opened the book and to my astonishment read on the inside of the front cover, in my Mother's own handwriting, "Constance G. Hardinge, 1909!" So this was the very book that God had used to bring the Hardinge family into His truth. What a find!

And as I sit at my computer retelling this saga, I hold the book in my hands. God works in strange and wondrous ways!

The Influence of a Consecrated Life

My parents remained faithful Adventists throughout their lives. Phyllis, my sister and the eldest, married Robert S. Joyce (brother of Mrs. Arthur S. Maxwell of *Bedtime Stories* fame) a successful evangelist in England. Later he moved to the United States and was a pastor in the Central Union, and then was President of Nebraska, Colorado, and Indiana Conferences. My brother Leslie was a pastor in England and Scotland. He also came to the United States and taught Bible at Union College, Nebraska, Columbia Union College, Maryland, and Pacific Union College, California. He then went to Philippine Union College and established the Theological Seminary at that institution. Mervyn, the writer of this story, was a pastor in Sheffield, England, then came to the United States, took medicine at Loma Linda University (then the College of Medical Evangelists) and taught there for over forty years. Following retirement he was called to the Seventh-day Adventist World Headquarters as director of the Department of Health and Temperance. My oldest brother Ivan, a physician, and Allan, an engineer at Northrop Aviation, both left the Church.

Foot Note

As far as my late brother Leslie and I can determine, the sales lady who brought the book to my Mother was Mrs. Luther J. Burgess, nee Georgia Anna Burrus. Not a lot is known about her but here is a delightful glimpse into the history of Adventism in India. She came from California (I believe San Diego), and as a single lady was the first regular worker to come to India. She reached Calcutta via England on January 23, 1895. First, she studied the Bengali language, but before a year was up, she arranged for a mission house at 154 Bow Bazaar Street. In March of 1896 she started a school for Hindu girls. This opened the way for her to gain entrance into homes so she could study with women. Thus she met Nonibala Biswas who became the first Adventist convert from Hinduism and later took the name

"Burrus." SUD News Letter, July 23, 1999. (Data excerpted by Barbara Wyman).

Georgia Burrus was born in 1866 and became a Seventh-day Adventist in 1882. She was graduated from Healdsburg College, the forerunner of Pacific Union College. She became interested in mission work in India, and as a single lady left California to be the first regular worker to come to India. She was married to Luther J. Burgess in 1903.

Thank you, Georgia Burrus-Burgess.

Chapter 2

MY SMALL WORLD

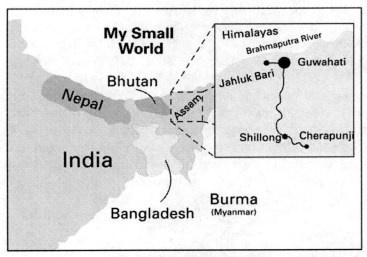

An approximate map of the small world in which I grew up, showing the countries which neighbor the Northwest portion of India and the Province of Assam.

The world in which I grew up, and in which I spent my boyhood and youth, was a small world. We traveled little for there was really no place to which to travel. Shillong was the capital of the Province of Assam, and was sixty miles by road from Gauhati (the city is now known as Guwahati), the largest city in the Province. There were no particular interests to attract us to that city. The road between the two towns was a winding narrow single track, gravel stretch with broadened areas sporadically placed for one vehicle to pass another. All traffic moved in one direction to the halfway station, Nunkpur. When all the down traffic and all the up traffic had arrived at the halfway point, each group was allowed to continue on their desired destinations.

Although Gauhati was only sixty miles away it took most of a day to negotiate the distance since one could start in either direction only at specified hours, and then had to wait at Nunkpur for the arrival of the slowest-moving lorry traveling in either direction!

Gauhati

Gauhati was only a few hundred feet above sea level and, except for the winter months, was hot and humid. As one traveled towards Shillong, at the elevation of five to six thousand feet, tropical forests at first covered the lower hills. Then the road passed through miles of bamboo forests, bamboo as far as the eye could reach. The scenery would then change to lantana covered hills, which stretched to the horizon. Hardwood forests came next, and finally conifers intermixed with oaks, poplars, birches and madrones. Rhododendrons were gorgeous in the spring. The ever-changing altitude provided a varying fauna and flora. Tigers, elephants, and monkeys enjoyed the warmer, more tropical climes, while deer of every sort and leopards inhabited the forests all the way to Shillong.

Shillong

During my boyhood years we lived in Shillong, which, although the capital of the Province, was a small town. The total resident European population comprised less than eighty families, for even at that time, the British Government was employing more and more educated Indians and fewer and fewer colonials. The major administrative elements of the government of the Province were located in Shillong, including the residence of the governor. Two battalions of Gurkha soldiers with their officers were stationed in town. A Pasteur Institute and an Agricultural Experimental Station were within the city limits. Early Catholic missionaries had introduced the growing of potatoes among the hill people. As a result, when I was a boy, potatoes had become a commercial crop and were an export commodity.

The roads were paved with gravel mixed with reddish clay, and there were no sidewalks or curbs anywhere! There was a post office. A hospital (physician's) assistant operated a medical clinic, and a six-bed "hospital." A small fire department had a relic of a fire engine. A water and sewer disposal system provided service only in the town's central area. There was a telegraph office but no telephone service except between the major government offices. There was a small library that was used by us to the limit. I was well into my teens before an entrepreneur installed a hydroelectric power station and electricity became available to the city and its environs. Prior to that time lamplighters at dusk would light carbide lamps and place them atop lampposts in the town's central district.

There was a social club, which operated two tennis courts, two badminton courts, a golf link, a polo ground, and a racetrack. Within the club building there was a billiard table, dance hall, and rooms for such activities as playing cards and socializing. My father was eligible to join the club; in fact he was expected to, but did not. The reason for this was that the common understanding among club members was that the loser in any game (my father played tennis and badminton) bought the drinks for the others. Dad, on principle, would not offer anyone an alcoholic beverage. He was, as result, ostracized and considered a social pariah! My brother and I would have loved to play tennis on the club's courts, and on occasion play a round of golf—but this was not to be. Visitors coming to town could rent these and other facilities of the club, but not the Hardinges!

As already mentioned, the medical facilities available for the town's folks were limited to the small government hospital and clinic, except for a Welsh Mission Hospital operated by a lone, but greatly beloved, missionary doctor. When he went on furlough periodically there were no physicians available except for an occasional army doctor who was not supposed to care for the civilian sick. Besides an itinerant Irish dentist, who visited Shillong once every three years, there was no one to care for dental problems!

St. Edmund's College

While there was a Protestant girl's school, the Catholic presence in Shillong was dominant. The church operated a seminary for training priests, a nunnery for training nuns, a girl's school taught by nuns, and a boy's school, St. Edmund's College, taught by the Irish Christian Brothers, a teaching order. The three schools took students from Standards 1 through 10 (or grade through high school). There was also a Catholic orphanage and an industrial school that taught trades to the hill folks.

Except for the seminary and nunnery, the students in the various schools came from cities in the plains of India. Parents, who could afford it, sent their children to schools located in mountain towns (Shillong, Mussoorie, and Simla) where the weather was not intensely hot and humid as in the low country. There were hardly any day students. Other than during the school year, between March and November, and during the summer months when people came up for a respite from the heat, the population of Shillong was quite small.

St. Edmund's College was the school I attended. And I hated school. In fact I hated school with a vengeance. The main reason for this strong dislike for school was that we, as students, were constantly under duress. The teachers were mainly Irish Christian Brothers, a teaching order, whose members were celibate and who wore long robes or habits. Strict discipline was the order of the day. Every teacher carried in his habit a leather strap, about 18 to 20 inches long, 1.5 inches wide, and 1/3 of an inch thick. To say the least, it was a formidable weapon, and this they used freely. Any infraction of the rules was punished on the spot. Generally the boy had to put out his hand, palm up, and was given one to several "straps," as we called them. Not by any means a pleasant experience. If the behavior was considered deserving of more severe punishment, both hands were strapped, or the strapping was on the buttocks and thighs.

And it seemed that we were strapped for all kinds of supposed misbehavior. If one could not spell a word correctly, or recite a recitation (from memory), or made too many mistakes in arithmetic, or in any way improperly finished an assignment, we were strapped. This constant "fear" galled me. To be late for any class was a real no, no!

Late for School

Let me give the reader one example. Most of the students in the school were full time residents. There were only a few boys who lived at home but attended school during the day. One morning, a boy who was about twelve years of age, we'll call him Bill, who lived in town, arrived about 15 minutes late. This was always punished with a strapping.

"What is your excuse?" the teacher demanded with an edge in his voice.

"There was a tiger in the way so I had to go way around it," Bill explained.

"Of all excuses that takes the cake," the teacher exclaimed with a tone of anger in his voice. "For such a made-up excuse I'm going to give you twice the punishment you deserve."

"No, no," Bill pleaded. "Honest teacher, I'm not making up anything. There was a real tiger in the way."

The teacher studied the face of the boy before him. He seemed to look and act sincere. Was he telling the truth? Did he really meet a tiger on his way to school? Leopards were plentiful in the forests around, but a tiger. No one had ever seen one in Shillong. Tigers tended to avoid high country (5,000 to 6,000 feet).

"All right," the teacher said to Bill, "show me the tiger."

Bill led the way to the window of the classroom, which over looked the football (soccer) field. Pointing towards the middle of the field he said with some delight, "There it is!"

The teacher, to his utter amazement, saw a large Bengal tiger rolling on its back as it enjoyed the sunshine. Turning to the class he whispered, "Stay absolutely quiet. I'm going to get a rifle."

Climbing out of a window in the rear of the classroom, he made his way to the living quarters for the teachers. He soon returned with a rifle and climbed back through the back window with gun in hand. Walking over to the front window and taking careful aim, he pulled the trigger. The sound of the rifle report brought every student and teacher out of the other classrooms to see what was happening. And there, lying in the middle of the field, they saw a beautiful tiger.

The whole town soon learned about this event. People came from every quarter and from miles a around. The rest of the day was declared a holiday to celebrate this unusual event. Bill, who had been late, was more than exonerated; he had become a hero!

Now there were other reasons why I hated school. The Hardinge family was different. Since my parents did not smoke or drink, they were ostracized from membership in the local club. Odd balls! We were also vegetarians, vegetable eaters, spoken with derision. We did not go to school on Saturdays, so we were Jews. We also would not box, so we were Japs, yellow, cowards. These and other epithets were constantly thrown in our faces. When sides were being picked for a game someone would often shout out that they didn't want a yellow or a Jew or a veggie on their side. We were left out of many activities we would have loved to be in, because school programs, tournaments, even graduations, usually came on Saturdays. And so it went. My parents would encourage us. Stick it out. Do your best. But always stand up for what you believe. And that is what we did. We got a good education and achieved academically. Now as I look back on those stormy years I believe they helped build characters that have stood the test of time.

Life at Home

Girls, from a practical standpoint, did not exist. During the summers there were plenty of them in the Catholic and Protestant girl's schools, but they were segregated, boys and girls never mixed. As for the local residents in Shillong, I never met a girl six years plus or minus my age until I went to Newbold College, in England! There just was none!

During the dry season, the winter months, Dad's work required him to travel frequently to different parts of the Province, especially into areas of the interior that were being mapped. Other than such trips, we seldom left Shillong. When Phyllis and Ivan, my eldest siblings, were ready for college, Dad took a furlough, and the whole family went to England. During the voyage, I had my sixth birthday. On returning to Shillong, I started school and never went further than Gauhati, Jahluk Bari, and Cherrapunji except for a one-week trip to Calcutta. After us boys became teenagers, Dad occasionally took us on trips into the interior of Assam. That was the world I lived in from a child to a young adult. And here is the experience of one such trip.

The Disobedient Engineer

Dad took Leslie on this trip. They were headed towards the interior of Assam, west of the border with China and north of the border with Burma. The train was traveling through a desolate section of country covered with jungles and grasslands. For no apparent reason, for they were nowhere near any station, the train slowed down and stopped.

Passengers were looking out of the windows up and down the track, but no one could determine why the train had stopped. As the minutes went by, by one and twos, passengers began to get off the train, most of them walked towards the engine and crew. Word soon came back down the line that a train was derailed from the tracks ahead of them.

Dad and Les decided to walk up the tracks to see what had happened. They found, as did others, a dead elephant entangled between two cars of the freight train that had preceded them. The accident had occurred just a few minutes before the arrival of their passenger train. This is the story that unfolded.

The freight train was proceeding down the tracks as it approached a cut through a hill ahead of them. With little warning a herd of elephants decided to cross the tracks. Elephant herds do not travel in a strictly orderly fashion, some stop to eat along the way, others just amble forward or stop to rest. The railroad authorities had strict orders that trains should be brought to an immediate stop when elephants were seen close to the tracks. Warning signs along roadways read, "Elephants have the right of way!"

But this particular day the engineer decided to ignore the rule. The tracks led up an incline through some low hills ahead and he did not want to lose the momentum he had. So instead of putting on the brakes he blew the engine's whistle. This startled the elephants and they panicked. Some ran one way, others another. One female elephant decided to run forward between the tracks.

The elephant could not outrun the train and although the engineer braked, the train kept gaining on the terrified animal. The elephant and the train reached the cut through the hills at the same time. Then the tiring elephant tried to avoid the oncoming engine by running alongside the tracks. But there was not enough room for the train to pass the elephant because the cut was too narrow.

Elephants, when walking or running, lift both feet on one side and then both feet on the opposite side. This makes them swing from side to side. The elephant would bang against the train and then bang against the hillside. It finally decided to try to go between two cars and charged, with head down, towards the opposite side of the tracks. Its neck was broken and the train derailed!

Nearby villagers, hearing the commotion came to see what had happened. The engineer gave permission to the villagers that they could have the flesh of the elephant. With great joy they each took their portion and departed to celebrate their good fortune. It was not till the following morning that the crane with a crew of repairmen arrived to right the cars that had been derailed, and replace the tracks that had been bent and twisted.

We often wondered what happened to the engineer who broke the rules. Was he fired, demoted, or fined? Whatever, the experience teaches us that when we play with fire we are much more likely to be burned!

Over the years my parents rented several different homes in Shillong. In 1924 they decided to build one for themselves. They bought five acres of hillside property on the out skirts of town. It was covered with pines and a scattering of oaks, and was adjacent to a reserve forest. The home, as I recall it as a boy, was spacious. We had no electricity, no running water (water had to be carried from a source three quarters of a mile away), no flush toilets, and cooking was done on charcoal fires.

The floors were planks without tongue and groove; when the wind blew the chairs kept the cotton rugs down! The walls were constructed with small bamboo used for lathe, plastered with a mixture of sand, cement, lime, cow dung, and grass. Walls and ceilings were whitewashed. It looked very nice! The doors and windows had no screens so whatever flew at night had a good chance of swooping in and out of our rooms. Mosquitoes abounded; we slept under mosquito nets. The roof was made of corrugated iron sheets, and the ceilings were of cheesecloth. It was built within Government specifications. No brick houses were allowed as some years earlier an earthquake had flattened every house in town. We lived in an earthquake zone and earthquakes were not infrequent.

Our Food Supply

We virtually lived off the land. There was no grocery store in town. There was a shop that sold rice, wheat, lentils, beans, and garbanzos. There was a major or bura bazaar held every ten days, and a minor or chota bazaar held every five days. Produce of all kinds was sold in an open-air area on a slightly sloping hill on the periphery of town. It was there that most of our food was purchased, vegetables and fruits as in season. Also, vendors went from door to door selling fruits and vegetables. Once in a while someone would bring honey for sale carried in a five-gallon can, accompanied by a large contingent of bees, wasps, and flies. After mother had bought some honey, it was heated, then filtered through a fine muslin cloth, and then boiled.

The kitchen was a room with a cement floor. There was no running water so the water used was held in two large galvanized buckets, which stood in a convenient place on the floor. On the brick-covered surface of a rectangular table were three charcoal burners on which the cooking was done. On the opposite side of the room was a large box-like structure, lined with bricks that passed for an oven. The cook's helper squatted on the ground outside the kitchen while he washed the dishes, pots, and pans; he also tended the charcoal burners. Since we had no refrigeration little if any food was kept over from one meal to the next. Some food was bought almost every day.

The Milkman

There was no dairy in Shillong. Milk was only available when one found a milkman whose cow was in milk. A new renter moved into the house next to where we lived and his mali (gardener) had a cow which was in milk. The mali came over and offered to sell milk to us. He brought a sample of his cow's milk, which proved to be rich in cream. So an agreement was reached as to how much milk we would buy per day and the price to be paid. In time, however, the amount of cream became less and less and the color of the milk became bluer and bluer. Dad accosted the milkman and told him he was watering the milk. "No, no, Sahib," he responded, "I would never do a thing like that. My father was a milkman, as was his father, and his father. We are all honest men. How could you bring yourself to think I would do a dishonest thing as to put water in the milk I sell?"

But the milk became more and more watery. So again Dad challenged the milkman. This time he replied, "Sahib, as I told you before, I would never think of putting water in the milk I sell. Please send one of your servants to watch as I milk my cow and he will testify to my honesty. So that is what Dad did. The servant returned saying the milkman took a pail, turned it upside down, beat the bottom to show there was absolutely no water in it. Rolled up his sleeves and went to work milking. He then handed the pail to the servant and asked him to take it to his Sahib. No cream, milk as blue as ever.

Calling both the servant and the milkman, Dad said in no uncertain terms, "Water is being added to the milk and you two are in cahoots. If I don't learn the truth, both of you will be fired." The servant did not want to lose his job and that morning he was especially watchful. And this is the report he brought back.

The milkman went through his usual routine. He turned the bucket for the milk upside down and beat the bottom. It was empty. Then he rolled up his sleeves and began to milk. At a critical moment he asked our servant, "Who was that who went by the door?" The servant looked at Dad and said, "Yesterday the milkman asked the same question and I looked out the door and saw nobody. Today, however, Sahib, I was fearful of losing my job so I did not look away from the milkman. As soon as he had asked the question, I watched the milkman with well practiced skill remove his puggree (turban), which I was amazed to see was soaked with water, and wring the water into the milk bucket. Then, in a flash, he had his puggree back on his head and continued milking as if nothing unusual had happened. Had I not being watching intently, he would have fooled me again. That is the truth, Sahib. Please forgive my carelessness yesterday."

There were a number of methods by which milkmen would adulterate the milk with water. One common way was for a milkman to wear a shirt or kurtha with long sleeves. He would place a balloon filled with water in one armpit. Attached to the balloon was a tube that ran down his arm into the palm of his hand. As he milked he would periodically squeeze the bag under his arm and put water into the milk!

Another way was to have a bucket with a double bottom, the lower portion filled with water.

A turban or puggree is a headdress commonly worn in the eastern Mediterranean and south Asia. It consists of a long cloth carefully wound around the head and gives the wearer a distinguished look.

One thing my Dad was adamant on, and that is, we boys were never to buy Indian sweets ourselves. Dad would try to check out the sweetmeat makers and select the one he believed to be the cleanest. Then at our periodic request, about every three weeks, he would order and then buy the particular sweet we had chosen.

Juicy Balls

This time we asked for juicy balls. There are a large variety of Indian sweets and we liked most all of them. Jalabies were our most popular ones. They were made largely of garbanzo flour and looked like a large pretzel, only they were larger and their hollow insides were filled with sugar syrup. Then came the ludoos, round balls of split garbanzos stuck together with sugar. There were other sweets made from milk curds, galabjamins.

It was a Tuesday when we made our request. Dad said he would order them and pick them up on the way back from work on Wednesday. Wednesday we were waiting for Dad to get home. When he arrived from work our disappointment was obvious, no juicy balls.

"You promised to get some. What happened?"

"Hold on, hold on. Let me explain." And this was his explanation.

Dad had stopped at the sweet-maker's shop to pick up the juicy balls. The sweet-maker apologized profusely that some problem had arisen which had delayed him, but that everything was ready and he would soon have juicy balls available. He knew Dad well so invited him into the "kitchen." He gave Dad a stool to sit on and went behind a wooden table, the top of which was about 3 feet long and 30 inches wide. Arranged on the table, side by side, was a pan full of milk curds, a bowl full of sugar syrup, a drainage rack to remove excess sugar, and finally a tray for the finished product.

It was a hot day and the sweet-maker had but his loincloth on. Standing behind the table he, with practiced skill, scooped up some curd with the tips of the fingers of his right hand and deftly tossed it into his left armpit. This was quickly followed by the taking of an appropriate amount of curd with his left hand and landing it in his right armpit. The third scoop of curd was kept in his hands. Before Dad's entranced eyes he had three beautifully shaped balls of curd which he dropped into the pan of sugar syrup. Without hesitation the procedure was repeated. Spellbound, Dad watched, and within a minute or so his order of juicy balls was complete. The sweet-maker said, "Let them soak a few minutes in the sugar syrup, then I will drain them a little so they will be ready to take, and you will find Sahib, they will be fabulously delicious."

Whether Dad bought them and threw them away or whether he somehow got out of the order, or possibly even ate them, we boys never were able to find out. The secret went to Dad's grave. Time tends to erase sharp memories. Les and I have eaten juicy balls since, but the above episode is still vividly imprinted in our minds!

Mr. Merrello was an Italian baker who had a store close to the middle of Shillong. He was a kindly gentleman who had a taste-tempting array of cakes and cookies. Whenever my folks would buy something from him we would like to go along with them. As little boys we would eye the cookies through the glass sides of the display case under the counter. Generally, after payments had been made, he would look at us and ask if we would each like to pick out one cookie? And would we! This was the moment for which we were waiting.

The Prick in the Boot

Mr. Merrello was a bachelor and lived alone in a house not far from his store. He had a routine, which he followed quite closely. He generally was at work around eight in the morning, and was at the sales counter waiting on clients until 5.30 in the afternoon when he closed shop and went home. He would be out of his store from noon until 2:00 in the afternoon during which he had his midday meal.

He was having part of his house remodeled and was unable to close out creatures like rats, and snakes from coming in to the part of house in which he lived. One morning he did not arrive at his store at eight o'clock as he invariably did. When nine o'clock came and he still had not shown up, one of his servants went to investigate. He quietly entered the house and peered into the bedroom. The master was asleep, or so he thought.

He returned to the store and continued his work. When ten o'clock arrived and still no Mr. Merrello had arrived, he became alarmed. He and another servant went to his house and entered the bedroom. They could not arouse their master, who was half dressed but still in bed, so they called the police. The police soon arrived and examined Mr. Merrello for foul play, but there was no evidence of anything out of the way. He was then taken to the local hospital.

When the doctor examined him he discovered the cause of Merrello's problem. His left foot and right hand were swollen, the skin was blotchy, and on close examination he discovered the two fang marks of the snake that had bitten him! He was in deep shock and nearly died. On his recovery this is what he said had happened.

He had gotten up in the morning and had eaten a light breakfast. He then returned to the bedroom to dress for the day. As he was putting on his left boot be felt a sharp prick on his foot. Strange, he thought. Was it a nail? So he put his right hand into the boot to see if he could locate the 'nail.' Then he got another sharp prick on his hand. He realized what had happened. But before he could call for help became sick to his stomach and dizzy. He flopped into bed and there his servants found him.

The police returned and found his boot and in it the snake that had bitten its owner. It was a banded krait, one of the deadliest snakes in the world! Morrello had failed to bang the heel of his boot on the floor to see if anything was in it. His failure to do this almost cost him his life. To this day I find myself, much to the amusement of my wife, banging the heels of my shoes on the floor before putting them on! Habits are hard to brake.

Not long after Merrello's experience, one of the gardeners of St. Edmund's College, where I went to school, while weeding a garden patch, was bitten on his hand by a krait. He, unluckily, was less fortunate than Mr. Merrello for he died within a few hours.

The moral of this story is bang the heels of your shoes on the floor before you put them on!

Hobbies

Dad was an avid stamp collector, and as you might imagine, Les and I had our individual collections. At that time the British Empire spanned the globe, and Dad specialized in the stamps from all the colonies. Thus our knowledge of geography and the world was imbedded in our minds. Although living in a little town in the then undeveloped province of Assam, we had a world-view.

My brother, Les, like to make things from an early age. He would make furniture, model airplanes, and he even put together a gramophone. I still don't know where he found the parts. One day he came up with an idea in which we both could participate.

The Boat We Built

Dad had read us a story about pirates and buccaneers, and our minds were filled with thoughts of sailing the seas someday. Then Les came up with a brilliant idea: why not build a boat and "sail the seas" in the river that was located about an eighth of a mile away? The thought of building our own boat further fired our imaginations. The folks had ordered something from Calcutta, which had arrived in a wooden crate. Wood was scarce, but if we could have the crate, presto, we would have our "ship." At the time Les was twelve and I was ten.

We went to our Mother and asked for the crate. She replied that she would have to talk it over with Dad, and they'd decide and let us know. Wood, as I already pointed out, was a scarce commodity. There were no lumberyards in town; in fact, nobody sold lumber. If we wanted some planks we had to find a "wood sawyer." He in turn would need to locate a tree that was suitable and available, and then, and then only, the process would start. That evening we got the good news that we could use the crate!

The first thing we realized was that the boat we had dreamed of had to be reduced to the size of the wood available. It would have to be much smaller than we had imagined. We measured and re-measured every inch of that precious wood. The final outcome was a boat two feet wide, four feet long, and one foot deep! We made the angles square, except for the front end, which had a slope of about forty-five degrees. Since the crate was made of the cheapest of wood the edges of the boards did not smoothly fit one against the other. But it was all that we had and the best we could do.

With triumph the last nail was hammered in and we carried "our ship" down to the river. We had no oars but we found a bamboo about ten feet long. It was just the right pole with which to punt. We placed our boat in the water, but before one of us could step into it, it filled with water and almost sank! The cracks between the boards and sides were so wide the water literally rushed in. In case we might lose our boat if it sank where the river was deep, one of us went back home and brought a length of rope, which we tied to a knothole in one of the boards at the back of the boat.

We carried the boat to a shallow part of the river. One of us got ready to get into the boat as soon as it touched the water so we could float at least for a minute or so. But it didn't work. The bottom was flat and had no keel. Unless we stood exactly in the center of the boat it would turn over. We tried over and over to ride in it but it was no good. We carried our precious boat back home with our eyes filled with tears.

Then Dad came to the rescue. He had a machinist in his office solder shut three empty five-gallon kerosene cans. They were rectangular and made ideal floats. One was tied to each side towards the front of our boat and the third was tied to the back. Wonderful! It floated like a swan! It would not turn over. It would not sink. It was like the Titanic! And the water that did fill the bottom of the boat we would bail out, keeping it from becoming too deep. But then we encountered a problem. Trying to push the boat forward with our bamboo pole was next to impossible because the flat ends of the five-gallon cans on the front two sides caused an enormous amount of resistance. Besides the current of the river was against us.

But even this problem we solved. The Umkhrah River in which we were trying to navigate had rocky fords about a half-mile apart. We would carry our boat to the lower side of a ford upstream and then float down to the ford below. Punting was just to try and guide the craft. Our boat, though crowded, would carry both of us. One would kneel in the front and the other would squat at the back. We, at last, were the mighty mariners we had envisioned as we floated down the river in a strange and wonderful craft that we had contrived! Then it happened one day. We had built the boat just before Christmas. The water in the river was anything but warm for we were at 5,000 feet altitude, and the river arose in even higher mountains.

I was at the back having my turn punting, Les in front directing the course. Being older, he of course, was the "captain."

"Pull over to the shore," he ordered. "It's my turn to punt."

It so happened that at that particular point the current was flowing towards the left bank of the river. The current was quite strong, and it was more the current, than my poling, that got the prow of the boat to the land. Les grabbed some long grass that was growing at the water's edge. At the point where Les was holding the grass, the current made a sharp turn outwards towards the middle of the river. The current was stronger than I could push against. Remember I was only ten!

The boat started to pull away from the bank no matter how hard Les pulled and I pushed with the pole. Soon his arms were at full length. "Punt, punt," he kept shouting. But our efforts could not compete with the force of the river. Slowly the boat moved further and further from the bank. It was hard for me to see what was happening because I was looking backward pushing as hard as I could, but when I did take a peek, the front edge of the prow had already passed Les' abdomen and was approaching his pelvis. He was still pulling on the grass and would not let go. Then I realized what was going to happen and began to laugh! This made me even weaker.

Les became desperate. "Punt, you chump," he kept shouting. But at that juncture my feeble efforts were worthless. Gradually, inexorably, the distance between the land and the boat was widening. He had already passed the "point of no return." I stopped punting and began watching him. The prow of the boat was now at his knees, then at his shins, and finally at his ankles. It was just a matter of time. My laughter did nothing to soothe his spirits. He, too, knew the jig was up! He was straight as if he had been lying on a level floor. Now it was only his toes that were holding him out of the water. Then he disappeared "beneath the waves!"

As soon as Les hit the water, the current shot the boat with its single passenger out into the middle of the river. And that was a good thing, for when Les emerged from his unwelcome bath, and had climbed up the six-foot riverbank, he was beside himself. He was like an angry male elephant trumpeting imprecations against his little brother. The reader is left to figure out what his words were because they cannot and should not be printed here or anywhere else. If he could only have gotten hold of me! I verily feared for my life. But the river saved me.

In a minute or two, though it seemed much longer, he turned and stomped off sloshing back to our house. It was on a Sunday so Dad was home. After several minutes Les returned in dry, clean clothes, though he was still not quite in his right mind. Dad was following him and they both arrived on the bank opposite the boat. Les insisted I had done it on purpose. I was just as insistent that it was not my fault and that the current was responsible for the accident. I could see that Dad was doing his best to keep himself from laughing. Finally Les calmed down and Dad had him promise that he would not lay hands on me. Things were made up and he and I carried "our ship" back up home. Prudently, I still kept my distance from him for the next 24 hours!

This event put a damper on our "boating" and our interest in becoming pirates and buccaneers became less and less. Finally "our ship" was dismantled and the wood used for a more useful purpose. Les and I never really quarreled; we certainly never hit each other. It seemed that when one of us was angry with the other, the other one was anything but angry. The old saying is true. "It takes two to make a quarrel."

About this time Dad read us a story about the forest dwellers of the Amazon jungles. The fact that they had blowguns, and poison-tipped darts with which they could shoot birds and animals high up in the rain forests, put a burning desire in our hearts to emulate them. But where could we get such 'instruments of destruction?' We decided to make them ourselves.

Blowguns and Darts

Aikra or small diameter bamboo (some are sold in nurseries to stake up young plants) was readily available. We each got a three-foot length, which was straight, split it in half, knocked out the joints and tied the two halves together. The blowguns were ready! The hole down the center was about 1/4 to 3/8 of an inch in diameter.

But fashioning a dart proved more difficult. We tried sticks of various kinds but could not blow them through; they were far too heavy. We reduced their size, got chicken feathers to attach to one end, and we wrapped thread around a straw, without the slightest success. We could not blow them through our blowguns, let alone shoot a bird high up in a tree! We gave up.

Then one evening while Dad was reading to us, Mother was darning a hole in a sock. Suddenly Les jumped up. "I've got it, I've got it," he shouted. "I've figured out how to make a dart that I think will work!"

His brilliant idea was to take a darning needle, leave a couple of strands of yarn (wool) in the eye, comb out the strands and cut them to about an inch in length. The "dart" would be inserted into one end of the blowgun, point forward. The wool would fill the diameter of the blowgun! It would be light, and had a sharp point. He could hardly wait to put his idea into reality. Mother lent him a needle and supplied him with some yarn (such as used for knitting sweaters and socks). It wasn't long before his dart was ready. He fetched his blowgun and inserted the dart. He gave one blow and out shot the dart, traveled several feet, and stuck in the wood floor! We were in ecstasy.

"Please make me one," I begged. "I'd like to shoot one myself." So mother gave him another needle and some yarn, and soon we both had our own darts.

Next morning, with blowguns and darts in hand, we went to the bathroom together. Now the bathroom was nothing like the ones we have in our homes today. It had a cement floor, which sloped to one corner of the room where a hole allowed the water to flow into an outside drain. At one end were two commodes, one for Les and the other for me. They faced the length of the bathroom. On the left wall was a small table which held a wash basin and a large jug of water (we had no running water). Beyond the table was an area that had a small wooden platform on the floor, a wooden stool at the far end, and a galvanized iron tub on one side. A small shelf on the opposite side to the tub held a bar of soap and an enameled mug. Hot water was brought in a can, emptied into the tub, and seated on the stool one used the mug to pour water over oneself. The whole procedure worked well and was quite efficient. A window was on the wall beyond the tub. The total dimensions of the room were about five by ten feet.

Each, seated on his commode, blew his dart into the side of the wooden table. The system worked perfectly. We did this several times and then Les came up with the suggestion that we try to blow our darts out of the window. Now the window was about 10 feet away, a distance we had never tried to cover before. Les tried first. He decided to take a real deep breath, deeper than he had taken before, and then blow as hard as he could. He raised his blowgun to his lips and then inhaled deeply. In the process he sucked the dart out of the end of the pipe and before he realized what was happening, had swallowed it!

A look of horror spread across his face, and I'm sure it did mine. We were both sure he was going to die. He coughed as hard as he could but the dart had gone down his gullet not his windpipe. Crying, we ran to Mother and told her, between sobs, what had happened. Mother told me to get Dad. I ran, most of the way uphill, to Dad's office a little over a mile away. Out of breath and still crying, I told Dad the whole sad story.

Mother was always calm about problems, but not Dad. His blood pressure would rise, he would become extremely agitated, and a torrent of words would come out of his mouth. As we ran towards home Dad kept reminding me how foolish we were, that we should never have made our blowguns and darts, that Mother shouldn't have aided and abetted us in the project, and should Les die his blood would not be on his shoulders! When we got home, Mother and Les were still crying.

Dad started in on Mother but she immediately stilled his tirade. "Take him to the hospital," she ordered, "all your criticism won't do any good!" The hospital was a mile away and the three of us covered the ground in record time. The hospital assistant examined his mouth and throat, which were normal. Since Les did not cough, he decided that the dart had gone down his throat. He ordered that Les be given no fluids for 24 hours and be fed dry bread only. "Watch his stools for the next week," he ordered, as we were leaving the clinic.

No forensic laboratory ever examined stools as closely as did we examine those of Leslie. Day after day nothing of the dart emerged. A week went by, and then two, but still no needle. Les was alive and doing well. Anxiety gradually lessened and eventually the whole incident was forgotten. What happened to the dart still remains a mystery. My brother died two years ago; he was almost ninety. I regret that I did not ask him to have a CAT scan of his whole body. Maybe the hiding place of the recalcitrant dart would have shown up!

Here is a little advice for the reader. If anyone wants to play blowgun and darts, remember don't use darning needles! And if you do, please don't take a deep breath!

As much as Leslie enjoyed making things, I enjoyed collecting them. I was born a collector. I still am. The other day someone asked me what I collected. My reply sort of startled him. "My wife collects everything, and anything she doesn't, I do!" I started collecting when I was in grade school. I collected stamps (my Dad was an avid collector), butterflies, moths, beetles, and bird's eggs. Rocks and fossils were also included. But the thing I liked most was collecting butterflies, moths and beetles.

During high school years we lived adjacent to a reserve forest, which separated us from the town and the school to which I went. To wander through this forest and others adjoining it was a pleasure, which I enjoyed whenever time allowed. I think I knew every tree and almost every bush! I kept a little notebook. In this notebook I wrote down where I found this beetle or caterpillar, and the time of year I caught it. This half-rotten tree had a nuthatch's nest in an old woodpecker's hole, and this other had a king crow's nest far out on a branch we could never reach. And so it went.

The Beetle Tree

Birch trees and oaks often had sap running down some injured part of the trunks. This sap attracted beetles and butterflies, and on occasion, hornets. There were two oak trees, perhaps from a single root, that grew side by side on a particularly steep hillside. Towards the top of one of them sap flowed quite freely and seemed to attract more beetles than did any other tree in the forest. Besides rhinoceros beetles, of which there were plenty, it attracted crocodile beetles. These are very active insects. Some of them were 3 to 4 inches long, about an inch wide, and rather flat. They had horizontal mandibles that could break a lead pencil without difficulty.

To get up to the beetles required a bit of effort. I would climb up one tree, Tree A. About fifteen feet off the ground I would switch over to the other tree, Tree B. Twelve or fifteen feet higher I would cross back to Tree A. Ten or so feet higher I could reach across and, if I was lucky, nab a beetle. I had climbed this tree every summer for years. The way down was quick and easy. Descend about 10 feet, cross to Tree B, and when I arrived at a branch about 15 feet lower, instead of crossing back to Tree A, hang from it and let go. I would drop about 3 feet and land on a branch that I could not reach otherwise. From there on down was very easy; it avoided scaling down.

The potential problem was that there was a gap of branches on Tree A; that gap was quite similar to that of Tree B. The difference being that if you hung from this particular branch and let go, there was no branch to arrest your fall three feet below! On this particular afternoon I had not been able to catch any beetles and was descending as usual. I failed to remember that I was hanging from the branch of the wrong tree, Tree A. A moment after I let go I realized my mistake. I threw my left arm around the trunk and swung spiraling down the tree for a distance of some fifteen feet. Fortunately a protruding branch broke my fall. Throwing my arms around the trunk, I sat there. Sweat was flowing down my face, I was shaking like a leaf, and my left arm looked like bloody cottage cheese where the rough bark had denuded the skin. But I was alive!

Had I not thrown my arm around the trunk or landed on that branch I would have fallen some twenty-five feet to a jagged pile of rocks below, and to certain death. I clung to the tree for a long time, and then slowly and carefully descended to the ground below. As I trudged home I thanked my guardian angel and the Lord for saving my life.

I climbed those beetle trees many times thereafter, but was always careful not to make that careless mistake again.

Our Social Life

As a family we had few friends, as our lifestyle was so different from those with whom we might otherwise associate. Work and play was the code of life. Since we were barred from the local club our friends were few and far between. Whenever possible my folks would study the Bible with interested parties and many of these became Seventh-day Adventists; however, with one exception, they all moved away. My father would play chess with a Mr. Mathews, a fairly deaf old gentleman! He was a bachelor. The thing we boys didn't like about him was that he smoked a pipe, incessantly. But in time, through my Dad's influence, he gave up smoking, then drinking, and eventually became a strong member of our church. He stayed on in Shillong until his death shortly before my parents left the country.

We had one or two other friends who, from time to time, would stop for a visit, but in general the family entertained itself. Mr. Marello, the baker, had a tennis court on his property which, my folks occasionally rented, but these occasions were rare. Les and I would entertain each other. My parents carved out of our hillside a level spot on which we played everything, football (soccer), tennis, miniature golf, and marbles! You name it. We played with each other and sometimes with one or two of our servants.

There was one event, which occurred once each year to which we children were not invited. This was a dinner with the Governor of the Province. When a new Governor was in office Dad would write a letter to His Highness explaining the facts that he and Mrs. Hardinge were vegetarians, did not use alcohol, and were nonsmokers. Without exception my folks were treated with deep respect on such occasions. It was not uncommon for the Governor, just before the meal started, to tell the guests of my parent's principles as an explanation for why they would be served special dishes and be given special drinks. God honors those who honor Him.

My parents were great readers and there was no book in our local library worth reading that they had not read. And what is more, they read them all to us children! From my earliest recollection they were reading to us. They subscribed to every magazine published by the Church. We grew up listening to *Our Little Friend*, the *Youth's Instructor*, the *Review and Herald*, the *Sabbath School Worker*, and the *Oriental Watchman* (*Signs of the Times*). Especially on Sabbath afternoons Mother would read to us from the Conflict of the Ages Series and *Christ's Object Lessons*. And we loved it. It was our joy and delight, especially during the winter evenings. During our holidays, whenever there was an opportunity, Mother and Dad would read; and we would listen. In fact, we grew up listening. Surprisingly they never asked us to read, they did the reading and we did the listening! And that ability to listen has proved an invaluable asset in all my after-years.

Another thing, which surprises me today, is that my folks never asked us to do anything "in public." We never stood up in the family circle and read a verse from the Bible out loud, no recitations, no performances of any kind. When we went to England this was something we had to overcome, especially since we were headed for the ministry!

Religion in the Home

A spiritual atmosphere pervaded our home. We had family worship morning and evening, plus our private devotions, which included reading from the Scriptures and personal prayer. I can still hear my father praying, as he often prayed out loud. Mother prayed quietly. They both were diligent students of the Bible. Mother was an authority on the book of Revelation, and Dad prepared a sermon for each late Sabbath afternoon service. Most of what Dad presented went right over our heads! However, the impact on Les and me was good. Off and on through the years they would give Bible studies, and a number of those with whom they studied became members of our church. Unfortunately they did not remain long in Shillong, but moved away, so the Seventh-day Adventist congregation in Shillong was, for the most part, Dad, Mother, Les and I.

Dad prepared a series of tracts in the languages of the hill tribes, Khasi, Jaintia, Lushai, and Naga. These he distributed by the hundreds as he traveled in his work. Dad was known as the Sahib who did not smoke, did not drink, did not eat meat, and his holy day was Saturday. He was highly respected and trusted by the populations among whom he worked. Months before I left for England, Elder and Mrs. Burgess, long retired missionaries to India, returned to start work in Shillong. They soon began a Sabbath School. Mrs. Burgess was the same lady who sold Mother the cookbook in 1909. In 1985 when I was holding a health workshop in Shillong I learned that there were 10,000 believers among the hill people! When my folks left Shillong for good, they set up a fund to build a Seventh-day Adventist school for the hill people. In 1966, on the way back from Africa, my wife, daughter and I visited the Adventist Training School, Jaintia Hills, partially funded by my folk's contribution!

Service for the Lord was constantly held before us boys. Although I dreamed of being an entomologist, I could not see how God could use such a person, so turned in the only direction I knew of—the ministry. It was the ministry that would give me the opportunity of being a foreign missionary. And with this goal in mind, I sailed from Calcutta, down the Hooghly River into the Bay of Bengal and on to Southampton, England to enroll in Newbold College.

Cherrapunji

It was really just a village, a cluster of small homes, about thirty miles by road from Shillong. It was, in fact, a famous place because the British claimed it was the rainiest spot in the Empire. The average rainfall was about 500 inches per year, the record rainfall in one day was 44 inches, and for a single season over 900 inches! Shillong averaged 100 inches during the rainy season. The village of Cherrapunji was between two and three thousand feet in altitude and overlooked the Sylhet plains (part of which are Bangladesh today). Moisture rising from these steamy flat lands was blown against the cooler mountains and would condense in the higher altitudes resulting in a torrential rainfall.

The area had no topsoil; it had long since been washed away. Rocky ground and stunted trees, with dense underbrush, formed the forests that surrounded the village. The area was infested with snakes, the trees festooned with orchids, and the forest floor abounded in ground orchids. The trees, because they were stunted, were generally not difficult to climb. The damp undergrowth and the moss hanging from the branches produced an abundance of orchids. Hunting orchids and Cherrapunji went together. In this, Dad would aid and abet us, and often would go with us into the forests. It was ever our hope that we could find a new variety!

The Orchid and the Snake

Snakes were everywhere. They seemed as common as the orchids what grew in the trees. It happened on a beautiful sunny afternoon. We had just finished lunch, so decided to go orchid hunting. Les didn't like climbing trees, but I did. So when we located an orchid which we wanted, he would lift me up to the lowest branch, and then it was up to me to get the orchid.

To our delight, on this occasion, we found one we had never seen before. It was growing on the top of a tall, somewhat, slender tree, which was bent over in a long arch, so the orchid was not far above us. It was, however, just beyond our reach even when I stood on Les's shoulders. The ground on which we stood was covered with a dense growth of bracken and other ferns. Lying at our feet was a fallen tree, or so we thought, about 6 to 8 inches in diameter. We have no recollection whether it was Les or I, for we were both looking up at the orchid, when one of us put his foot on "the tree." "The tree" took off thrashing through the forest floor in one direction, and we, thrashing though the bracken and ferns, in the opposite direction. When we finally stopped at the forest edge the hair on the back of our necks was still standing out like the bristles of a toothbrush!

Giant pythons were not uncommon. To kids who are 12 and 14 years of age memory tends to make things appear larger than they really were. However that may be, we conservatively estimate the snake was close to eighteen or more feet in length. We visited Cherrapunji many times in the following years but never went near the "snake tree" as we called it. The orchid doubtless died of old age as did the snake!

Jahluk Bari

The meaning of this name is rather interesting. "Jal' is spicy hot; 'luk' is a small indigenous pepper, about the size of one's little finger nail. It is inedible because of its excessive 'heat,' for it burns the lips and tongue producing blisters. If eaten it causes a severe gastroenteritis (an inflammation of the stomach and intestines): resulting in violent diarrhea, bloody stools, and, if not immediately treated, shock and death. 'Bari' is the Indian name for a garden. Therefore 'Jahluk Bari' means 'a garden of jalhuks.'

The village consisted of rice paddies and a few scattered small parcels of land separated one from the other by coconut palms, plantain patches, papaya and pepal trees. A deep but narrow high-banked river flowed through the village emptying into the Brahmaputra. The only way to cross the river was on an occasional old dead single palm tree that had been placed from bank to bank. There were no handrails or ropes to hold on to! On the north side of the village flowed the Brahmaputra River, while a mile or two to the south ran a single lane gravel road which extended westward eight miles to Gauhati and eastward to towns in the interior of the Province.

Across the road began a series of rounded hills covered with dense forest and undergrowth. These were the foothills of the mountains that extend southward forming the Khasi and Jaintia ranges in which Shillong is located. Just west of where these hills began was the Assam Survey Training School, the campus of which extended to the edge of a swamp. This swamp, composed of lakes and wetlands, ran parallel to the road and extended some thirty miles to the east. It was two to five miles wide, forming a vast wintering ground for millions of water birds of every kind.

The Surveyor Training School

The Assam Training School was a Government owned and operated institution for training surveyors. My father's responsibility in the school was to give a few lectures prior to holding qualifying examinations for certifying the completion of the course. These activities required his presence on the campus every three months, and during the cool season he would bring the whole family with him. Since there were no living facilities except for students and teachers, tents were pitched on the upside of the campus for us. Tents were provided for Dad's supporting staff as well. Each surveyor was provided a squad of eleven men to help pitch tents, gather wood, carry water, and do the many duties of camp life. All of these tents formed a little encampment overlooking the campus and the swamps beyond. When Dad traveled to the interior his squad of men went with him. Our cook always accompanied Dad.

At the time of my boyhood it was an ideal area for hunting. The coming population explosion had not as yet reached this relatively remote region. In the dense underbrush of the forests, which clothed the low rounded hills, lived various animals: tigers, leopards, monkeys, wild pig, porcupine, and a large variety of deer from small to large. At the edges of the forests game fowl abounded, such as jungle fowl, partridge, pigeons and doves. On the lakes and marshy wetlands that extended beyond the campus geese, ducks of every stripe, snipe, and plover were plentiful. Besides these, non-game birds abounded. Vultures, kites, storks, egrets, parrots, kingfishers, woodpeckers, hummingbirds, and many other species were for us to enjoy and identify. The crowing of jungle fowl cocks, the cooing of pigeons, and on occasion, the roar of a tiger could be heard in the morning and evening hours. And all this was for us alone! It was rare to see another hunter.

Now I should explain something. The experiences about to be related happened over a period of years. There were many visits to Julhuk Bari, which we enjoyed, but no event worthy of record occurred. The happenings recounted below are to provide the reader, in story form, the environment and activities in which my growing-up years was lived.

My Father's Elephant

The Province of Assam in which Dad worked, was in my boyhood days one of the most primitive in India. Away from the few roads and highways one either walked or road some beast of burden. The Government had provided Dad an elephant. It could not only transport a number of men, but it could carry the tents and other essential equipment needed by the surveyor and his men to live, camp, and work. The animal was constantly in use, if not by Dad, then by one or other of his surveyors who were working in primitive areas.

When my brother and I were about eight and ten years old, we would love to take rides on Dad's elephant. Since it was stationed at the Assam Survey Training School, some eight miles from

Gauhati, in the village of Jahluk Bari, it was only when Dad took the family with him to the school that we got a chance to ride the animal. A pad would be placed over its back and a rope strung from the root of its tail to around its neck. To stay on its back we had to hang onto the rope because sitting on an elephant's back is like sitting astride a dining table! A howdha is a wooden frame with a bench on each side. The howdha is placed over the back of an elephant and will allow a number of people to sit on each side, back to back. For everyday use a pad is easier to apply and is the common covering for the back.

The pad did not cover the entire back so some of its skin could be seen. Elephants have stout hairs about an inch and half long scattered over the back. These hairs fascinated us. What is more we liked to pull on them. When we thought the mahout was not watching we would reach over the edge of the pad and give a hair a gentle tug. Immediately the elephant would make a sound like thunder! The mahout would glare at us and we would try to act innocent. Then we would do it again, but never more than two or three times. We were afraid of what might happen if the elephant got angry.

The Disobedient Elephant

Dad was out on one of his trips into the interior. It was an area where no roads of any consequence existed, so Dad took his elephant to carry the tents and other equipment needed to live and work. It happened on a weekend. It was the day of rest, Sabbath. The campsite for Dad and his men, along with the surveyor he was supervising and his staff, was adjacent to a small lake, part of a larger swamp. Two men were generally needed to care for an elephant, the mahout, who was the main keeper of the animal, and a grass-cut, who was responsible for feeding and bathing the animal. Earlier in the day the grass-cut had taken the elephant into the swamp where it had collect enough grass and weeds to provide enough food to meet the animal's needs for that day. He now was bathing the elephant in the lake. Elephants are rather delicate animals and must be kept scrupulously clean. Dad was reclining in his chair watching the procedure.

Elephants love water. They roll in it, fill their trunks and spray themselves all over. The grass-cut had been rubbing his elephant down with a brush, something the animal enjoyed. It was time to take him back where he was tethered. The elephant would not get out of the water. Try as he might, the animal just would not move. The grass-cut became frustrated and yelled at the beast. It ignored all his efforts. Finally in disgust the grass-cut left the elephant in the water and strode angrily to where he could ask help from the mahout.

A minute or two later the mahout appeared, and slowly walked in the direction where the elephant was lying in the water. He was muttering to himself as to how wicked the animal was, that it was disobedient and worthless, the son of an elephant that must have been like him, and that he deserved a beating such as had never been given to any elephant before. Approximately 20 feet from the elephant the mahout reached down, picked up a little stick about the size of a pencil. Shaking it in the direction of the elephant he demanded in a loud voice that it should get out. The elephant promptly stood up and, looking sheepishly toward the ground slowly came out of the lake and walked towards his master. The grass-cut now took over and took the disobedient animal to his corral.

Dad's Elephant Gets Sick

Our elephant (my Dad's hanthi) was sick. He had a large sore on his back that would not heal. The mahout or his helper, the grass-cut, had been careless when loading the elephant and something sharp had pressed down through the pad and rubbed a hole in the animal's back. So Dad had ordered that it should not be allowed to do any work until the wound had healed. It was slowly recovering and the sore, the size of a small plate, was getting smaller.

The elephant was stationed at the Survey Training School where Dad went at regular intervals to give lectures and hold examinations. I know exactly where the incident happened. As you leave the gate of the campus and travel towards Gauhati, the hill that backs up the campus is at your right while rice paddies lie to your left. The hills in this region are carpeted with dense undergrowth and small trees. Wildlife of every kind abound, tigers, leopards, small and large deer, wild pigs, wild foul, pigeons, and doves.

The Elephant Takes Revenge

It was a hot, humid day and the elephant was standing under a large shade tree swishing dirt with its trunk onto its back to keep the flies off. Its large ears were flapping to help keep it cool. The mahout and grass-cut each lived in two small huts nearby. Three men, carrying large bundles, approached the mahout, who was lying in the shade of a mango tree.

"Is this a government elephant?" one inquired.

"Yes, sir," the mahout replied.

"Then take us," he replied "to Gauhati. Our bundles are heavy, we are hot and tired, and we, as government workers, have a right to the use this elephant when it is not being used by the "bura Sahib," referring to my father.

"Unfortunately I cannot help you at this time," the mahout responded politely. "The elephant is sick. See that large sore on its back. And besides, the Sahib has given me strict orders that it should not be used under any circumstances, until the sore has healed."

"You lazy scoundrel," the traveler shouted, "all you want to do is lie around and do nothing! Now get going. Put the pad on the elephant's back, and tie our bundles up there too. We are in a hurry and need to be on our way."

"I'm sorry, sir, but I cannot disobey my Sahib. He has given me strict orders that no one is to use the elephant until the sore has healed. I am not a lazy man. Please do not insult me."

The traveler was beside himself. He angrily ordered the mahout to get the pad, put it over the elephant's back, and to tie up their bundles securely. "That little sore is no problem. You are using it as an excuse so you can stay in the shade and do nothing. If you don't do as I tell you, I'm going to report you to the higher-ups."

"All right sir, I will do as you say, but I want to warn you that I cannot take responsibility for what the elephant might do. Elephants are very intelligent animals, and when they are not treated well they often do strange things. You have demanded that I disobey my Sahib's orders, and beyond that I am to put the pad on the tender wound which you can see with your own eyes is a serious injury!"

The mahout and his grass-cut then got busy and soon had the elephant loaded. With its trunk the elephant picked the men up one by one and helped them get settled on its back. The mahout mounted the elephant sitting on the animal's neck with his toes tucked behind its ears. By prodding the ear on one side or the other he could direct the animal in the direction he wishes it to go. With an order, the elephant set off for Gauhati eight miles away.

Elephants are four legged animals but they do not walk like horses, dogs, or cats. They lift both the legs on one side and then both legs on the opposite side. This makes them swing from side to side as they stride along. The party had gone about a quarter of a mile and had arrived at the spot I described earlier. The densely forested hill was at the right and the rice paddies to the left. It so happened that the rice paddies had recently been flooded. This allowed the soil to become soft so it could be easily plowed in preparation for planting the rice seedlings.

The elephant abruptly stopped. "What's the matter?" the men nervously inquired of the mahout.

"How can I know," the mahout answered. And then it happened. The elephant swung its back to one side and then to the other. It did it again and again, each time a little harder. Then with one mighty swing it sent the three travelers and their bundles flying through the air, landing them with a terrific splash right in the middle of a rice paddy. With angry shouts the men picked themselves up, collected their bundles, and, covered with mud and dripping with water, sloshed to the road. Shaking their fists in the mahout's face they yelled: "You made it do it on purpose!"

"Sirs," the mahout replied, "I warned you that the animal might be unpredictable. When they're injured one can never tell what might happen."

Grumbling and complaining the three travelers turned towards their destination. Finally, as the mahout recounted the story to my Dad, they disappeared in the distance.

"Did you make the elephant do it?" my Dad asked. With a twinkle in his eye, the mahout responded, "Sahib, in this life strange things can happen! And by the way, elephants are very intelligent animals."

Les and the Baby Monkey!

We were again in Jahluk Bari. On that particular morning Les and I had decided to go our separate ways. He went in the direction of the river (Brahmaputra) while I set off in the opposite direction to the area of the rounded hills. When we were having lunch, this is the experience Les related.

He and two of Dad's men had reached the small river that flowed through the village, and were walking along its right bank, when they reached a rice paddy probably two hundred yards long and one hundred and fifty feet wide. Along the river's edge grew a lone medium-sized willow tree. The edges of the paddy field were bordered with large pepal trees. The rice had recently been harvested so the field was dry. Feeding on fallen grain was a large troop of monkeys. There were perhaps twenty adults and almost the same number of babies.

Now Les and I had wanted a monkey of our own. On numerous occasions we had begged Dad to buy one in a local bazaar, but Dad would have none of it. He believed that even a pet monkey was a treacherous animal and might bite its owner at any time. As Les watched the baby monkeys frolicking around an idea jelled in his mind. Perhaps he could catch one of the babies and then we would, at last, have a monkey of our own. He talked it over with the two accompanying men. They decided to stampede the troop and hoped to separate the babies from the adults.

At a given signal they rushed towards the surprised monkeys, waving their arms and yelling and shouting. The troop scattered, and just as they had hoped, all the adults ran to the large pepal trees, while six babes climbed the willow tree by the riverbank. Now they were sure they could catch a least one little fellow! But to their surprise, one by one, five of the baby monkeys climbed to the end of the branches which hung over the river, jumped in, and swam to the opposite bank. But one little fellow found himself on the end of a branch that leaned over the rice paddy. Aha! It should be easy to catch him!

One of the two men climbed to the branch on which the baby monkey was sitting while my brother and the other man stood just below the monkey. Then the man in the tree gave the branch a tremendous bump with his foot. This jerked the baby off the branch and as it fell Les grabbed it. The baby monkey let out the most pathetic scream you ever heard. Down from the pepal trees came its mother and father, its uncles and aunts, its older brothers and sisters. In fact every older monkey was on the ground coming towards my brother. They were screaming and chattering. With glaring eyes and bared teeth they rushed towards Les. He and the man with him ran for their very lives.

But as fast as their legs would carry them, the monkeys could run faster. Closer and closer they came. My brother finally realized that he could not outrun the angry monkeys. The mother monkey was at his heels and the others were not far behind. So he threw the baby monkey over his shoulder towards the oncoming monkeys. The mother caught her baby, and suddenly everything was quiet! The whole troop stopped, turned back, and slowly walked away.

That experience taught us a lasting lesson. Our mothers and fathers love us just as much as those monkeys loved their babies. And what is more, our God in heaven loves us even more, and will come to our help if we call to Him when we're in trouble.

The Fish Tale

Again we were in Jahluk Bari at the Assam Survey Training School. It was a beautiful Sabbath morning. We were sitting in front of my folk's tent. It must have been some type of holiday for it seemed that the entire village had gathered by the nearest lake that was situated in the swampy area. They were there to fish. There must have been some fifty villagers in all.

The villagers were using especially designed baskets with which to catch the fish. Each basket was a woven bamboo dome and if two were placed so that their greatest diameters met, would form a ball some five feet in height. In the sides of the basket were holes through which the hand and arm could be thrust. The technique used was for three or four men to wade into the swamp holding the basket with its wide mouth just above the surface of the water. They would then stand perfectly still until they thought that fish had arrived and were under their basket. At a given signal they would plunge the basket down to the lake bottom as fast as their strength would permit. Inserting their arms through the holes provided they would feel for the fish that hopefully they had trapped. This would be repeated at intervals. Sometimes they were successful but most often not.

The fishing was going on about a half mile away. Periodically there were shouts of joy as someone had caught a fair sized fish. Suddenly a tumult erupted; men and women were yelling and shouting. Within minutes the villagers had divided into two groups, each facing the other. With angry voices they were cursing one another and waving sticks in the air. Finally things quieted down and the groups slowly dissolved.

It must have been some twenty minutes later when three men approached our encampment and stood quietly to one side. Our cook went to speak with them and returned to tell my Dad that they wished to talk to him, and to present him with a fish. "Tell them to leave. I don't want any fish," my father said with some disgust.

"No, Sahib, the cook almost pleaded. I think you should hear them out."

Dad sat quietly pondering the advice the cook had given. "All right, tell them I'll listen to what they have to say."

The cook nodded to the men and they came up to where we were sitting and bowed in respect. The spokesman approached a little closer. "Sahib, we have brought this fish which the villagers wish to present to you as a present. We are most honored that you are staying among us, and please accept our humble gift."

"No, I don't want the fish. What do you really want?" Dad suspected that they were making him indebted so they could ask some favor from him. Dad was a government official and had to be careful not to make any commitments that might compromise the government.

"We have no requests of any kind to make, Sahib," the spokesman replied. "All we have come to do is to present you with this fish which my people desire you to have. You would indeed be doing us a favor if you would kindly accept it."

Dad was adamant. Then the cook came close to Dad and whispered something in his ear. Dad's face broke out in a smile and he graciously accepted the fish from the men, asking them to express his deep appreciation and thanks to his fellow villagers. The men quietly departed leaving the fish with the cook.

Turning to us Dad explained his change of mind. This is the story that unfolded. One group of four villagers had caught the fish they had given Dad. Once the basket was plunged to the bottom of the swamp they realized they had caught a prize fish. It was about five feet long and about a foot in its greatest diameter. It was a beautiful specimen with distinct markings along both sides. The Hindus recognized it as a sacred fish, called a cowfish, and so would not eat it and wanted to let it go. But some of the men who had helped catch it were Muslims, who had no qualms about eating it providing they could bleed it before it died. But the Hindus did not wish to have it killed. A struggle ensued. Neither of the parties could get control of the fish, and the fish died without having been bled. Now neither sect would eat it, and the fight erupted; Hindus formed a group, the Muslims an opposing group.

Then some sage among them spoke up. "Why should we fight one another? We are neighbors; we have lived together for years; our children play one with the other. Why not give the fish to the visiting Sahib?" And so Dad had accepted their offer.

The cook proudly sat by the fish as he divided it among Dad's squad of eleven men. That night and the following everyone had all the fish they could eat. Their castes (or possibly because some of them may have been outcastes) did not prevent them from enjoying the treat. And treat it was!

My Double Barrel

Jahluk Bari and hunting went together. Les and I had each gone our separate ways in the morning but without either of us even seeing a single game bird. At around two in the afternoon we decided to go together southward from the campus where there were a series of low rounded hills covered with dense jungle. From there a tiger had roared in the morning! In the late afternoon jungle fowl liked to come out from the dense underbrush and eat in the rice paddies, which filled the valleys between the hills.

We had gone perhaps half a mile when a deer began baying on the hill nearest to us. The sound was like a dog barking; hence the common name applied to it was a "barking deer." We decided to go after it, but who was to get the first shot? We tossed for it and I won. That meant that I would lead and be in front of the others.

We decided to follow a well-used animal track to enter the otherwise virtually impenetrable underbrush. The hill was steep; I was in front, Leslie behind me, and then two of our men. Whenever the deer began to call we walked towards it up the trail, as the animal seemed to be straight ahead. We arrived in easy range when the deer stopped calling. It must have either heard us or sensed our presence. We waited awhile but all was silent. Then Les spoke:

"Let's de-cock." Both of us had ancient guns with full hammers. Before one could discharge the gun it was necessary to place a cartridge in the breech, pull back the hammer, and then pull the trigger. Just before we had heard the deer "barking," Les had asked if he could use my double barrel while I was to use his single barrel. So we had exchanged guns. I had put buckshot into the right barrel and a ball cartridge into the left. He had loaded his gun with buckshot.

When the deer stopped calling us we all stopped. The hill was very steep. I was standing on the highest ground. Les stood behind and below me, so the barrel of his gun was pointing upward and slightly forward. Now I should emphasize the point that in a double barrel, there are two triggers one in front of the other. The front trigger controls the right hammer to the right barrel, while the rear trigger the left hammer and the left barrel. As soon as Les had suggested we de-cock I looked down to locate the single hammer, as I was unfamiliar with his gun. At that very second the hair on the back of my head was blown off! About tent feet ahead of me the bark of a tree shattered as the ball struck it.

Slowly I turned and looked at Les. All the blood had drained from his face and he was as white as a sheet. He had held the right hammer but pulled the rear trigger so the left barrel had discharged! Had I not tipped my head downward at that very moment, I would not be narrating this story. Then Les, with a pained expression, looked at me and slowly but deliberately handed me my gun.

"Take it, this is the last time I'm ever going to us it." He spoke in a soft but emotionally filled voice. With a short prayer of thanks to the Lord, I handed him his gun and I took mine from him. We never traded guns again!

The Assam Survey Training School

Jahluk Bari, as already described, was a village consisting of a small cluster of thatched roof huts scattered between rice paddies, small sugar cane plantings, coconut palms and bananas, with large pepal trees growing between holdings. Along the south boundary of the village began a series of small rounded hills covered with forests with dense undergrowth, teeming with all types of wild life. Between the hills and the village a road ran westward to Gauhati, some eight miles distant. Gauhati was the largest city in the Province of Assam, a province which in the year 1930, was one of the least developed. About two to three miles north of the road and paralleled to it, flowed the Brahmaputra, one of the three large rivers of India, and the third longest in the world.

Turning eastward from Jahluk Bari, on the left side (south) of the road and for some 30 miles were lakes or swamps, which stretched to the hills two to three miles away. This enormous wetland provided an ideal hunting ground. Millions of water birds of every kind wintered between the river and the swamps. Jungle fowl abounded in the forests and green pigeons in large flocks enjoyed the fruit of the pepal trees. Small deer to large samba, along with monkeys of several types, wild pigs, wild cats, leopards and tigers could be seen and heard in the early mornings and late afternoons.

As mentioned before, in this setting the government had built a school to train surveyors. The school campus was across the road from the village and to the west of a moderately size hill. Adjacent to the campus the trees and shrubs had been cleared to the brow of the hill. The cleared hill revealed large granite boulders jutting outward towards the campus. The campus itself consisted of scattered buildings for classrooms, for student residents, and faculty homes. It gently sloped from the hill to the nearest of the swamps, some half mile distant.

Whenever Dad visited the school the family would accompany him. We looked forward to these occasions for we lived in tents and the hunting opportunities were boundless.

Our temporary encampment was at the bottom of the cleared hillside I have already mentioned. Dad and Mother lived in a fairly large tent, Les and I in a smaller one, and then there were tents for the cook, and Dad's squad of eleven men, who were provided every surveyor to aid in his fieldwork. Duck, snipe, jungle fowl, pigeons were our common game, but the thing we dreamed of bagging most was "the leopard."

The Leopard of Jhaluk Bari

There were many leopards that abounded in the forests. The leopard that we dreamed of bagging was one that enjoyed visiting the school campus. It was believed to be a male, and had ravaged the dogs and goats that the faculty had attempted to keep. Despite every precaution taken, sooner or later, their animals disappeared. The village animals had fared no better. Hunters among the faculty and among the ever-changing student body, some of them experienced shikaris, had all had their "go-at-it" without success. Many a machan had been built in forest and campus trees, and long uncomfortable nights spent watching for the stealthy approach of this cunning predator to a tethered goat. Shots had been fired and claims made of mortally wounding the animal, but soon the preying on goats and dogs would continue.

The villagers had come to believe that it was no ordinary leopard but an evil spirit or shitan, and that no effort to kill the animal would be successful. This belief also had permeated Dad's squad of eleven men. It was late one afternoon, February 17, 1932, when it happened. My brother had left about 18 months earlier for college in England. I was to leave in three months for the same purpose since I had completed my high school examinations in November. It would be six months before I would turn eighteen. This was my last chance at the wily leopard.

I had just returned from hunting pigeons, and the sun hung low in the western sky. The short tropical twilight would quickly fade into night. One of my father's men could perfectly imitate the call of a leopard. Using a brass lota, a vessel for carrying water with a narrow neck and large rounded bottom, he would place it on the ground. Crouching over it, he would cup his mouth over the mouth of the vessel, and produce the sounds, haa-harr, haa-harr, haa-harr, breathing out with the first sound and in with the second. It was like sawing wood with a hand saw, the first sound coming from pushing the saw forward, and the second from pulling it backward.

I decided I would try making the call of a leopard. Borrowing a lota, I got down on my hands and knees, cupped my hands over the vessel's mouth, and placed my mouth to my hands. I made two or three calls. To my astonishment, the leopard answered from the direction south of our camp along the lower side of the cleared hill, perhaps two hundred yards away! Calling for the man who was the expert "caller," I grabbed my gun and making the least noise possible, we set off cautiously in the direction of the animal. My man would call and we would then wait. When the leopard answered, perhaps a minute later, we would quietly advance. Then we would stop, wait about a minute, and call again. While the leopard was responding, we would walk in the direction from which the sound came as rapidly as caution and rough ground would permit.

The sun had set by the time we approached a large granite boulder some 30 feet long and 15 feet high. The leopard was on the far side. Since the boulder merged with the hill on the upside, and would disclose us should we track the animal from above, we decided to approach from the downside with the rock rising abruptly to our left.

Sitting on a machan 20 to 30 feet above the ground and taking deliberate aim at a dangerous animal some 30 to 40 feet away is quite different from stalking one on foot. We were now no more than 10 feet from where the returning calls were coming. An outcropping of the rock hid the animal from view. I decided that my man should call once more, then I would wait for the answering call unless the leopard advanced on its part. If it did not, as soon as it began to call, I would step around the rock out-crop and shoot.

The time for which I had waited for years had come. My heart was pounding furiously; my hands even trembled. I kept telling myself, "calm down." I had never done anything like this. What would my friends say? How would it be announced in the papers? "Young man bags long-sought-for leopard on foot!" But what if I missed? Could I get in a second shot in time? I had read many blood-curdling stories of what a wounded tiger or leopard would do. Was I foolhardy and should I turn back? My mind was racing full of irrelevant thoughts, as the seconds ticked off. The whole camp was watching from a distance as darkness rapidly approached. Objects could still, however, be seen reasonably well.

And then the leopard began to call. With gun to shoulder, I stepped around the jutting rock, and there, no more than two inches from the muzzle of my gun was the muzzle of another gun pointed by a hunter in my direction. Behind him, crouched over a lota, was a man making the call of a leopard! Our eyes met, slowly, unbelievingly, we lowered our guns. Then, as we faced each other, burst into laughter. The hunter was one the teachers and we had been stalking each other!

I left in May for England, and never heard of anyone ever shooting the Leopard of Jahluk Bari. Perhaps it died of old age, or perhaps, as the villagers all believed, it was indeed a shitan or evil spirit. Long years ago I gave up hunting and became a conservationist. I have been an ardent birdwatcher for nigh on 40 years. I often think if only someone, when I was a boy, had placed in my hands a pair of binoculars and a bird book to help identify them, how differently I would have approached the wondrous things that God created.

Chapter 3

MY STAY IN ENGLAND

At Newbold Missionary College

I arrived on the campus in September 1932. It was the first time I was to attend a co-educational institution. I had just turned eighteen and, as I may have mentioned earlier, I had never met a girl six years younger or older than me! There just had not been any. My small world was a thing of the past and my education was progressing at a breakneck speed. To sit down at a table for four, with two girls and two boys, was a real experience. I soon fell "in love" with a girl only to discover in a few weeks that she had six other young men on her line! My sex education was abrupt, vigorous, and challenging!

The country was still deep in depression and I still wonder how the matron financed the food we ate. While some complained, I enjoyed my food and had plenty of it, even though we had cabbage and potatoes at least five times a week! The students were assigned to "tables." Two boys and two girls ate together for two weeks and then a re-distribution occurred. One of the boys was the "host" and one of the girls a "hostess." Cafeterias had not been discovered in England at the time. Fellow students served the food to each table and they earned a little for their efforts. During the Sabbath hours the work of the kitchen was done on a voluntary basis. I thought it was a splendid idea.

My brother Leslie was spending his third and last year at Newbold, and chose me as his roommate. It was like old times and he taught me much. The college had been moved from Watford, Hertfordshire, about 20 miles east of London to

Newbold, an old mansion five miles from Rugby. The mansion had been purchased and converted into a school. It was adequate for one hundred and twenty students, teachers, and staff. The boy's dormitory was in the servant's quarters while the girls had the luxury of living in the main building. An artificial lake of some size was in front of the mansion, and the whole estate was surrounded by rich agricultural land. The college was beautifully located.

As much as I hated high school, I loved college. My pleasure was to study in an atmosphere where duress did not exist. To be left to explore to the fullest the parameters of each subject, and to sit at the feet of godly teachers, whose interest in life was to prepare us students for a place in God's work, was for me out of this world. And I enjoyed every moment of it. I took a double major, theology and business (accounting).

Music in our Family

I grew up in a family in which all my siblings had musical skills. My sister, the eldest, obtained her L.R.A.M. (equivalent to a Ph.D.) from the Royal Academy of Music in London. Piano was her instrument. My brother Ivan never tried hard to play any instrument, but he did own a banjo. If he heard a tune, even once, he could, days later, play it perfectly. Leslie, according to my sister, was the most musical of the family. He also made most of the instruments he wanted to play: Hawaiian and Spanish guitars, ukuleles, and the mandolin, which he never cared for. He could play the piano, write the scores for a choir (although he did not sing), and seemed to have the magic touch when it came to music. And then I came along.

My Musical Skills

Everyone expected the same of me. I took piano lessons starting at an early age but did not progress very well. Then my parents bought me a melodeon, but with it I did no better. Finally I was given a mandolin! But no matter how hard I tried, my hand just wouldn't move fast enough to give it the sound of a mandolin. Then

I decided to try a Spanish guitar, one of Les' older models. It seemed one of the real problems was that I could not tune an instrument. I would tune it, but if anyone came along and heard my musical attempts they would immediately say, "Shut it off! Why don't you tune it?"

The first year at Newbold I determined I would master the piano. I faithfully practiced three quarters to an hour and a half per day, five days per week for a full nine months. At the end of that time I couldn't play "Jesus loves me this I know..." without making mistakes! So I gave up trying to make my own music. And then the final blow came.

A new music teacher arrived on the campus. He was a German, young and enthusiastic. His instrument was the violin but he could play the piano, organ, guitar, in fact any instrument you put in his hands. He could both yodel and sing, and, by the way, he had perfect pitch! He wanted to start a choir and announced that anyone who wanted to make a joyful noise was welcome. I had never sung in a choir but the idea sounded good. I joined.

The music teacher and I became good friends. About three months after his arrival we were out for a walk one Sabbath afternoon, when he turned to me. "Mervyn," he said, "I surely appreciate your faithfulness at choir practice, but I wish you weren't so faithful!" And that did it! I gave up music but still enjoy listening to others making it. Now that I have studied biology I realize my DNA never had a musical gene!

Keeping Physically Fit

For reasons I cannot explain I entered upon a program of physical fitness. My brother could not have cared less and that was the attitude of most, if not all the English students. However, the "Keep Fit" programs were spreading from one European country to another, in which the governments encouraged their young people to gain and maintain health and strength for their Motherland or Fatherland. In 1935 the British government sent a delegation to evaluate these programs. They returned with the following summary: "The burning will to achieve strength and physical fitness cannot be maintained other than for some cause greater than self!" World War II was looming on the horizon and the rulers of the European nations were preparing their youth for what lay ahead.

A large number of students, from all over Europe and Scandinavia, came to Newbold to study English. Among these were graduates in physical fitness. In the late afternoons the gym was crowded with these young people engaged in various forms of physical activity. I learned many things from these "teachers." My program started each morning at four. The first twenty minutes was spent in personal Bible study and prayer, after which I took up the studies of the day. At five-thirty I went for a three mile run, and on my return got ready for morning devotions and breakfast. Classes started at seven-thirty.

Learning to Canvass

The college could provide little work for students, so the majority went canvassing (selling religious books) on Sundays. I usually went with a fellow student named Dudley Emma, a superb athlete and a very successful salesman. We would generally select a suburb of some town twenty to forty miles away, bicycle there, do our work until around four in the afternoon and then bike back to Newbold.

However, before a student could graduate from ministerial training he had to have two summers of colporteuring or canvassing experience, which is, as I mentioned above, selling religious books. The method at that time was to go door-to-door. The student colporteur was given an undercoat or sleeveless jacket with two large pockets, one on each side. On one side he usually carried a prospectus, or abbreviated copy of the large book he was offering for sale, and in the other pocket a few small books or booklets which generally sold for a shilling (equivalent to a quarter). The large book could only be sold by colporteurs and was written for the public with this purpose in mind. The smaller books which were used at the time were *Uncle Arthur's Bedtime Stories* (the first four booklets were then available), and *Steps to Christ*.

My First Summer

The first summer of colporteuring required that the student go with a fellow student who had previously canvassed. I went with my future roommate, Eric Zinns, a German boy. We arrived by train at our beginning point, the City of Windermere, in the Lake District of northwest England.

After retrieving our luggage, which included our two suitcases and two bicycles, I asked Eric how we should find a place in which to lodge?

His reply shocked me, "I don't have any idea."

"But didn't you go canvassing last summer?" I inquired with growing apprehension.

"Well, yes, but this is what happened. Because of my German accent, the other two decided to leave me at the station to watch our suitcases and bicycles, while they went to find a place to stay!"

Trundling our bikes we set out to find a rooming house, our small bags strapped to carriers over the rear wheels and our suitcases perched between the saddle and the handlebars. After numerous inquiries and considerable walking we found a place which provided food and lodging (except for lunch). The next day, it was Monday morning, we cheerfully set out to sell our books. We worked long hours, but by Thursday evening neither of us had sold a single book. Friday was the day we were to pay our landlady but we had no money. So we decided we would concentrate on selling shilling books. When we returned that evening we had enough to meet our obligations.

The following week I got one order for the large book, but Eric got none. Friday arrived and we had no money, so again we sold the little books and by evening had sufficient to pay the landlady. We tried the colporteur book one more week with no more success. So we decided to sell shilling books all the time, and show the large book only if the customer showed any interest in current events. We wrote desperate letters to the Publishing Secretary begging for help, but received no response. He was the one in charge of all the canvassers. We found out later that he was swamped by requests for help from all over the field! Others were having the same experience we were.

The problem with the large book was this. The author, Arthur Maxwell, was indeed a brilliant writer. His articles for magazines and journals and his numerous books have been well received. His stories for children, the series of *Bedtime Stories*, are classics, as is also, *You and Your Bible*. These books have been read and appreciated by young and old. But the book by him which we were trying our best to sell, *This Mighty Hour*, described the events associated with the end of the world and the final Battle of Armageddon. When we knocked at a door and the man or woman of the house opened it, our approach was to introduce ourselves as students from Newbold Missionary College (now Newbold College), and that we were selling a wonderful book and would like to show it to them. This usually resulted in an invitation to "come in." As we showed them the contents of the book with its many pictures, using the prospectus as a guide, things went well till we mentioned the possibility of a forthcoming conflict or war. Then things abruptly changed.

"Don't you dare speak of a war. I lost my two sons in the last one," and with angry tears we would be shown the door, which was often slammed behind us. Or it might be, "My husband was killed in 1918; I and my children are without support, and you come here to tell me of another war." With grim looks we would be ushered out. Or perhaps even worse, when we entered a room we would find a sickly-looking man desperately trying to breathe. His lungs had been badly ravaged with the poisonous gas chlorine or mustard gas used during certain phases of World War I. In other homes we would encounter men with no arms or no legs, veterans striving to adjust to the realities of a life with incurable handicaps. And this was in the midst of the Great Depression when healthy men could not find a job! Although Hitler was on the move in Europe, the atmosphere in England was "Peace at any Price!"

So Eric and I decided we would sell the shilling books full time. This meant long hours of canvassing each day. We would often be at work at five or six in the morning, especially when working the farming areas. Farmers get up early and we found it was a good time to meet them. In the towns we often worked till ten at night. Because we were at so high latitude, the sun shone from 3:00 in the morning till ten or eleven at night. Canvassing with the small books burnt up a lot of territory so we covered most of the Lake District. The country was beautiful and the people friendly. We each earned over a half scholarship.

During the next year my plans for colporteuring the following summer slowly formed. A matter that troubled me was the requirement by the Press that a canvasser, to be eligible for a scholarship, must put in a minimum of 400 hours of actual canvassing time during the summer. These hours were not to include travel time, really an impossible task if one was strictly honest. Some of those canvassing would select a block of homes close to where they lived, and would make a call at one of these homes to start the day's work, and then cycle for an hour or more before they actually began to work house to house. Then before returning home at the end of the day, they would make a call at the house next to the one that had been visited first thing in the morning. All the hours from the first knock to the last good night were included in hours worked that day. One schoolmate had a more ingenious plan. He discovered that the house across the street from where he boarded was vacant. So he would knock at the door, wait a minute or so, and the first canvass of the day was logged. In the evening he would again knock at the same door, wait a minute, and not receiving a response, would cross the street and record the hours between his first and last call as actual hours worked!

I was able to stir up enough interest among the students planning to colporteur the next summer to request the Press to give the scholarship on the basis of the amount sold, without the time requirement. To my delight the request was granted.

My Second Summer

The second summer I wanted to sell a book that was strongly Bible oriented, and so I chose *Bible Readings for the Home Circle*. And I hoped that I would be allowed to canvass alone. I was tired and wished to be free to work each day as long as I felt sharp, and not pressured by a companion to do this or that. But this latter desire did not work out. A fellow student, an Indian whose name was Philip and who was a chartered accountant, about 40 plus years of age, was assigned to go with me. He was a fine fellow, but turned out to be a disaster as a sales person. Fortunately he did not like to cycle. So we split the territory assigned us, he took the city in which we set up our base, together with the small communities in the surrounding countryside. I took the more distant towns and communities. It actually worked out quite well.

A Simple Woman

I decided to start my work in the City of St. Andrews, a city famous for its University and its golf course. It was about 50 miles from our base, a beautiful ride through farms and small forests. On my first day, as I arrived at the outskirts of the city, I came to a spinney. A spinney is a relatively narrow forest that may run for several miles following a rather strait course. On occasion a stream may meander in it. Parking my bike, I found a secluded spot among the trees and kneeling down asked the Lord to guide my paths. I did not know how to start, but He did. I rode into the city to find myself in a below average community. The homes were stuck to each other and there were no front or side yards, the front doors opened directly onto the sidewalk.

I had walked 30 or 40 feet down the street when an elderly woman, who was sunning herself in a chair just outside her front door, wished me a cheerful, "Good morning, lad." I stopped and returned the greeting.

"Are you vacationing?" she inquired.

"No," I replied, "I'm working."

"What kind of work do you do?" was her next question.

"If I might step into your home I will be happy tell you," gesturing towards the door.

"Come in, come in," was her immediate response, and arising from her chair led me into her home.

It was a small room. There were two couches facing each other with two or three smaller chairs arranged comfortably. She pointed me to one couch while she sat down on the other. "Now what is it that you are doing?" she once again inquired.

"I'm a student from Newbold Missionary College, near Rugby, England, and am selling religious books in an effort to earn tuition for the upcoming year."

A knock at the door interrupted our conversation. Excusing herself she went to speak to the visitor, returning a couple of minutes later. While she was talking to her friend my attention was drawn to the coffee table directly in front of me. Under its top was a shelf filled with books, and there, right in the center was the book entitled, *Bible Readings for the Home Circle*. Wishing her friend a "goodbye," she returned to her couch and sat down. Apologizing for the interruption, she asked, "Now what were you saying you were doing?"

"Before I answer you, may I ask you a question?" I queried. She nodded her approval.

"While you were talking with your friend I was looking over the books you have under this table, and happened to see a book with the title, *Bible Readings for the Home Circle*. What do you think of it?"

"It's a wonderful book, and one I treasurer. I don't know what I'd do without it," she enthusiastically replied.

"That's the book I'm selling," and pulled out my prospectus so she might see for herself. We were smiling at each other. Finally I asked, "Would you have some friends who might be interested in having a copy of this book?"

"I believe I do. Now let me think." Rising from the couch she went into the kitchen and came back with a pencil and pad of paper. While I watched, and made small talk, she wrote down seven names with their addresses. I thanked her and then asked if she would object if I used her name as a reference.

"Oh, of course you can! In fact, I'll make a point to let them know you'll be coming!"

We shook hands and wished each other goodbye. How could I thank the Lord enough for His wondrous guidance? I sold a copy to every name she gave me. Beyond this each customer gave me other names, and in turn they gave me still other names. I worked about one third of the summer in St. Andrews and remained there until the last name I had been given was visited. The results were fabulous!

"Where next do you want me to go?" I prayed the Lord.

"Go down to Leaven," was the impression I got. Leaven was a coal-mining town along the coast some fifteen miles south of St. Andrews. So I headed for Leaven. The weather was beautiful and as I entered the town at about two in the afternoon, I noticed a grade school to my right. "Perhaps I can sell a few *Bedtime Stories* to the teachers. They might like to have some stories to share with their pupils," I thought to myself. So I rode to the entrance of the school and parked my bike.

A Lowly Custodian

As I entered I noticed a custodian seated in a room to the left. The room had sliding glass windows and overlooked the lobby. As I approached him he asked what he could do for me. I told him I was selling some small books that contained stories that might interest the teachers of the lower grades.

"Please may I see them," he asked. I took out the five books, four *Bedtime Stories* and *Steps to Christ*, and laid them on the counter before him. Glancing at them he picked up *Steps to Christ*.

"Are you interested in religious things?" I inquired.

"I surely am," was his prompt reply.

"Do you study the Bible?" I asked.

"Yes I do."

"Then I have just the book for you." I pulled out the prospectus for *Bible Readings for* the *Home Circle* and handed it to him. From the expression of his eyes I could see at once that he was interested. He looked at a few pages and then, handing it back to me, said,

"I'm on duty now, so cannot pursue the matter further. But I'm interested. Would you be willing to come to my house so I can look it over?"

"I surely can. Please give me your address and I'll be there." He wrote down his name and address and handed it to me.

Just then the bell rang indicating recess time had arrived. "You may go see the teachers now," nodding in the direction of the classrooms. I sold four *Bedtime Stories* and then wished the custodian goodbye saying I would be at his home at a quarter past five.

I rode down to the beach and watched the waves rolling in and the sea gulls floating in the air or standing by the surf making their raucous calls. I strolled up the beach praying that God would bless this contact and give me a start in this new town. Little did I comprehend what lay ahead.

At five-fifteen I knocked at his door which he immediately opened. He ushered me towards the dining table and pulled out a chair for me to sit on. He then sat down and asked for the prospectus and I handed it to him. Slowly and with keen interest he looked it over. "How much is it?" he inquired with obvious anticipation. I told him the cost of each of the three bindings. Without hesitation he ordered a leather-bound copy. "When can I get my copy?" was his next question. "In about ten days I should have it for you," I replied.

As I was writing out the sales slip I turned to him, "Would you know anyone else who might like a copy?" He then explained to me that he was the secretary of a Bible Study Club of thirty-two members, and then added: "Would you like their names and addresses?" And would I! For the next hour I copied the thirty-one names and addresses of the other members of the club. Then with almost uncontrollable joy I bade him goodbye. God had opened before me a path strewn with roses!

Every member of the club bought a book. Of the thirty-one I delivered thirty. One was unable to raise the money. Several of the orders were for the deluxe binding. I obtained numerous names of friends of the club members which, of course, I followed up. What a summer! Just as the names on my list were coming to an end, God had yet another blessing planned for me.

A Battered Looking Insurance Salesman

Where we roomed, the landlady, who was about fifty years of age, had a grown up daughter some twenty-five years old. They were very kind and gracious to us and we enjoyed our stay in Coopar. A life insurance salesman, Ralph Thornbrook, representing some large established company, visited the landlady's home almost every evening. We could not decide whether he was interested in the daughter or mother, or both! He was about five feet

MY STAY IN ENGLAND

seven in height, had buckteeth, was most unprepossessing, always appearing a bit unkempt, tie awry, hair in disarray, but was a most affable fellow. And besides all this he drove a dilapidated Morris Minor car, a two-seater with a fold-back hood.

One evening Philip and I were seated in the front room, having finished our evening meal, when Ralph came in. He greeted every one cordially and sat down. He then said, "Well, me lads, what do you fellows do anyway?" I explained to him that we were both students at Newbold College and were selling books to earn our way through college.

"What kind of books are you selling?" he queried.

I turned to Phil and suggested he show Ralph the books. Phil went to our room and returned with a copy of *Bible Readings* and one of each of the five smaller books. Ralph looked the big book over and then asked: "What's the price?" Phil explained the price of each of the three different bindings.

"I'll take the standard binding," and reached for his wallet.

"Why don't you write it up," I suggested. Poor Phil had sold precious few books.

An Unbelievable Experience!

Ralph turned to me, "Would you like me to introduce you to some of my clients?" he asked with a twinkle in his eye.

"I surely would. When can you do it?" He thought a moment." Would next Tuesday be all right with you?" That's fine with me. What time can we get together?"

"Would eight o'clock be O.K.? I'll be by to pick you up." And with that Ralph began to tell me about his clients.

"You know, lad, my clients are high grade. No common stuff. They're earls and baronets, and knights and lords. High class, you know! You'll see," and with a little chuckle he leaned back in his chair and surveyed the ceiling. I was convinced the guy was a blow hard.

Tuesday morning arrived and he was there promptly at eight. I got into his car and off we went into the country. The hood was down and the wind blew through our hair. "Great morning, I'd say. You'll meet some real high ups today. My clients are the best, earls and baronets, and knights and lords. You don't believe me, do you? But you'll soon see."

In my heart I didn't believe him but I hoped for the best. Soon he slowed down and turned through ornate cast iron gates into a curving driveway that led to the front entrance of a huge mansion. He parked right in front of the steps and ushered me to the door. With a flourish be pressed the bell. A few moments later the door opened and a maid appeared. "Oh, Mister Thornbrook, I'm so glad to see you. Won't you come in? I'm sure Lady Manly will be happy to see you. She's in the library. I'll go see if she will."

With that, the maid ran up the curving staircase and disappeared into a doorway. She was back in a moment. "Won't you come up? Lady Manly will be happy to see you." We mounted the stairs and were led into a large room, the library. Lady Manly arose and walked towards us. "So glad to see you Ralph, I wondered when you would be by. How are you doing?" They exchanged greetings. Then Lady Manly spoke: "Do please sit down, won't you. And who is this young man with you?" Ralph did the talking.

Lady Manly interrupted Ralph's flowery introduction. "So you're a college student trying to earn your way. And isn't that noble of you to sell books all summer? I'd like to see what kind of books you have." I pulled out my prospectus and showed it to her. She looked at it with but little interest and than asked, "How much does one cost?" I mentioned the price of the three bindings, and immediately realized I had made a mistake. "I'll take the standard binding," and opening her checkbook, wrote out a check. "Deliver it at the tradesman's entrance,' and with that she turned to Ralph. They both chatted away for a few minutes and then she arose and walked with us to the head of the stairs. "Come again when you can, Ralph. You know you're always welcome." Then with a smile she said to me, "Young man, every success as you pursue your college education."

The maid ushered us out and watched us drive away. We had only driven a few yards when Ralph turned to me. "You chump! Only the best for my clients; the leather binding!" I didn't need to be told. I had seen my mistake. And that was the story the rest of the day, mansion after mansion, the same welcome, the same cordial greetings, and a leather bound book, paid for, and to be delivered at the tradesman's entrance.

Ralph stopped at a country Inn and paid for my lunch. The afternoon was like the morning, doormen, butlers, and maids; Lords and ladies, knights and earls. It was unreal; unbelievable; a lovely dream; something out of this world! As he left me off at our lodging, he asked with a chuckle, "Would you like me to take you out again?" I didn't have to answer. He took me out for two more days. My sales sky rocketed.

What a God! The verse in the Bible rang in my ears, "Commit your ways unto the Lord, . . . and He will direct your paths." And another lesson engraved in my mind and one that I have never forgotten, don't judge by outward appearances. God uses the humble of this earth to do his bidding. A simple woman, a lowly custodian, and a battered looking life insurance agent were instruments of God to encourage a young student to trust His guiding hand.

Graduation!

My folks visited relatives in Australia after they left India. They arrived in England shortly before my graduation, and watched the ceremonies with both interest and joy. Anyone who has had a child or close relative or friend graduate knows just how it feels. It was a great occasion as I received my diplomas in Ministerial and Business.

Dad and Mother were living with my sister and her husband in a suburb of London, East Finchley. It was their plan to become acquainted with different areas of England, and then to buy a home for their retirement years. But this was not to happen as events in my life, and experiences in theirs, changed our destinies beyond our wildest dreams!

Soon after I was graduated from Newbold Missionary College in May 1935, I received a call from the President of the British Union Conference (of SDAs). He wondered if I might be interested in doing Ingathering during the summer. The proposal was that I would be employed at the salary of a starting minister and my responsibility would be to work with the pastors of some of the large cities in South England. I would then do Ingathering among the wealthy homes of the particular city where the local church members did not do so. All contributions received would be forwarded to the Union office, half the proceeds being retained by the Union and the other half sent to the local church. Among the cities I worked in, were various suburbs of London, Bournemouth, and Bristol.

A Summer of Ingathering

I dressed like the young graduates of other colleges, a white shirt, tie, gray flannel trousers, a blue blazer with the emblem of the school from which I was graduated (in this case Newbold Missionary College, Rugby, England), black belt and black shoes. To reach the wealthy an appropriate approach was necessary. My brothers Leslie and Arthur Maxwell of *Bedtime Stories* fame prepared a booklet and a can with the aide of the Stanborough Press.

The document consisted of a small loose-leaf booklet, containing about eight pages of heavy glossy paper, bound in black morocco leather with the words printed in gold on the cover, "British Advent Missions – For Humanity's Sake." Inside the front cover was my permit from the police. The pages carried photographs of the various aspects of the work of the Church with appropriate captions. It covered the physical (medical work), mental (educational activities), and the spiritual mission of the church. The last two pages provided space for the donor to sign his/her name and the amount given. One page was for contributors (one-time donors), the other for subscribers (those who would donate the amount specified year after year). The can (5" by 3" by 1") bound in black morocco leather had the same logo on the front of the can as was carried by the booklet. This was for those who, when contributing, did not wish to be identified by name. An appropriate slot on one side of the can allowed for the deposit of both coins and paper money.

Should a cheap looking Ingathering magazine be presented, the outcome was usually a total refusal to give, or the offering of a few paltry coins.

The Blockade of the Wealthy

To reach the wealthy residents of these large cities required much prayer and considerable courage. Maids and butlers were paid to keep salesmen and solicitors out! To get past these "barriers" became quite a game. I remember clearly one such residence. My brother Leslie had tried every year for three successive years without gaining access to the master or mistress of the home. After Les was graduated I took over his district in one of the suburbs of London.

When I rang the bell, the butler Les had described appeared. He looked at me quizzically.

"You were here last year and I told you you're not getting in. In fact, you've been here three times in all. Thank you and good day."

With that he started to close the door but I immediately responded: "I beg your pardon but this is the first time I've ever rang this doorbell."

He stopped short, stepped outside the half-closed door onto the porch, and carefully studied my face. "Oh, yes you have," he said.

"No, I haven't, and please tell your master I'm waiting to see him."

He was somewhat taken aback. He hesitated. "Do you have a twin?" he inquired.

"No, I don't," I said.

"Then you must be his brother?" (He was referring to Les).

"That I am," I replied with a smile.

We both laughed. And with a broad smile he said: "I want to tell you, young man, I'm paid to keep 'thems like you out, and that's what I'm a-doing." And with a smile he bid me a good day and closed the door.

I rang his bell the next year and the next. He would always greet me with a warm smile but I never got by him! However, whenever one did reach the master or mistress of one of these mansions, the harvest was usually a bountiful one.

Ingathering on the Island of Guernsey

About mid-summer I received another call from the Union President asking whether I would do Ingathering on the Island of Guernsey. The Islands of Jersey and Guernsey or Channel Islands are famous for the milk cattle that were raised there. The islands are not far off the coast of France, but are owned by the British. In the thirty's they were still regulated by ancient religious laws. The president had attempted the previous year to do Ingathering on the Island of Jersey. However, towards the evening of the first day he was apprehended by the police, his books were confiscated, all donated money had to be returned, and he was placed on a ship that evening and sent back to England! "With this in mind," he inquired, "would I try the Island of Guernsey?" I agreed.

Arriving in Guernsey by boat, I found lodging in the home of a widow. She provided my morning and evening meals. She turned out to be an excellent cook, and the milk provided had a fat content of 7%! The richest milk I have ever had to drink! And was it good! Those were the days when nobody was aware of cholesterol, fatty acids and arteriosclerosis. Ignorance was surely bliss, or was it?

I walked to every home on the Island starting with the homes along the coast and the farms. Finally, I did the major city on the Island. I had no problems with the police or anyone. It was a delight to meet people who had rarely if ever been solicited. And they were generous. Each day, the contributions exceeded what I collected in a week in England, and often very much more.

A Great Experience

One day I came to a large mansion that faced the ocean. The view was magnificent. I rang the doorbell. A maid opened the door and I greeted her.

"May I see the man of the house?" I inquired.

"Please, will you step in? The master is in his study. Let me see if he will see you." With that she went up a sweeping stairway. She soon returned.

"Please follow me. The master will see you." She led me into a large room, the library, with bookcases of various sizes placed in and around the room. Towards the front of the room was a huge curving window that looked out to sea. A large mahogany desk was strategically placed so as to exploit every point of the magnificent view. Behind the desk sat a large man in a gigantic (it seemed to me) high-backed leather upholstered chair. He pointed to a chair placed at one end of the desk.

"What is it that brings you here, young man?" he inquired in a deep voice. I told him and briefly showed him the pictures in the leather bound booklet. Leaning back in his chair and looking me in the eyes, he said, "I'm not interested in missions. But since you took the time to tell me about what you are doing, I'll give you a trifle." There upon he took a check book from the desk drawer and with fascinated eyes I watched him write a check for £5 (a handsome contribution of $25 during the depression. In today's exchange it would doubtless be equivalent to $250). Then in large letters and with a flourish, he signed his name, "Ernest Hemingway!"

Needless to say, my experience on the Island of Guernsey was not only profitable, but also immensely enjoyable. As I boarded a ship for England I thanked and praised the Lord for his multiple blessings.

My Sheffield Experience

While still Ingathering during the late summer after graduation, I received a call from the British Union President informing me that I had been hired by the North England Conference, and was to work with a Pastor Madgwick in Sheffield, England. I was to start my duties on the first day of October. The news was a delight to my ears! Thank you, Lord, I prayed; for during those depression years, few if any, new pastors were being added to the work force. I arrived in Sheffield a few days early, found a suitable lodging place, and then introduced myself to Pastor and Mrs. Madgwick. They turned out to be delightful people.

My responsibilities were to be the assistant pastor of the Sheffield church, and work with Pastor Madgwick in an already planned evangelistic series. October 1 that year was on a Monday. I met Pastor Madgwick at eight-thirty that morning. He drove a Morris Minor. In it we toured areas of the city and studied billboards where advertisements for the forthcoming meetings might be advertised. He let me off about twelve-thirty and I took a streetcar that took me to within a few blocks of my lodging.

God Spoke to Me

I had walked two of the five blocks to my home and was crossing an intersection, when a voice said to me, "You must take the medical course!" It stopped me in my tracks. I looked in all directions and there was not a soul in sight. I'm not sure how long I stood there, perhaps a minute, perhaps longer. As I started again towards home I decided it was the Devil who was trying to sidetrack me. I did my best to banish the command from my mind and threw myself into my work with everything I had.

I had never thought of taking the medical course. My eldest brother, Ivan, was a physician and a graduate of the University of London medical school. He was practicing in the City of Wimbledon. I had visited with him on several occasions, but the idea of medicine never entered my mind, and if it did, I rejected it immediately. My goal from the age of sixteen was to be a foreign missionary. I had committed myself to the Lord to do just that. My ministerial education was over, I was embarked on my two years of training in the British Isles, after which I planned for service abroad. And now the Devil was after me!

All through October, November, and most of December the battle raged in my mind. Was it the Devil or was it the Lord? Was the Devil determined to lead me away from what God wanted me to do? If I took medicine I would make more money, but money had never tempted me. Was it all a figment of my imagination? But try as I would, every waking moment when I was not concentrating on something I was doing, that voice would ring in my ears, "You must take the medical course." The Divine directive was unequivocal; it was clear, concise, and commanding! I would awaken in the night with the voice saying, "Mervyn, you must take the medical course." Had I not been the first and only member of my graduating class to be hired? God had signally blessed me in my Ingathering and Colporteur work. Why should I take medicine? There were others I knew who would give anything to be medical doctors. Why me? Then, one day, the thought entered my mind: "Maybe God wanted me to be a medical missionary." I still did not want to do what I had been bidden, and had serious doubts as to whether it was God or Satan? I told no one of my experience.

A Long Delayed Decision

Christmas that year (1935) was on Sabbath and the plan was that we were to have a family reunion at the home of Phyllis and Bert. They lived in East Finchley, a suburb of London. Bert was then the president of the South England Conference. My parents were living with them at the time, planning to purchase a retirement home in the spring.

Thursday (December 23) had all but passed. It was nine o'clock. I had been studying and praying that God would help me to make the right decision regarding this strange command that I should take medicine. These verses in Scripture were spinning in my head, "Commit your ways unto the Lord, and lean not unto your own understanding. In all your ways acknowledge Him and He will direct your paths." Could I bring myself to do that? What would people think?

Then I got down on my knees as I had done many, many times before, and lifted up a prayer to heaven. "Lord, you know all about the struggle I am having. You know I want to do what you want me to do. But Lord, I don't like the thought of taking medicine. However, if You want me to do it, I'll do it, and I'll do it as if it was the only thing I ever wanted to do in life. I have no money and I assume you would want me to take it (medicine) in "Your medical school" (I knew the Church had a School of Medicine somewhere in the United Sates but did not know its name or where it was located). It's now in Your hands, and if I am doing the right thing, please open the way. Thank you, thank you, for hearing my prayer. In Jesus name."

I rolled into bed. My mind was at peace. I slept better than I had for many months.

The Evangelistic Meetings

The Evangelistic meetings were going well, and Pastor Madgwick seemed to have no difficulty in holding his audience to a full house. One of my responsibilities was to make weekly visits to a number of the most interested attendees. My economic state was tight, to say the least. Even to ride a streetcar was most of the time too expensive. And then many of the homes were some distance from a bus or a streetcar stop. So I rode a bicycle.

A Cat and a Dog

The City of Sheffield is built on a number of hills and some of the roads are quite steep. I had just completed a "call" and was riding down a very steep street. I noticed a woman with a dog on a leash coming up the sidewalk to my right. And then it happened. It seemed like a flash! The dog spotted a cat that had just decided to cross the street, and dashed towards it and the leash slipped from the owner's grasp. The cat sped for its life and shot straight into my front wheel.

The next moment I was sailing through the air having left my bike behind. To my utter amazement I landed on my feet, ran a few steps forward, and regained my balance! I turned to see the cat extricating itself from the spokes, and the dog, with a curious look on its face, looking on!

The cat got free and dashed to the opposite side of the street while the lady regained the leash. I examined my bike and, to my joy, it was still in perfect shape. I continued on my ride with a few cat hairs still clinging to the spokes!

The moral is, don't get mixed up with a dog and a cat!

A Slip of the Tongue

It was during one of Pastor Madgwick's sermons. The meetings were held once each week in a large YMCA convention hall, seating some six to seven hundred people. One of the regular attendees was a very large man. He was well over six feet tall and doubtless weighed at least four hundred pounds! He had an enormous belly, and always sat in the back row next to one of the entrance doors. The sermon, I cannot remember what the subject was, was dealing with Christ's feeding of the five thousand. The pastor was in a serious mode, when quite abruptly he summarized what he had been saying by referring to Christ as having fed the multitude with "three small loaves and two barley fishes!"

A wave of merriment swept over the audience but because the Pastor was oblivious to what he had said, everyone tried to suppress their laughter. I was seated on the platform and was having a difficult time myself. Others were also struggling with their emotions. And then of all things, I happened to look at our obese friend. He too was obviously desperate. On his face was an agonized look. Suddenly he slapped one hand and then the other over his mouth and heaved up and down. His whole frame undulated and shook like a gigantic bowl of Jell-O!

And that did it. I burst out laughing and when I did, everyone in the room roared with laughter! It was some time before things settled back to normal. Meanwhile the preacher, with only a surprised look and merely a slight hesitation, continued on his subject.

When the meeting was over and the guests had left, he came over to where his wife, a Bible worker, and I were standing. Turning to his wife he queried, "What was so funny about what I said?" She looked at him and replied, "You and your three small loaves and two barley fishes!"

And this reminds me of what my mother would tell us boys from time to time:

"A slip of the lip is no fault of the mind,

And those who remark it are very unkind!"

The First Elder of the Sheffield Church

A few days after arriving in Sheffield I received an invitation to have tea with a Brother Casson (as he was called), the first elder of the church. The purpose of the get-together soon became apparent. He let me know that all the major decisions regarding church activities were to be made by him! He ran the church! I learned later that what he said had been true. If the Pastor, for example, crossed him in any way, he started meetings in his home and more than fifty per cent of the members would follow him! He had run out the past three pastors assigned to the Sheffield church! He meant business.

Two or three weeks later I was elected to be the Sabbath School superintendent. The church had sixty or seventy attending members. I called the teachers of the various divisions together. One of the things I emphasized was that the Sabbath School should start on time. All agreed and there were no objections raised. Whenever I had been superintendent of a Sabbath School, I always studied the lesson and would teach if a teacher did not show up. So I went to Sabbath School all prepared. The teachers were all present five minutes before nine-thirty, the time Sabbath School was scheduled to begin.

Nine-thirty arrived and I said to those going up on the platform, "Let's go." Nobody moved!

"What's the matter?" I asked in surprise.

"Brother Casson has not as yet arrived and we never start Sabbath School until he's here." They spoke in unison.

"When does he usually arrive?" was my next question.

"We never know; sometimes ten o'clock, sometimes ten-thirty, and on occasion it might be as late as eleven."

To say that I was shocked is an understatement. I could not believe what I was hearing! "Its past nine-thirty and we must not be late. Let's go." I spoke with as much authority as I could muster. As we walked down the center isle all eyes were on us. When they looked around for Brother Casson and realized he was not there, the looks on the faces of the congregation were incredulous. The program went as planned. I noticed the surprised look on the faces of all late comers as they came and found that Brother Casson was not present!

When we separated for classes all the teachers were there except for Brother Casson, so I taught his class. The study time was almost over when I saw Brother Casson enter the church. It was now his turn to look surprised. He stood there surveying the scene. Then he came over to his class. He wished each one good morning and made the circle shaking the hand of each member. He then came over and stood beside to me.

"I'll teach the remainder of the lesson." He tried to push me aside.

"No, Brother Casson, would you please sit there (pointing to an empty chair), and I'll finish the lesson." I finished the lesson, but I don't think any member of class heard what I said. Their looks told me how unbelievable were the events transpiring before their eyes.

There was no hesitation the following Sabbath to start Sabbath School at nine-thirty. I noticed a new spirit among the members. Again I taught Brother Casson's class. Again he came late, but not as late. Again he tried to push me aside and start teaching. I again asked him to sit down and that I would finish the lesson! He never came to Sabbath School at nine-thirty but was always there when the members separated to go to their classes. I never had to teach his class again!

The attitude of the entire church changed for the better, for he never regained the control over the church that he had exercised through the years. Sixteen years after leaving Sheffield I met a Mr. Morris Mustoe, one of the deacons of the church while I was there. He told me that Mr. Casson had died a few years back, but that he had never run the church from the time that first Sabbath School was held on time!

A Miracle of Miracles

It was Christmas morning and the whole family went to Sabbath School and Church. We then returned to Phyllis' home for Christmas dinner. Dinner over everyone wanted to go for a walk except Mervyn; I just didn't want to go. It was a beautiful afternoon, and although snow covered the ground, the sun was shining brightly.

"Aren't you feeling well?" they all inquired with surprise and concern.

"I feel fine, but I just don't want to go for a walk. You go and have a good time. I'm O.K."

Then Mother spoke up. "I'll stay with Mervyn. You folks go along."

"No, Mother, you don't need to stay with me. I'm fine; there is nothing wrong with me. I just don't want to go for a walk." I felt like Peter on the housetop before the Gentiles arrived!

"Son," my Mother spoke in her quiet but firm voice, "I have decided to stay with you. Let the others go for a walk." Everyone knew that that decision was final. They left, and Mother and I returned to the house.

Mother and I were seated in the front room by the small, coal fire. I could not understand why I felt like I did about the walk. I was considered "Mr. Exercise," as I was the one who was forever promoting some form of physical activity. Then mother spoke:

"Mervyn, now that the house is quiet and everyone else has gone, I want to share with you something that no one else knows except Daddy (she always called my father 'Daddy'). Daddy and I have decided that we are not going to stay in England. It's too cold. We hate it. Daddy doesn't like to wear an overcoat; he won't put on his gloves, or go outside. He just sits by the fire from the time he gets up till he goes to bed. If we don't go where it's warmer, he is going to die."

She paused for a moment. "Phyllis and Bert are settled, so is Ivan and his family, and Les and Molly are happy where they are. You are the only one who is single and not settled. Now we don't want you to do anything that would upset your plans for the future. You are old enough to plan for your own career. But we would like to take you with us."

Neither of us said anything. We sat gazing into the fire. Then she spoke again. "We have written to Australia where we have relatives, and to South Africa where we also have relatives, and to California where we have friends. We have checked the climates and the exchange rates for our finances."

"Mother," my voice was filled with surprise and wonder, "if I were to leave England now, nobody knows me. I haven't established any kind of reputation for myself."

"I know, son. We have thought of that. If we go to Australia we will send you to Avondale; if we decide to go to South Africa you can go to Helderberg; and if we go to California and you want to take the medical course we will help you!"

I could not believe what I was hearing. Was I having a dream? I sat looking at the flames of the fire for a long time. Then I told

Mother what had been going on in my life since the voice spoke to me on October 1, and the decision I had made last Thursday evening.

"We are going to California." Mother spoke with finality. "We should plan on it for next summer. I'll write to the medical school and tell them you are coming."

The Beginning of an Unexpected Life

That Christmas in 1935 was a drastic turning point in my life. God had spoken and He had worked it out in a way in which I would never have dreamed. My obligation to my parents was to repay the cost of my medical education, payments to begin following graduation. I sold everything I had, my stamp collection, my butterfly, moth, and beetle collections, and my collection of birds' eggs. The money I thus raised was exactly the cost of my ship fare from Southampton to San Francisco. My parents, my younger brother Allan, and I traveled on a German freight boat. The average number of passengers was eight people, four of whom were Hardinges! After leaving England the ship stopped at various ports, loading and unloading. It passed through the Panama Canal and up the western coast of North America. What a delightful trip we had. It took forty-nine days!

And now a new life began at Pacific Union College.

Chapter 4

PREPARING FOR MEDICINE

My Year at Pacific Union College

It took my parents, Allan, and I all day to get through customs, immigration, and the Department of Agriculture. Everything we owned was opened and checked. My Dad was so angry by evening that he was all but ready to go back to England! A Dr. Cobb, a Professor of English, was acting as finance officer for the College at the time. He was there at dockside when we arrived and stayed with us all day long. He took us at 10 PM for our first meal of the day. Dr. Cobb was a prince of a man.

In those days it took over two hours to travel from San Francisco to the College. We were about an hour away from PUC when Dad asked Dr. Cobb if he had a house reserved for us. I believe Dr. Cobb drove probably ten miles before he answered. When it had been decided I would attend Pacific Union College Dad had written asking that a house be reserved for them. Dr. Cobb had replied that if a deposit of a certain amount were sent he would reserve a house. This Dad had done. But Dr. Cobb had forgotten!

No houses were available to rent or buy in the Pacific Union College area! Dr. Cobb took Dad and Mother into their home, while Allan and I stayed in the guest room of the boy's dormitory. The following evening Allan and I were invited to the Cobb's home for supper. During the meal Mother wanted to show Mrs. Cobb some artifact she had brought with her; it was in my suitcase in the guest room. Since the dorm was just across the street from the Cobb's home I ran across to get it.

When I arrived at the front steps of the dorm some twenty to thirty boys were on the porch and along the stairs. They were talking and laughing. The lights were out. I knew where the guest room was and had no trouble finding my suitcase. But rummage around as I would I could not find the artifact. So I went out to the porch and innocently asked, "Would someone please lend me a torch?" There was silence and then some tittering.

"What's a torch?" someone asked.

"It is what you hold in your hand, push a switch and a light comes on," I replied. There was general laughter.

"Torch, torch, whatever is a torch?" There was a chorus of voices.

Then from the depths of the lobby a voice boomed out, "Lend that bloody Englishman a flashlight!" I later met that "voice." It belonged to a boy from South Africa called Gerald Ingle, who was also taking pre-med. We became friends.

Next day Dr. Cobb came up with a solution to our house problem. There was a piece of property that had been given to the College on which was a tumble down shack, or so he called it. The school would rehabilitate it for us. And they did. It was twenty by twenty feet outside dimensions. There were three rooms, the living-dining room area, a small kitchen, and an even smaller bedroom. A back screened-in porch, five feet wide, ran the full length of the house. Part of the porch was used to construct a bathroom; it had not had such a facility!

Two or three weeks later we moved in. Allan slept in the dining area, I in the back porch, and the folks squeezed into the bedroom. We loved it. It was the best house we had ever lived in! It had screens on the windows and doors to keep the flies and mosquitoes out. It had a wood-burning range and cook stove in the kitchen, hot and cold running water in the kitchen and bathroom, and a flush toilet! What more could one ask for!

Starting Classes

We arrived two weeks late for the school year. I had never taken a course in science or biology so had to take all the major science courses required for pre-medicine: general physics, general chemistry and its sub-groups, and biology or zoology and its sub-groups. This required I take a full load. Dr. Raymond Mortensen, who was head of the science division and my pre-med advisor, informed me I was required to take one religion course. It was finally decided that I take the "Spirit of Prophecy" class.

The studies at PUC were a dream come true. I loved every minute of every class, and drank the information in as dry land does water. I especially enjoyed chemistry. The "Spirit of Prophecy" class was taught by Dr. Mary MacRenolds, a physician by training. As I reported earlier, we arrived two weeks late and all the courses were in full swing. The first class of hers I attended was an enigma. Dr. MacRenolds spoke of the Spirit of Prophecy as a person. Other strange terms were used: the Messenger of the Lord, the Modern Prophet, and the Servant of the Lord. Who was she talking about? Everyone else in the class seemed to understand. Being a stranger in a strange land I hesitated asking.

When I went home that evening I asked my folks if they had ever heard of the "Spirit of Prophecy?" They hadn't. How about the Modern Prophet, or The Servant of the Lord? The Lord's Messenger? All these titles drew a blank. In the next lecture I fared no better. But again, I was hesitant to inquire. It was during the third lecture that it suddenly dawned on me that Dr. MacReynolds was speaking of Ellen G. White! I thought it was blasphemy!

Now I knew of Ellen White. I had one or two of her books, and as a religious author I enjoyed reading her literary works. But that she was inspired? A prophet of God? No, no! I was shaken and so were my parents. We all diligently studied my notes and all reading matter provided, and we all could easily have received A's in the class! But at the end of the course I was not convinced. I accepted her as an excellent religious writer, enjoyed reading her books, but that she was inspired, no. It is interesting to note that Leslie, my brother, and I had both taken theology at Newbold Missionary College and we had never heard that Ellen White was inspired. Also, we had met missionaries in India from the United States and Australia, were acquainted with a reasonable number of ministers in England, and never once had we heard of the possibility that Ellen White was inspired!

Purchasing a Car

The home we lived in was a mile from the college if one followed the direct route. However the road was not paved and part of it was up a steep hill only navigable with a truck. Another circuitous route was approximately three miles in length, too far for my folks to walk. They decided they would buy a car. After counseling with friends they decided to buy one delivered at the factory in Detroit, as cars in the east cost far less than did those in the west. So I was to go back east during my Christmas vacation and drive the vehicle to California.

Obtaining a License

But now we had to get a license. Dad had driven in India so had a license from there. Since one had to be eighteen years of age to obtain a license, and I turned eighteen after arriving in England, I had obtained a license in England. One of our neighbors was a Canadian lady who had a car and was also seeking to get a license. So it was agreed that the three of us would go down to Saint Helena and get licenses.

At that time the Motor Vehicles office was only open two mornings a week. Mrs. C drove over to our home with great difficulty. She was just learning to drive and unable to park or back up! My Dad was never a good driver and was extremely nervous. So I was delegated to drive to the office. On the way it was decided that I was to get my license first, then Dad, and finally Mrs. C.

When we entered the office the officer was chatting with two gentlemen and the secretary was listening to the conversation. I approached the officer:

"How can I help you?"

"I would like to get a license," I responded.

"Have you ever driven before," he inquired?

"Yes, in England."

"May I see your license?" I presented my license. It was something he and the others in the room had never seen. A little booklet, about 3" by 2.5," with a black shiny cover with a gold crown imprinted on the cover. They began to laugh as did another couple who happened to come into the office. They were still laughing when the officer said to his secretary

"Give him a license!"

As I stepped to the side and towards where the secretary worked, Dad faced the officer. "I would like a license too," Dad said nervously.

"And where did you drive last.?

"India." There was a titer of laughter.

"Do you have a license?" he inquired.

"Yes." And Dad produced his Indian license. It too resembled my English license, but it was much larger, probably 5" by 3 ¼", black with a large ornate gold crown imprinted on the front cover. The group fell apart, handing it from one to the other. Stifling his laughter for a moment the officer almost shouted to his secretary, "Give him a license!"

And then Mrs. C stepped to the counter.

"And where do you come from," the officer spoke while restraining his merriment.

"Canada," she responded. And that was it. The room, now almost full of the curious, roared with laughter. This seemed the funniest thing they had ever seen. Still laughing the officer turned towards his secretary for the third time: "Give her a license!"

Fifteen minutes later the three of us drove back up the hill to Pacific Union College, each with an American license. The relief Dad felt was only exceeded by the relief Mrs. C was showing. She could but barely restrain herself while tears coursed down her cheeks. "Wonderful, how wonderful," she kept repeating. And, indeed, how wonderful it was!

The Loaded Revolver

Sometime during the school year, between Sabbath School and the Church service, Gerald suggested I come to his room after Sabbath, as he had something he wanted to show me. I arrived at his room later that evening. He asked me to close the door. Going over to his dresser he reached into the lowest draw and from under some clothes pulled out a hand-gun, a .22-caliber revolver. He then began flourishing it around. Pointing at this object or that, he would say, "Bang, bang!" Then he began pointing it at me, at my head, my heart, at all parts of my body, each time saying, "Bang, bang!"

"Don't point it at me," I said in a loud voice. But he continued. "Don't," I shouted. "Don't point it at me again!" He would not listen. Then I yelled, "If you point it at me again, I'm leaving." With that he swung the gun up above his head and came down in an arc. As the gun barrel was directed to the floor between us, he pulled the trigger. The revolver discharged! Slowly he turned towards me. He was as white as a sheet. All the blood had drained from his face.

"I'm sorry," were the words that came from his lips. "Please, I'm so sorry. I was sure I had unloaded every chamber." Then I pointed to the hole in the linoleum where the slug had entered.

"Wonder what the ceiling downstairs looks like?" I remarked.

The blood that was returning to his cheeks immediately vanished. He looked at me with a scared look. Generally the exit point of a bullet makes a much larger hole than where it entered. Gerald understood this and he and I pictured a large rupture in the ceiling of the room below. This would put him in real trouble. Perhaps he would be kicked out of school.

"Let's go and take a look," I suggested. "You make talk with the student whose room it is, and I'll survey the ceiling."

So we went down and at his knock and the call from within, "Come in," we entered the room. I have no idea what Gerald and his fellow student talked about, but I carefully examined the ceiling. It was perfect. Absolutely nothing had happened! The slug had hit a floor or ceiling joist, and, as we checked later, had only gone a short way into the wood. What luck!

I don't know what happened to the handgun. Gerald never brought the subject up again, and neither did I, but I'm sure

Gerald never pointed a gun at someone else again. I thanked the Lord that my brains had not been blow out.

In mid-summer my family and I moved to Loma Linda, where another chapter in my life began to unfold.

Courtship and Marriage

In the spring of the year, while still at Pacific Union College, I set my eyes on one of the girls, Margaret Feldkamp. She was a junior student and graded papers for the physics department part of the time. We began to go out with one another, then to date regularly, and by the end of the summer became engaged. She returned to college and completed her senior year. Following graduation, with a major in chemistry, she trained as a lab technologist. Two years following our engagement and after I had finished my first two years of medicine, we were married. That was 65 years ago! And she has been a faithful wife ever since and may her tribe increase.

Our Honeymoon

Let me tell you about our honeymoon! We were dirt poor, so we decided to go camping in the mountains about 10 miles from Loma Linda. Margaret borrowed from relatives and friends everything we would need, a tent, folding iron camp bed, some blankets, cookware, cutlery, plates, and a gasoline stove on which to cook our food. I had bought a kerosene oil lantern (which our daughter keeps as a keepsake). Everything was loaded in our car and following the reception we headed for the hills. We spent the first night in a motel. Next morning, we found a campsite and pitched our tent. It was Friday and we were all set up for Sabbath and a few days to follow.

At around five in the evening Margaret asked me to light the stove. I had never used a gasoline stove before. "Take it a little distance from the tent and pump it up before you light it," my wife instructed me. As I pumped it and the pressure in the gas tank increased, streams of gasoline shot out at several points of the stove. "This doesn't look right," I called to my wife. "Come and see."

She came over and gave one look. "Better turn it off. It will be dangerous to use. We'll need to have cold meals until we can collect some wood on Sunday."

She returned to the camp table and then exclaimed, "Oh, no! All the cutlery, knives, forks, and spoons were never transferred from my brother Bud's car to ours! Now what are we to do?" There were no other campers in the campground from which we might borrow an implement or two. We searched through all our belongings and found a metal shoehorn and a bread knife. The knife had been handed to us as we were driving away from the reception. At least we had something!

We enjoyed our supper although it was not on the planned menu. We then went for a walk by the lake that adjoined the campground and returned ready for bed. The site on which the tent was situated sloped slightly so we had found some stones to put under the legs of the camp bed to level it. The bed, now a relic of the past was composed of two halves, hinged together. Each half was about 2 feet wide by 6 feet long made of heavy angle iron. Wire mesh made taut by springs supported the mattress. The double frame was held flat by latches top and bottom. It stood on four iron legs. It was a work of art but not conducive to be carried more than a few feet from a motor vehicle! It was heavy! On the "wire mattress" a thin pad was placed and then the blankets. It was before the sleeping bag era.

The Folding Bed

It was the second night of married life! It was decided that Margaret was to get into bed first. In due time, I came along and lay down on my half of the bed. It immediately folded down the middle where it was hinged! With some difficulty we extricated ourselves from the contraption. "You didn't latch it right," was Margaret's comment.

So we righted the monster, and very deliberately I latched it top and bottom. She got in and then I did. The bed's response was immediate, it folded, and once again we were intimately together!

As we struggled to free ourselves from our unintended embrace, Margaret said with a tinge of irritation in her voice, "You didn't latch it right."

When we had straightened things around, I suggested that she latch it this time. She did. Then she got in and so did I and immediately we were face to face and side by side! Things were heating up, and we were gaining experience in untangling ourselves! "I think the thing is broken," was Margaret's controlled remark. "Let's sleep on the ground." And to this I heartily agreed.

But the floor of the tent sloped! I took the down side and spent much of the night trying to push my dear wife off. It was quite a night. Believe me.

But aren't honeymoons to get acquainted?

My Years of Medical Studies

In those days Loma Linda was a small village and the majority of the residents were employees or ex-employees of the Sanitarium or the Medical School. Besides the first two years of medicine, there was a School of Nursing, and a School of Nutrition and Dietetics—the latter with a very small student enrollment. The number of students to be accepted for the freshman year of medicine was ninety-six.

The spiritual atmosphere on the campus was strong. That was what the College of Medical Evangelists was all about. Although the majority of students did not work for the Church after graduation a significant number did. The contribution of the school's graduates was worldwide. The staff of all our medical institutions in North America and abroad were graduates of CME. First class hospitals could be found in Penang, Singapore, Manila, Hong Kong, Tokyo, in China, in Sydney and Melbourne Australia, and many of the capitals of countries on the African continent, besides Inter- and South America.

For the first few weeks of study we students felt like we were being asked to drink from a fire hydrant of information. But in time we got our stride and the studies were both pleasant and profitable. The third and fourth years of medicine were taken in Los Angeles, at the Los Angeles County General Hospital, an institution of some three thousand beds, and at the White Memorial Hospital and Clinic respectively.

It happened during our junior year. The class was divided alphabetically into groups of four and each group rotated through the clinical areas of Medicine and its subspecialties, Surgery and its subspecialties, Obstetrics and Gynecology, and other disciplines of medicine. Exposure in the various areas was each from two to four weeks in duration. My group consisted of Gilbert, Harris, Hartzell, and Hardinge. We would each study the same patient and then one of us would report to our attending physician. The attending physicians were all specialists in their fields and volunteered their services to teach the students.

Doctor Pride and Doctor Pomp

We were on the Chest Service and had as our attending physician a Doctor Babcock (a pseudonym), an excellent chest man, famous all over Southern California. Our fellow students all agreed that we were indeed lucky to have a man of his caliber to instruct us.

It was Monday morning, the first day of our two-week chest service. Dr. Babcock was waiting for us when we arrived at 9:00 AM. He was immaculately dressed, and looked like a picture-book example of a successful physician we hoped to be. He directed us into a ward holding about 12 patients. In the middle of the room was a patient seated on a stool with his back bared and directed toward us. On his left lower scapula area (left upper back) he had made a two-inch circle with a pen.

"One by one," he said, "I want you men to place your stethoscopes in the circle and then tell me what you heard." We all listened in turn. None of us heard anything abnormal. He was somewhat miffed. "Listen again, and listen carefully," was his command. This time two thought they heard something unusual, but two of us didn't. For some reason he picked on Freeman Gilbert, a quiet spoken, very bright fellow student. In a loud voice, while all the patients were both listening and watching, he more or less yelled, "Put your stethoscope right here, and tell me what you hear."

Gilbert did as he was told and turning to Dr. Babcock, and in a quiet voice, said, "I don't hear anything abnormal."

Dr. Babcock, now completely out of control emotionally, shouted, "Follow me," as he angrily strode out of the ward to the nurses' station. Reaching for a large envelope on the counter top, he pulled out the x-ray film of the patient's back. Slamming it into a viewing box, with jaws clenched, he hissed through his teeth, "See that!" It was an outline of a large cavity that we should have easily recognized by the breath sounds such a hollow makes.

Gilbert looked carefully at the x-ray, and then to Dr. Babcock. With a clear, but assured voice, he answered, "Dr. Babcock, you had us listening to the left upper chest. This cavity is on the right side."

The silence was deafening! We were all looking at Dr. Babcock. The color of his face turned a bright red. He stood there in silence looking at the x-ray in front of him. He then yanked the x-ray out of the viewing box, shoved it into the envelope, walked towards the nurses' station and slammed the envelope down. We watched as he strode down the hall and disappeared around a corner. We never saw him again, even though, for the rest of that week and the next, we came every morning and waited for him to arrive.

Later in the year we were on the Urology Unit. Our tutor was Dr. Brown (a pseudonym), an urologist. He was short, plump, and jovial. Although somewhat pompous he was, indeed, a very friendly fellow. We soon learned that he had trained at Edinburgh, and found it difficult to forget that fact as he reminded us of this several times each morning!

One day as we arrived on the ward he was waiting for us. "I want you gentlemen, one at a time, to look carefully at the patient in that room," pointing to a closed door a few feet away. "Please don't go close to him, just look carefully at his face, ask no questions, and then determine what his illness is." He then lectured us as to how we, the modern generation of physicians, are not taught to be keen observers. We rely on tests, x-rays and the laboratory, to make the diagnosis.

"When I was young we had none of these newfangled procedures. We had to rely on what we could see, and hear, and touch. As I learned in Edinburgh, use the senses God has given you. Be observant!"

One by one we each opened the door and looked carefully at the patient as he lay propped up with pillows. We carefully scrutinized his face. Although he did not look well, he did not appear seriously ill, that is, as far as any of us could tell. When we all had had our turn, Dr. Brown asked: "Well, what's your diagnosis?" None of us had the slightest idea. "That's just what I expected; no idea as to how to use your powers of observation. Just go around hoping the lab tests will tell you what's wrong with your patient. Now go back and look once more. His diagnosis is written all over his face."

Again we looked as carefully as we could, but with no better results. "What is the diagnosis?" we asked in chorus.

With a twinkle in his eye, he responded, "Typhoid fever! It's obvious to anyone who has learned to be observant. 'Typhoid fauces,' it's written all over his face." We looked at him in amazement. But Doctor Brown began again: "When I was in Edinburgh…"

He was cut short by one of my classmates (I thought quite boldly), "Dr. Brown, have you had a blood titer done?"

"There you go again, tests, tests, and more tests. But for your sakes and to confirm my diagnosis, I will order one done."

After the session was over, and as we were going back to our other assignments, we all agreed to come a little early next morning, and to check his chart to find out the results of the test. When a patient has typhoid fever certain antibodies (proteins) increase in the blood stream. The measurement is spoken of as "the blood titer."

When we arrived on the ward next morning and looked at the test results, they were negative! Dr. Brown arrived soon thereafter. "Good morning fellows, glad you're here a little early this morning," he spoke in a cheerful voice, "let's go to such and such a ward."

"Not so fast," we spoke almost in unison, "what about the lab test?"

With a slight smile on his face he replied, "So you've looked at the lab report, haven't you?" We all burst into smiles with nodding heads.

Then with a wide grin, he looked at us, and this is what he said, "Just goes to show that sometimes even the greatest of urologists can make a mistake!" And off he went, down the hall, with us following.

We respected the man.

We were on our "inside" obstetrical service at the Los Angeles County General Hospital. In those days we also delivered babies in the homes of people which we called "outside OB." We were divided into groups of three. Number one was on first call, a 24-hour shift; the next was on second call, a 24-hour shift; and the third had a day off. I believe we were on the service for three weeks. The one on first call delivered all the babies whose mother's delivered on his shift, unless more than one mother was delivering at the same time. In that event the one on second call was called into service.

Not a Joke

The three of us were Jim, Tom, and me (names are fictitious). As we approached the end of our service Tom and I had delivered over 20 babies each. Poor Jim, I think he had worked the hardest. On his shift large numbers of mothers were admitted. This meant he had to work them up, take histories and do physicals. But only two had delivered while he was on first call! They all seemed to deliver when Tom and I were on first call.

To give Jim a break we suggested he sleep in the intern-resident room during his day off and we would call him when a mother was ready to deliver. This would enable him to get a little more experience. He was single and therefore had no home responsibilities. He was elated; in fact, he would even give us a hand while on his day off.

One night, around one in the morning, a mother who was supposed to deliver began to show signs that the time for her baby's arrival was imminent. I dashed into where Jim was sleeping and shook him awake.

"You had better hurry, a baby is on its way," I informed him. So we rushed to the delivery area. He began to scrub his hands.

"That's enough," one nurse remarked. "You don't have time to do a thorough job. Dry your hands and we'll get you gowned and gloved." One nurse stood ready with a gown, another with a pair of gloves. Hurry! Hurry! was the word on every one's lips. Now I should explain to the reader that Jim was a cut up. He had been joking with and teasing the nurses mercilessly! He lost no opportunity to play a trick on one or other of the girls.

He was wearing the loose shirt and baggy pants worn when doing surgery, making deliveries, and other such procedures. As he raised his hands to get his gown on, his pants fell off! "Mervyn," he called, "pull my pants up."

"Oh, no you don't," the nurses chorused. "It's our turn now." One nurse got a towel and pinned it across his lower back! Everyone was laughing and things were hilarious. With great triumph he was conducted into the delivery room.

The mother had been given a little ether, and the baby was born without delay. It was a beautiful baby boy! As the mother was coming out of labor she asked two commonly asked questions: "What is it? and is it all right?" With a chuckle in his voice Jim replied: "You have a lovely baby boy, but the only problem is that he has three legs!" The mother gave a little grunt, and lapsed back into unconsciousness. Under the circumstances it sounded funny and the merriment continued.

In due time, the baby was taken to the nursery and the mother to the ward. Things normalized and each one went their several ways. Next morning when her baby was brought to his mother, she took one look and refused to accept it. The nurse, who was on the morning shift, knew nothing of what had happened during the night. She then asked the mother what was wrong.

"That baby has two legs. It isn't mine. The doctor told me mine had three legs!" The startled nurse, taking the baby with her, went to her supervisor and reported what had happened. The night shift was called back and everyone was gathered together. The head of the nursing department and the superintendent of the hospital were present. The details of the night's episode all came out.

Jim, the nurses present, and I went to see the mother. By this time she had figured out what had happened. Her baby had died and another mother had died at the same time. The nurses had taken the live baby from the dead mother, and were claiming it was her baby. But she wasn't going to hear of it. She wanted her baby who had three legs even if it was dead!

Jim apologized profusely. He told her what had happened and did his best to explain that he had only been joking. We corroborated what he said but she would have none of it. A counselor was called in. He talked at length to us and to the mother but could not convince her that the healthy baby was really hers. She did, however, take the healthy boy home. Whether she ever really believed that the baby was hers, I cannot tell you. The days of DNA testing were years in the future.

The experience sobered us all. We certainly learnt a valuable lesson and that was that an inappropriate joke is never a joke!

We were rotating through the services at the Los Angeles County General Hospital, a huge institution of over 3,000 beds at the time. One of my classmates, Ellsworth Wareham by name, was in one of the groups of four. In his group was another of my classmates, Jack Whieldon. Jack was slightly different, but he was a keen student, and one who would stand by his opinions.

The Fly in the Stethoscope

Just before the session began Ellsworth asked Jack if he could borrow his stethoscope for a couple of minutes. Jack was happy to oblige, and the instrument was returned to him promptly. The group was taken to a patient who Doctor Baker, the preceptor that day, had selected. Dr. Baker asked each of the four to listen to the patient's heart. Each was then asked what they heard. All but Jack heard only a slight murmur. Jack on the other hand heard all kinds of irregular sounds.

Dr. Baker asked the students to listen to the heart again. Again it was three to one. Jack insisted that the sounds were so clear and strong that he couldn't understand why the others couldn't hear what he was hearing. Dr. Baker then listened to the heart and agreed with the three—only a slight murmur. Jack was indignant. Dr. Baker and the others must be ganging up on him! His voice in decibels was rising. It was then that Dr. Baker asked to borrow Jack's stethoscope. Jack handed it over.

As Dr. Baker listened with Jack's stethoscope a smile came over his face. He began to chuckle. He then screwed off the diaphragm of the stethoscope and there in the bowl was a fly with one wing off! That is why Ellsworth had borrowed the instrument! By then everyone was having a good laugh. Jack took it well but the story went around.

It was in my senior year in medicine and my rotation through the White Memorial Clinic that was giving me experience in the Eye Department.

Sincerity is Not Enough

One afternoon a young girl, perhaps 13 or 14 years of age, led an elderly gentleman into the examining room. She was his

PREPARING FOR MEDICINE

granddaughter and lived a block or two down the street from where he lived. This is the story that unfolded. It was the custom for the old gentleman, whenever the weather was propitious, to sit in a chair sunning himself in his front yard. He knew all his neighbors and all his neighbors knew him. On the morning of the day he came into the clinic, he had gone out as usual to watch the world go by from his usual seat in his front yard. Jim, one of his neighbors on his way to work, greeted him cheerfully. "Hi, Grandpa (the nickname he had been given), how are you doing this day?"

"Just fine, you would know," he replied. Just then he brushed the back of one hand over his eyes.

"Having a little trouble with your eyes?" Jim inquired.

"Not that I know of," was Grandpa's response.

Coming over, Jim looked in his eyes. "They look a little red. If I was you I'd wash them out with a little 'murine'." With that he turned and headed for his commute that was already honking for him.

Grandpa happened to have some 'murine', so he went to his bathroom, found the 'murine' and put drops in both his eyes. He then returned to sun himself. He had hardly sat down when Mrs. Jones who lived up the street came along. "What's the matter with your eyes?" she inquired. "They're tearing." She came over to take a closer look. "You know what I would do if I were you, I'd rinse them out with salt water. It works every time. Just put a little salt in some warm water and bathe your eyes with it. Works like a charm." And off she went to catch the bus.

Grandpa got up and headed for the house. He was getting worried. Maybe there was something wrong with his eyes, he pondered. Now Mrs. Jones had not told him just how strong to make the salt solution. Just how much was "a little salt?" And how much water should he add it to? After a minute or so he decided that if the solution were a little strong it wouldn't hurt him. So he filled a glass with warm water and added a couple of teaspoons of salt. Then he stirred it thoroughly and washed his eyes with it. He then went outside wiping his eyes, which were still wet with the salt water. Bill, his neighbor who lived across the street, noticed Grandpa wiping his eyes, so came over to see what might be the problem.

By this time Grandpa's eyes were really red. "Looks like you have conjunctivitis, Grandpa. How long have you had it?" Grandpa didn't know what conjunctivitis was, but it sounded bad. "What have you been doing for it?" he inquired solicitously.

"Just washed it out with a little salt water," was Grandpa's response.

Bill's response was immediate, "Grandpa, salt water! That's the worst thing you can do for conjunctivitis! All it does is irritate the eyes. I'll tell you a treatment that has never failed. Clears up conjunctivitis in a flash. My mother used it on us kids and so did her mother. Sort of a family secret. But I'll let you in on it. This is what you do. Slice a small onion in half and squeeze a couple of drops of juice into each eye. They will sting and water a little, but then things will clear up right smart." As he left he called after him, "See you this evening, Grandpa. You'll be OK by then."

Things were sort of getting out of hand. Now what was he to do? Should he call his daughter? She was at work. His granddaughter was in school. Onion juice sounded like a natural treatment. It had worked for Bill's family. He would give it a try. Nothing to lose, he mused. So into his house he went, found a small onion, pealed off the outer layers, cut it in half, and lay down on his couch. He then carefully squeezed two or three drops of juice into each eye. Did it burn and did they water! Phew!

After a few minutes he decided to go outside again. His eyes were still smarting and a tear or two would run down his cheeks every now and then. He reclined in his chair enjoying the warmth of the sun. He felt relieved and was sure things would clear up. Now it was Nancy Jones' turn to pass by. She was always nosey as to how her neighbors were doing. She walked over and looked at Grandpa.

"My! My! You have a real problem with your eyes! They look red and swollen. How long have you had this problem, and what have you been doing for it?" If he was already alarmed, the tone of her voice alarmed him still more.

"Only since I came out this morning, the way I always do," he replied. He recited the several things he had done. Nancy Jones took a deep breath and stood to her full height. "Onion juice, of all things! Who ever suggested that needs to go to kindergarten to learn a few things; that he does!" She stood there in deep thought as if wondering what she should do. Then her face brightened:

"I'd like to suggest something different. In my experience onion juice never works. But I have a treatment that has been a wonderful blessing to me. It sounds sort of harsh and if you don't want to try it, I'll understand." She watched as an expression of expectancy swept over Grandpa's face. "Would you like me to tell you?" She sounded like she was about to disclose a dark secret.

"Of course. Of course." Grandpa could hardly wait. "I'm getting to the stage where I'm willing to try most anything! Tell me what you do."

Nancy leaned down and in a hushed voice said, "Take a pinch of black pepper and put it in each eye. It will burn like fire and hurts awfully bad, but it kills every germ in your eyes. Never fails to heal a sore eye!" With that she was on her way.

Thoughts of alarm and thoughts of relief both contended with each. Dare he try one more treatment? If pepper burns one's mouth what might it do to his eyes? For a long time, with his eyes closed, he turned Nancy's suggestion over and over in his mind. He finally got up and headed for the house. He would give it a go!

He lay down on his couch again and bravely put a pinch of black pepper in each eye! He immediately regretted what he had done. He was in agony! Buckets of tears seemed to flow from his eyes, but the burning continued. Rubbing his eyes seemed to make them worse. What should he do? And then there was a knock at his door. Mary, a nurse, who lived up the street, was returning a shovel he had lent her the day before. As she stood by the door she heard Grandpa moaning so came in to see what was the matter.

There was Grandpa lying on the couch, his eyes shut, a pepper shaker and two halves of an onion on an end table beside him. "Have you been treating your eyes with these things?" Her voice was incredulous!

"One of my neighbors thought I had conjunctivitis. Others suggested things they do for their eyes when they redden. What should I do?" Grandpa sounded desperate.

After a moment or two Mary responded, "I'll go over to the school and take Sharon, your granddaughter, out for the rest of the day. I'll make an appointment for you to go to the White Memorial Clinic so they can treat you properly. Your granddaughter can take you there. In the meantime, to soothe your eyes, I'll get a couple of wash clothes dipped in warm water to put over your eyes. I'll tell Sharon how to change them every few minutes; the warm moisture should give you some relief." With that Mary was on her way.

But the tragedy did not end there. Sharon made the water in which she dipped the wash clothes too hot and blistered Grandpa's eyelids! Later that afternoon she led Grandpa into the examining room and between the two of them I got the story I have recounted. As it unfolded I could hardly believe what I heard. I put some anesthetic solution in Grandpa's eyes to give immediate relief and an ointment to soothe his maltreated eyes. As he left the clinic I admonished him to take the advice of neighbors and friends with a large pinch of salt. When he returned for a checkup the following week the only remaining trauma were the healing blisters on his eyelids! What an incredible experience and one I doubt Grandpa ever forgot!

From this saga we can all learn a lesson. Sincerity is not enough, one must be sincerely right!

NOTE. To any who read this story and believe it is fictitious (and for this I would not fault them), I would suggest they check in the archives of the White Memorial Clinic, Eye Department records, in the spring months of 1941. If these files still exist, the record should satisfy the most ardent skeptic!

The Stubborn Patient

I was an intern and would soon be graduating from medicine. One of my last rotations was Surgery. I had admitted a 45 years old man, we'll call him Joe, who had been an uncontrolled diabetic for some time. One of his toes was red, swollen, and extremely tender. One tiny area was duller than the skin immediately surrounding it. This spot was slightly soft and moist. The first signs of gangrene, I thought!

Antibiotics had not as yet been discovered and the use of sulfonamides was still in various stages of clinical trial. His family physician had tried the single sulfonamide available to him without any beneficial effect. He was now under the care of the chief of the Surgical Unit at the White Memorial Hospital, who carefully examined the offending toe as well as his foot. He agreed with my diagnosis and turning to Joe spoke in a very kindly manner:

"I'm sorry to report to you Joe, that you have the early signs of gangrene. Your family doctor has tried sulfur drugs without improvement so the only treatment I can offer is amputation of your foot at the ankle."

"Why at the ankle," the patient remonstrated? "The problem is just a little spot on one toe and you want me to lose my foot! No way, that's ridiculous!"

"Listen Joe, I know it sounds too radical but when we see that little spot on the surface of the toe it tells us that the gangrene has already traveled up your foot and is approaching your ankle. Just removing the toe would do no good. I will assure you I will not remove any part of your foot unless absolutely necessary."

"Forget it, doc. I'm not giving permission for the removal of my foot, and that's final."

After the chief had left I tried to explain in some detail what was going on in his foot. All my appeals fell on deaf ears, as did those of his wife and other family members. The patient was adamant.

Next morning it was obvious to all, including Joe, that the gangrene had reached his ankle. He was now ready to have surgery. When the chief made his rounds and had again examined the foot, he spoke kindly to the expectant patient, "I'm sorry to say that we will have to remove your foot and leg at a point just below your knee."

Joe exploded! "Yesterday you wanted to take my foot off, and today when I give you permission to do that, you up the anti and want my leg too!! I'm no fool. You can take my foot but not an inch further."

"It's too late just to amputate at the ankle, for the gangrene is already approaching your knee. I assure you again, I will leave as much of your limb as possible." But it was no use and Joe rudely turned his back to the surgeon.

Again the support staff urged him to take the advice of an experienced physician, as did his weeping wife and anxious loved ones. But all the pleas were rudely rejected.

Next morning the gangrene was below his knee and Joe was repentant of what he had told the surgeon. When the chief had checked him carefully he again, in a soft kind voice, said "Joe, yesterday the gangrene was visible at your ankle but had already traveled part way up the tissues of your leg. That's why, to be of any benefit to you, the amputation had to be just below the knee. In the last 24 hours the gangrene has passed your knee and is now in your lower thigh. Today I would have to amputate at the hip."

Joe response was angry and abusive. "Now I give you permission to take my leg and what do you demand, my thigh! Doc, I hate to say it, but you're crazy. You can take my leg off at the knee but not any higher. Do you understand?"

The chief understood all to well. As he turned to leave he looked at Joe, "Joe, experience tells us that the gangrene has already traveled further than what the surface shows. I wish I could convince you!" But Joe would have none of it.

Next morning his entire thigh was a mess! When the chief arrived, the tone of Joe's voice showed his regret for not heeding the pleading of the chief. "Take my thigh, doc, and go as high as you want. I've been one big fool!"

The chief looked at Joe for a long time, and when he spoke you could tell the sorrow in his voice, "Joe, the gangrene has now passed your hip joint. I will remove as much as I possibly can of the rotting tissue, but I'm afraid it is too late!"

The surgery was unsuccessful. The gangrene was already in his pelvis and there was no way to stop its progress. Joe died soon thereafter.

As I reflect on this sad episode I have come to realize that sin, like gangrene, is ever pushing to expand its territory. The physician's advice may appear drastic but experience tells him it is the only life saving way. As Christ discussed this type of problem with his followers, he advised that "If thy right hand offends thee, cut it off. If your eye offends thee take it out!" If you are sinning by what you do, or watch, or even think, allow the skilled Surgeon to remove every trace of the soul destroying malady. The gangrene of sin must be eradicated.

Christ is telling us that as much as we would hate to lose a most precious gift like a hand or eye to save this life, that sacrificing the passing pleasure of our most cherished sin is not worth the loss of eternal life. It is a matter of life and death. You cannot compromise. Christ, the Great Physician, never makes a mistake in His diagnoses. His recommendations may sound drastic but he sees where our "besetting sin" will lead. Joe thought he knew better, and we, like Joe, too often think we know, but let us follow the advice of our Heavenly Surgeon and allow His Holy Spirit to do the drastic surgery of removing every trace of soul destroying sin and thus assure us of eternal life.

A Time of Trial

My folks had agreed to lend me the tuition for my four years of medicine. On graduation I would pay them back, and this I did. But things did not work out quite as we had planned. World War II was raging and things weren't going well with the Allies. The British Government froze all funds in England in 1940, so Dad no longer received his pension. This put my folks and me in a double bind. They could no longer help me with my tuition, and we (my wife and I) had to start paying them back for the tuition already lent. This would allow them enough to live on. The only way to get this extra money was for me to find a job.

The Lord opened the way and I secured the position of doing the emergency laboratory work at the White Memorial Hospital. The requirement was that I must be on call from Saturday night through Thursday night, 6:00 PM, to 7:00 AM.. I was off every other weekend. However, the weekends I was on call began at 4:00 PM, Friday and went through until 6:00 PM, Saturday! Then the routine started again.

But the income I earned did not cover the amount we needed, so I found additional work from 6:00 PM, when classes were over, to around 10:00 PM. How the work came in was a miracle. It consisted of doing cabinet work and finishing jobs, such as hanging doors and putting on trim on the inside of homes. The pay was good and the people I worked for could not have been nicer. But this caused a problem for it required my good wife, a lab technologist, already working full time at the White Memorial Laboratory, to cover for me. And this she did.

When I came home at ten at night she was often on a call. Before she got back I had been called out. Often we never saw each other all night. The hospital was taking advantage of us but we were hesitant to complain as jobs were not that plentiful. Then one weekend when I went on call at 4:00 PM, Friday things became really busy. A patient was brought in needing blood transfusions. In those days there were neither blood banks nor any way of providing stored blood.

The procedure was as follows. A sample of blood was obtained from the patient (the recipient) and matched with the blood of a would-be donor. This took considerable time, and as one might expect, many of the donors did not match the blood of the recipient. After a match was found, the donor went from the lab to the hospital. The patient would be lying on one bed, the donor on an adjacent bed. Two physicians with the assistance of a couple of nurses now began the task of transfusing the patient. Large caliber needles were inserted into the appropriate blood vessels in the arms of both donor and recipient. Syringes holding fifty milliliters of blood were used to withdraw the blood from the donor. The syringe was then handed over to the physician standing by the patient. He, in turn, would inject the blood into the patient. The procedure would be repeated over and over again until the appropriate amount of blood had been transfused.

The recipient of the blood was a man who, with five others, had gone deer hunting at Big Bear Lake, a mountain lake about 60 miles east of Los Angeles. On the way back, while still in the mountains, one of the hunters thought he saw a deer. The driver of the car in which they were riding pulled over to the side of the road. As the now patient was getting out the back door his rifle caught in something and discharged, blowing a hole in his right groin, and severing a large vessel carrying blood to the lower limb (femoral artery).

The wounded hunter must have belonged to a club for members came out in droves, offering to give blood. At 8:30 PM, I called my wife for help. Together we worked non-stop through the night until the last call for blood came at 9:30 next morning. The hunter survived. It was 3:30 that afternoon when we caught up with the requisitioned tests and were just leaving the lab when Doctor Pratt, the head of the lab, came in.

"How is it going?" he asked, in a cheerful voice.

I told him what had transpired. "Are you always kept busy?" he inquired.

"Not as bad as last night, but without my wife's help I could not keep up with the work load."

He looked at me quizzically. "Keep a record of the tests you do and give the list to me," was his comment.

"I have a list already," and handed him a little booklet in which I had a record of all tests requested.

"May I have it for a day or two?" he asked as he accepted the proffered record.

"You surely may." Margaret and I went home. We hadn't eaten since noon the previous day!

A few days later Dr. Pratt called me to his office. "You have been asked to do numerous tests that are not emergencies. I have talked to the medical staff and informed them that only emergency tests are to be requested." He handed me a list of tests that I was to refuse to do. Then with a twinkle in his eyes he said, "And by the way, Mervyn, we are doubling your salary." For the rest of the year the workload dropped unbelievably and we entered upon our year of internship with high hopes of a more normal life.

From the Frying Pan into the Fire!

But that was not to be. The workload during the internship was, if anything, worse than had been the night job at the Lab! We interns were to be on duty at 6:30 each morning, and by the time we got through the patient load it was generally 10:00 to 11:00 PM. Most of my fellow interns were just as tired as I was. The surgical service was perhaps the worst. We started at 6:30 AM, and usually got out of surgery around 1:00 PM. During any breaks we had to start IV drips, watch the patients as they were recovering, and admit new patients. Besides doing a history and physical on these new arrivals, we were required to do a blood count on each one; sometimes there were as many as seven new arrivals, and to make each count required at least 20 minutes.

The intern-resident room was a beehive of activity all evening. My good wife would come by around 8:30 PM to see how things were going. I usually was still busy checking on patients and finishing up the charts. Every patient's chart had to be completed, including a blood count, before we left for the night. Out of the goodness of her heart she would draw the blood from each of my patients and do the blood counts. We would get home by 10:30 PM.

The program was such that it made honest interns dishonest. One evening, it was near 10:00 PM, a fellow intern returned from the ward with a syringe full of blood. Walking to the sink she turned on the water, and squirting its contents into the sink, washed the blood down the drain. Then sitting down she opened the patient's chart and made up the blood count. Turning towards me she said, "I don't have a husband to do my blood counts!"

Other interns never even bothered to take any blood from their patients. They just made up the counts! This changed with the next group of interns who were no longer required to do any blood counts; otherwise, the program remained the same.

Spiritually Dead

My wife and I were tired. Bible-study and even prayer went by the board. Weekends, when I was off, we spent in bed. One afternoon it happened we were both off for a couple of hours. I remember sitting on the bed, my wife beside me, and turning towards her I said, "Margaret, we can't go on like this. Emotionally and spiritually we are dead. We either take time to worship and practice our religion, or we quit it all together. I can't be a half-hearted Christian any more!"

"How do we regain our spiritual life?" she inquired.

"Try to help someone else in theirs. Give Bible studies."

She looked at me. "How do we find someone to study with?"

"I have no idea but the Lord can provide someone if we ask Him. Why don't we decide to truly serve Him and ask Him to revive our parched souls?" We then got down on our knees and poured out are hearts to the Lord. New commitments were made that have never been broken.

We both had to go to work, I a little sooner than she. We kissed and said we would see each other later. We lived a block from the hospital. On approaching the hospital I ran into a teenage girl and her mother. The girl had been a patient of mine; I had assisted in removing her appendix. She had just returned for her final checkup.

"How are you doing?" I inquired with a smile.

"Just wonderfully," was her reply. And then her mother spoke up, "What would you do with a girl who wants to read continually?"

"It all depends on what she reads," I replied.

"Oh, she reads only good books, in fact, mainly religious books."

"Then I would encourage her," and we all laughed.

"Would you like to study the Bible?" I asked.

"Oh, yes, yes. When can we start?" They both spoke in unison.

So the following Friday evening we started studying the Bible together. Less than five minutes after Margaret and I had arisen from our knees, Bible studies had been arranged! What an answer to the prayer of two desperate souls!

Two interesting things followed. When I was on duty Friday evenings I had to arrange for someone to cover for me. It was not difficult, as I would agree to take the other intern's duties some subsequent evening. When my fellow interns learned I was giving Bible studies they refused to allow me to make up the time. "It's the least I can do for a good cause," was their usual reply.

Now the Bible studies continued until my internship ended and we moved away from Los Angeles. The relationship of the family to the Lord was strengthened and so was ours. We hope, someday, to meet them in God's eternal kingdom. God works in the most wondrous ways.

Back to Loma Linda

I was nearing the end of my internship when my wife and I read, in The Review and Herald, of an urgent need for doctors in three of our Mission Hospitals on the continent of Africa. We paused and looked at each other. Then we asked ourselves, "Shall we go? Wasn't this the reason I was taking medicine in the first place? Had not Margaret prepared for such a calling by becoming a Laboratory Technologist, and had even gained experience in delivering babies, an opportunity provided by the White Memorial Hospital?" And so we decided to speak with Elder Branson, the then Secretary of the General Conference, who, it happened, was visiting a camp meeting in Southern California.

It was a hot Sabbath afternoon when we met the Elder in a tent! I can still see the beads of perspiration on his forehead. We told him of our qualifications and that we were ready to go where the need was greatest. Turning to me, he asked, "How much surgical experience do you have?"

"I will have all the experience a good internship provides."

"Well Brother Hardinge, I think you should get more experience in surgery. I'm sure that when you do, the Lord will have a place for you in His work." Our meeting was over. To say we were disappointed is an understatement. It had never entered my head that I should become a surgeon, but if that was the way to get to go the mission field, a surgeon I would become.

The next morning I talked with Dr. Tomlinson, the Chairman of the Department of Surgery. He looked at me as if I was out of my mind. I could see the astonishment written all over his face. Then he spoke. "There isn't a chance in the world! We have already selected one of your fellow interns and will be taking his name at the end of this week for confirmation by the Intern Resident Committee. Did you know that we have been receiving applications for the past twelve months and there are sixty qualified applicants left over from last year? We can, unfortunately, only take one resident a year and that position is filled."

"May I have an application for the residency?" I inquired.

"Of course you can, but you will be wasting your time and effort if you fill it out. The Department's decision is final." His voice had a tinge of frustration in it.

I picked up the application and headed for the office of his associate, a Dr. Stafford. He listened to me with a half smile and then indicated in no uncertain terms, that the one opening for the current year was filled, but if I wished to apply for next year's opening, it would be appropriate. The third man on the totem pole was a Dr. Jorgensen. He was quite receptive to my desire but let me know that he was new in the department and had no influence whatsoever as to the selection of the next resident.

I went home and filled out the application, making clear why I wanted the training. I sent copies of my application to Dr. Orville

Pratt, the chairman of the committee, and to Dr. Tomlinson, department chairman. With the application I earnestly asked the Lord to guide in the decision that was to be made. Friday morning Dr. Jorgensen sought me out. He urged me to indicate to the committee that on completion of my training I would be willing to work in the clinic for two or three years. That it was very difficult to fill this position and that such a commitment would put me in a more favorable light. I thanked him sincerely but said I could not do such a thing.

The suggestion bothered me for I was committed to leave for the mission field immediately on completing my training. So I wrote a letter to the committee stating that on completion of the residency I would not only be leaving Southern California, but I would also be leaving the country! I did not want to leave any doubt as to my plans.

The committee met Saturday evening. Sunday morning I was asked to go to the chairman's office. He greeted me with a smile and congratulated me that the committee had over ruled the department's recommendation and had selected me to be the next resident! The department's recommendation had never been overruled before, and as far as I can gather, has never been overruled since. God knew what He wanted me to do

Our First Refrigerator

At the end of my internship we were preparing to move from Los Angeles to Loma Linda. A year earlier, after starting my internship, and no longer having to pay for tuition and for books, Margaret and I decided we would splurge and buy a refrigerator. We went to the General Electric Outlet Store that sold both old and new refrigerators. We decided on a $35 model. It was well used, had a huge finned cylindrical arrangement on the top of the refrigerator to cool the compressor, or so I thought. To appreciate what we took home one needs to go to the Smithsonian Institute to see a replica of the contraption we purchased!

It worked for a few days and then quit. We lugged it back to the GE Service Department and invested another $10 in the appliance. It again worked off and on for a couple of weeks and then died of old age. We had been taken. But we bought 25 Lb. blocks of ice and used it as an ice box. Just before leaving for Loma Linda we purchased a new Westinghouse refrigerator. The appliance store told us they would give us $5 as a trade in.

One afternoon a senior medical student who was just going to start his internship at the White Memorial Hospital came by and asked it we planned to sell our refrigerator? I told him about the trade in we had been offered and I would sell it to him for $5. He accepted the offer and that evening came over with some friends and took possession of the machine. I had explained to him that he would have to use it as an icebox for the cooling system would not work.

A year later I ran into him again. He was leaving the next day to start a residency program in an eastern city. We greeted each warmly and were saying our goodbyes when he remarked: "Do you remember the old refrigerator I bought form you a year ago for $5?"

"I certainly do. Any problem?"

"No, no. Just thought I'd let you know what happened. I took it home and arranged it in our kitchen. Then I told my wife I was going to buy a block of ice.

"Why are you going to do that," she asked in surprise?

"Because the cooling system doesn't work and I bought it as an icebox. Only paid $5."

"Well," she replied, "If it's a refrigerator why don't you plug it in and see what happens."

"So I did. I plugged it in and it worked up until a week ago when it quit cooling. Just sold it for $5 to a classmate of mine. He's planning to intern here!"

And so is life. Can't win for losing.

And so on July 1, 1942 I was in Loma Linda again where the first year of resident training was to begin.

Back in Loma Linda

I loved every minute of that year. The first six months was spent working in the Department of Anatomy, while the remainder of the year was spent in the Department of Pathology. Before many months had passed both departments were offering me a position in their respective departments. I was promised if I taught for the duration of the war (World War II) that I would be guaranteed to have the opportunity to complete my residency at the end of the conflict. But how could I do such a thing since the Lord had miraculously provided me the residency. No, I must go through with it.

Following my six months experience in Anatomy, I moved over to the Department of Pathology. Dr. Small, the Chairman of the Department, had contracted with the San Bernardino County Coroner's Office to do the postmortems for his office. The coroner was responsible to determine the cause of death of people who died without having a regular physician, of those killed in accidents, and all deaths in which foul play was suspected. The bodies were available in the local mortuaries.

Mr. Peptic Ulcer

There was one mortuary that my fellow resident and I dreaded to be called to. It was in the City of Colton. The mortician, Ken Balder, was the crabbiest individual we had every met. He grumbled and complained about any and everything we did. Why did you do this or why did you do that? You always leave a mess that I must clean up. We bent over backward to be cooperative, but nothing would please him. We nicknamed him, "Peptic Ulcer!"

One afternoon it was my misfortune to be called to this mortuary. I entered the autopsy room with dread. To my surprise "Peptic Ulcer" wasn't there. A new man, we'll call him Bob, greeted me with a smile and asked if he could be of help? I was tempted to ask him where "Peptic Ulcer" was but refrained, remembering the old adage, "Speak of the devil and he will appear." The work that afternoon was as pleasant as such a procedure would allow.

Sometime later I was again assigned to a case in the Colton mortuary. Again there was no sign of "Peptic Ulcer." With difficulty I curbed my desire to know where he was, and refrained to ask about the new man's former colleague. But the next assignment to that mortuary I could not hold my curiosity any longer and asked Bob what had happened to Ken."

"Ken," he replied, "had not been feeling well so went to his family doctor. After a thorough examination he was found to have, of all things, a peptic ulcer! The harsh words and cutting remarks he constantly spewed from his mouth were just as corrosive as the acid that had bored a hole in his stomach's lining. What a lesson for all of us!

The Muffled Bell

I was on my way back from Blocmington, a small town west of Colton, where I had just signed a death certificate. In my mind I was going over the events which had made the autopsy necessary. On my arrival at the mortuary I had been informed that it was an accident case.

The cause of death was easy to determine. There were fractures of all the bones on his right side, skull, right shoulder, arm and forearm, pelvis, and the bones of his right lower limb. His liver and bladder had also been ruptured. As I was signing the man's death certificate, I inquired of the mortician as to how the accident had occurred. Let me recount what I was told.

The dead man, Jack Johnson (pseudonym), lived in what was then the north part of Bloomington. The home that he occupied was one of those through the backyard of which an electric train passed. The right of way had been granted to the Railroad Company some time after the houses had been built. As a result his garage was on one side of the tracks, his home on the other. An alleyway provided access to his and other garages in the block. And finally Jack had a corner lot that faced north.

The Railroad Company, as required by law, had installed a bell that clanged whenever a train was to cross the road to the west of his property. The loud "clang, clang, clang" began to irritate Jack. He sent a letter to the Railroad Company requesting that the bell be removed. "Everybody in the neighborhood," he wrote, "knew where the crossing was and also knew the time the trains would pass." As one might expect, the company politely replied that the law required them to place a bell at the site and that they could do nothing about the matter. Jack became more and more disturbed. He wrote several letters, each increasingly abusive. Nothing happened. Then he got an idea. He would circulate a petition and ask all those who lived within earshot of the bell to sign requesting that the bell be removed. Surprisingly he obtained a large number of signatures. So the railroad did do something. They could not remove the bell so they muffled its sound. Now instead of going "clang, clang, and clang" it went "click, click, and click." Jack was delighted, as were his neighbors.

A year or two went by. On the afternoon of the accident, as Jack was returning from work, he stopped at a supermarket and bought some groceries. He drove to his back door and carried his purchases into the kitchen telling his wife he would put the car in the garage while she was fixing dinner. He turned onto the street and headed for the alleyway. His mind must have been on other things for he apparently did not hear the clicking sound the bell was making. He ran head-on into the side of the train. His car turned a full circle and hit the train again. By the time the ambulance arrived, Jack was dead. And I signed his death certificate.

Do we, like Jack, want God's still small voice muffled so it will not disturb our tranquillity? Are there things we do that dull our senses, or do we listen to the sounds of this world that drown out God's clanging bell? Jack thought he knew better, and the Railroad Company compromised their obligation. To compromise is a dangerous thing.

It cost Jack his life.

Joining the College Teaching Staff

As the first year of my residency was drawing to a close I began to realize that the Church was not sending missionaries overseas, but was trying to bring foreign missionaries back to the States. The war was not going well for the Allies.

I was an English citizen and not subject to the draft laws of the United States. It seemed I could help the Medical School. So I decided to accept the proposition and selected Anatomy as my area of teaching. It was a Friday morning when the agreement was made. At midnight Friday night the Government of the United States announced that all residencies for specialty training were abolished! The army needed doctors! So I completed my first year of training and began teaching.

I had never thought I would enjoy teaching, but it became my joy and delight. Several months passed and again one Friday night (all major announcements of policy were made midnight Friday or midnight Saturday), it was announced that the Allies had agreed on the policy that all friendly aliens living in a country were subject to the draft laws of that country. On hearing this news I turned to my wife and said, "I'm in." Ten days later I received a notice that I should go to such and such a location for my pre-induction physical. I complied and then waited for my classification.

Others who had been processed at the same time received their assignments in short order but mine did not come. Every mail was examined for the paper. Weeks went by, then months. I kept teaching. Two years later the long-looked-for paper arrived. It read, "Medical training is part of the war effort. Since you are an experienced teacher you are in an essential industry and have been so classified." Little did I know then that I would be teaching for the next forty years!

Chapter 5

TEACHING ANATOMY

Due to the desperate need for physicians for the Army, in the spring of 1943 the US Government canceled all residencies for specialty training, and my first year of surgical training ended on June 30. On July 1 I began my teaching career in what at that time was called Gross Anatomy. The term "gross" separated it from the term "micro," for there was also a separate Department of Microscopic Anatomy. Simply put, anatomy was divided into what could be seen by the unaided human eye and what was discerned through a light microscope. The electron microscope had not as yet been invented.

As a student I enjoyed gross anatomy very much. But now that it was my full time job I enjoyed it even more. Human bodies, after embalming, were dissected by both teachers and medical students. Studying in detail the structures and organs of the human body was to me an inspiring experience, for under my very fingers was unfolding the handiwork of God Himself, when, in the Garden of Eden He made man, the masterpiece of all His creation.

Muscles and tendons, blood vessels and nerves, all were present lying in perfect relationships one with the other. The design of the bones, their shapes and curves, their knobs and crevices, each and every part was there for a purpose. The locations of the organs, the heart and lungs, the liver and spleen, the stomach and intestines, were all arranged so as to carry out their ordained tasks most efficiently. There were no vacant spaces anywhere, for everything was of the appropriate size and shape to do its appointed task.

Gross anatomy was in essence surgical anatomy. The size, shape, and location of every structure and organ was essential knowledge for a skillful surgeon. But what was not emphasized was the function of these very structures. It gradually became apparent to me that structure was designed for function. The reason for every bump on a bone was not happenstance, but carefully crafted to accomplish a foreseen purpose. To me the concept of functional anatomy was gradually emerging, the idea that to accomplish a certain function, a specially designed structure was needed. To move the hand a certain way, for example, required the bone or bones to be a certain shape and size, and the muscles to be so arranged as to move them in the desired direction. It was not until some thirty years later that I taught such a course, a requirement for a doctoral degree in the health sciences.

I became interested in bone healing and then bone growth, how weight was transmitted through a bone, and then how this weight passed through a joint. Since nutrition, of which I knew little, influenced growth, I became interested in nutrition. This research in turn produced papers, and the papers allowed me to become a member of the American Association of Anatomists, and other parallel scientific organizations. Everything I seemed to do prospered, and life was a joy.

Improving on God's Design

During one of my lectures I made the statement that "one could not improve on God's design of the human body." Later that morning I was in the dissection laboratory, a large room that housed twenty-five tables. Each table had an embalmed body for a group of four students to dissect. They worked in pairs, two on each side. I noticed an enlarging group of students at the far end of the lab so I ambled over to see what was going on. One student was standing on a stool informing the others that it was easy to improve on the design of the human body, and seemed to have convinced his classmates that that was so. As I stood on the periphery of the group he caught my eye, and turning asked, "Did you really mean what you said—that one could not improve on the body's design?"

"Yes, I did," was my reply.

"Then I can prove you wrong." He spoke confidently. Now it should be mentioned that the students were in the beginning of their freshman year, and had been dissecting for less than three weeks! "Now," he continued to speak, and he had the rapped attention of his fellow students, "take, for example, the pronator terres. If you lengthened the muscle so it's tendon attached one inch further down and wrapped around the radius a little more, wouldn't that increase the strength of pronation?"

"It surely would," was my response.

"Then there it is. It's easy to improve on the body's design." The students all seemed to agree.

Now I should say a word about pronation and supination. The forearm has two long bones to support the muscles that attach to it. The ulna, on the side nearest the body, is relatively fixed, while the radius can partially rotate around the ulna. When your hand is placed on the top of a table and your palm faces downward, the hand is pronated. When your palm faces upward it is supinated. The muscles that accomplish these movements are called pronators and supinators.

Then I asked the student, "What will you do with the structure which is already attached to the space an inch lower down and a little further around the radius?"

"I hadn't thought of that." He spoke in a somewhat less confident tone of voice.

"Well let's assume there is a vacant space where you wish to attach the lengthened muscle. This would strengthen pronation. To counter this increased force of pronation you would have to proportionally increase the force of supination, otherwise the balance between these two functions would be lost, and your hand would remain pronated! But let's assume you can increase the strength of supination, then you would need to increase the mass and strength of the bones to which these more powerful muscles attach. Now the muscles of the arm would need to be strengthened to support the increased mass of the forearm. This in turn would require stronger arm muscles and a heavier bone in the arm (humerus). Now, don't forget, that the arm is integrated with the shoulder, and one shoulder with the opposite shoulder, and on and on. I think you ought to leave things the way they are!"

Soon after I began full time teaching, I was requested by the Dean to teach a course called Bible Hygiene. The professor who had taught it previously had died so I filled the need. As a student we considered the course neither Bible nor Hygiene! I changed its name to Health Evangelism. At the time the medical students were encouraged to speak, on Sabbath mornings, in the small churches in the little towns on the periphery of Loma Linda. The format of the service was that a medical student would give a ten minute health talk, a nursing student or students would then provide special music, and finally a ten minute spiritual talk presented by a medical student would end the service. The program was organized by a retired minister and was entirely voluntary. I believed that I could provide the students with information to help them in these presentations, and with the help of my wife, prepared two syllabi, one on Spiritual Talks and another on Health Talks. The course promoted a healthful lifestyle and was well accepted. It continued for the next forty years under a variety of names, finally being given the designation, A Philosophy of Health.

The early years of my teaching coincided with World War II. All the medical students were in uniform and a cadre of soldiers was located in the men's dormitory to direct the activities of the students. The students were under tremendous pressure. Any student who failed was immediately shipped off to boot camp, and from there sent either to the Western or Eastern theaters of war. The pressure was so intense that some of the students began to break in health, either physically or mentally, or both. I was at the time the faculty sponsor of the freshman class. How could I help them maintain their well being?

The understanding of healthful living as we know it today had not crossed the thinking of either the medical profession or the laity. So with prayer, an investigation of the scientific literature (which my good wife did), and the searching of the writings of Scripture and Ellen White, the course in Medical Evangelism became in essence a course in healthful living. For the well being of the students they were encouraged, among other things, to exercise, get adequate rest and sleep, eat appropriately, and take time to provide for spiritual nourishment. And with the blessing of God it worked.

The Failing Student

One day I called a student who was failing hopelessly into my office. He had started his freshman year with good grades but by Thanksgiving his performance was a disaster. I asked him, "Do you study?"

"Doctor," he replied, "that's all I do."

"Give me your schedule then," I queried. He was one of the few students who were married so he did not live in the dormitory. And this is what he reported.

"I get up at 4:00 AM, regardless of what time I go to bed. I study until six, then get dressed, have family worship and breakfast, and I'm at school for the first class at 7:00 AM. My wife makes me a lunch so I study while I'm eating. When the last class ends, usually at 5:00 PM, I go home, play with my children, have our evening meal, then family worship, and by seven, I'm hitting the books. I study till ten, eleven, and sometimes 12:00 or even till one. But I always awaken at four!"

"Do you get any exercise?" I inquired.

"Exercise! I don't have time to exercise."

"How many hours of sleep do you need to feel completely rested?" was my next question.

He thought for a few moments, and then replied, "About eight hours a night."

"Then why don't you get some form of physical exercise for at least 20 minutes a day, and get eight hours of sleep each night?"

"But I can't do that! I'll flunk for sure," he exclaimed. "Do you really mean what I heard you say?"

"If you keep on your current program you're off to boot camp. You've hit bottom, and the only way you can go, is to go up. Why don't you give it a try?"

He thanked me and left. I watched his grades. Two weeks later he got a passing grade, and from then on he did better and better ending his year in the top third of his class! Some months later he came to my office.

"Doctor Hardinge, I want to thank you for the counsel you gave me. When I went home my wife asked me what you had advised. I told her what you had suggested and added, "Absolutely ridiculous!"

"Now hold on," she spoke in no uncertain tones, "you've only had a few weeks of medical classes and you think you know more than Dr. Hardinge? You've tried your own program and it isn't working. Don't you think you should give his advice a try?" And I did, and I can hardly believe how well it's worked. Thank you again. It's the best advice I've ever had!"

It worked then and it still works today! And there were many others who were helped by simple changes in their living habits.

A Major Choice

The war ended and I received a visit from Dr. Stafford, now head of the Department of Surgery. He encouraged me to complete my resident training in surgery, and then added, "We are planning to organize a new department called Surgical Anatomy. We would like you to be the Chairman of that department, and you can take your residency on the salary of a department head not just that of a resident!" What an opportunity and what an offer!

At the same time the administration of the medical school came urging me to remain at Loma Linda. There are scores of physicians who want to go into surgery, they said, but we have difficulty finding one who is willing to teach in the basic sciences. Besides you are doing extremely well in anatomy, the health of Dr. Samuel Crooks, the current Chairman, is failing fast, and we would like to groom you to replace him as Chairman when he can no longer teach. Please feel that this is your call to the mission field. After considerable prayer and searching of heart, I decided to remain at Loma Linda and continue in anatomy. However, I made one proviso, and that was that if I received a call to serve in the mission field, I would feel free to accept it.

Back in the Lab

One afternoon I was in the student dissection laboratory, a large room that housed one hundred students, divided into groups of four, each group assigned a table with an embalmed body for dissection. It was my turn to monitor the lab. When monitoring we would walk up and down helping students to find or identify structures. On some days we would question the students as to what they had dissected, name this artery, or what does this nerve supply, and so forth.

The Humorist

At one table there was a student who was an inborn humorist. He had the ability to turn most any discussion into a laugh. Chuck (pseudonym), my associate, and I were monitoring the lab that afternoon. We happened to be at the humorist's table. The cadavers were in the prone position, that is, face down, and the assignment required they dissect the gluteal region, commonly called the "buttocks" or "sit-me-down!" Their dissection had revealed the gluteus maximus, one of the largest muscles in the body.

One of the "hen medics" in the class was a very large girl, overweight, and with distinctly protruding buttocks. She happened to be one of the four at the adjacent table. Turning towards the humorist, Chuck pointed to the large gluteal muscle, and asked him to name it. The student looked at it as if he had never seen it before. He allowed the fingers of one hand to pass over it. Then he did the same thing with his other hand. He seemed to be deep in thought. Then he brightened up and turning towards the "hen medic" referred to above, and cupping his hands as if he were holding a very large watermelon, said, "gluteus, gluteus," and then paused. After a few moments, and with a twinkle in his eyes but still absolutely dead pan, blurted out, "gluteus tremendous!"

Experiences such as this are among some of the bright spots of teaching.

Orthopedic Clinics

During War II there was a shortage of physicians on the home front. I had been granted the General Surgery Resident training program at the White Memorial Hospital, in Los Angeles. However, because of the need of physicians in the armed forces all residencies had been suspended. The White Memorial Clinic was in desperate need of an orthopedist so I was urged to accept the position, which I did. I was still employed by the Medical

School at Loma Linda, but devoted one and sometimes two days a week at the White (this was in the afternoons). In the mornings I would do volunteer service in an orthopedic clinic at the Los Angeles County General Hospital. I had no specialty training in orthopedics but was ready to learn. Both institutions were ready to take almost anyone!

At the County the major clinic started at 7:00 AM, Thursday morning with a review of the problem cases, which were presented to the staff by the senior resident. Following the review of the difficult problems, the group would make ward rounds, following which the clinic patients were seen. The group (all volunteers) was made up of five orthopedists, called junior attending men, and one senior attending man, or the chief. Since I did not have an independent practice I served on a 12-month basis, that is, on two services of six months each.

Toenails

At this particular time, the chief was Dr. Mosser Taylor, an orthopedist renowned in Southern California. The first problem patient that morning was a cowboy who worked on one of the large ranches located south of Los Angeles. It was around two in the afternoon. While harnessing a horse, it rose up on its hind legs and attempted to come down with its front hoofs and strike the cowhand. He fortunately stepped aside but one hoof struck the forefoot of his left foot. This knocked three of his tarsal bones completely out of his foot and sent them flying to different areas of the corral. The blow from the hoof also broke all the metatarsal bones. These are the long bones that support each of the toes. Please remember this happened in a horse corral with horse manure all over the ground!

His companion helped him into a pickup truck and then collected the three bones wrapping them in a newspaper. They headed for the Long Beach General Hospital. Arriving there they were seen at the emergency room after approximately two hours, at which time they were informed that he had better go to the Los Angeles County General Hospital as they could give him better care. By the time they got there and were admitted it was 8:00 PM. Six long hours had elapsed since the accident.

By the time he was in surgery it was 10:00 PM. While the chief resident and his assistants were cleaning out his wound and appraising the full extent of his injury, the three bones were taken from the newspaper and placed in a disinfectant solution. The three bones were later replaced into their original positions and the wound sutured. Embedded in the cast into which his foot was then placed was a rectangular wire extending about three inches beyond his toes; a tiny hole was drilled through the outer limits of each of his toenails, through which was placed a small wire hook. A rubber band extended from the hook to the rectangular wire mentioned above. The pull of the rubber band provided forward traction on the fractured metatarsal bones. This would help to keep them aligned and healing would be promoted. This method of using a wire hook and rubber band was replaced following World War II by an invention made by the Japanese. This consisted of a woven "finger cot" placed over the toe. When pulled forward it gripped the toe and worked extremely well.

Following the conference we went to see the patients who had been presented for discussion. When Dr. Taylor and I entered the ward in which the cowboy was lying, he had a cradle covering his injured foot so the bedclothes would not put pressure on it. A towel was thrown over the wire cradle. The cowboy was smoking a cigarette and laughing and talking with the patients on either side of him.

"How are you doing?" Dr. Taylor asked.

"Just wonderful," he answered with a chuckle. "Best holiday I've ever had. Just lie around and have to do nothing. When I want a drink of water or a cup of coffee, I just press this here button and a pretty girl brings it to me! Never dreamed I'd ever have a vacation like this. It couldn't be better, Doc!"

Dr. Taylor lifted the towel that covered the wire cage. I don't know what my expression was but it was probably similar to that of Dr. Taylor's, one of disbelief, amazement, and horror, all put together in one! Dangling from the rubber bands were the wire hooks, each with a toenail hanging from it! The tension exerted by the rubber bands had been sufficient to pull off all his toenails! Slowly Dr. Taylor replaced the towel and turning to the others in the group, said, "I want each of you to take a look at his foot."

One by one they came by and on raising the towel each face showed the same look of amazement and horror. No one said a word. When everyone had looked, Dr. Taylor turned to the patient. "Do you have any pain?" His voice was calm and controlled.

"Naw, Doc, not the least. This whole thing is a picnic!"

When we were back in the conference room Dr. Taylor turned to the chief resident and with a quizzical look admonished him, "Next time use less powerful rubber bands!"

The story of this cowboy continues as if it was a fairy tale, no complaints, no infection, even though at that time there were no antibiotics, and no problems of any kind. We saw him again six months later. One would never know that his foot had had any injury.

Gang Warfare

After Pearl Harbor the Japanese, the majority of whom lived in the western portion of our country, were summarily deported to detention camps for the duration of the war. A large segment of the population who lived in the area of the White Memorial Hospital was Japanese. They were good citizens and the area was one of the safest in the City of Los Angeles. However when they were forced to vacate their homes, undesirable elements from Chicago and other large cities in the east, migrated west and replaced the Japanese.

The Flail Arm

At the time, on certain days of the week, I worked in the Orthopedic Department of the White Memorial Clinic. One afternoon a patient was presented who had become involved in a gang fight the evening before and had been surrounded by three members of another gang. One member of the gang got on each side of him while the third stood behind ready to help if needed. The patient was a heavy set, bull-necked individual as strong as an ox. But he was no match for those who attacked him.

The one on the left grabbed him around the head locking the fingers of his right and left hands together over the patient's right ear. The one on the right locked his two hands over his right shoulder. At a signal they both came into action. His head was jerked as far to the left as possible while at the same time, his right shoulder was depressed. The result was that the large nerves that traveled from the neck via the shoulder to the arm and fingers were torn apart. When I examined him I found that his right arm was hanging limp with only patchy sensation here and there. Movement of the extremity was virtually nil! What a tragedy!

At the time this happened, repair of nerves was in its infancy. Had the nerves been clean-cut the problem would not have been as grave. But even today, with microsurgery available, shredded nerves like a broken rope would be extremely difficult to repair. I was surprised to learn that the gang world knew enough about the anatomy of the body to do serious injury to a rival without killing him. Stab wounds were directed towards vulnerable areas such as under the arm, behind the knee, and in the groin.

A Close Call

But not all the injuries that were seen in the clinic had such a sad ending. I recall another patient who was in his late teens. He came in complaining of extreme pain at the lower border of his left shoulder blade (scapula). He had been seen in the general medicine clinic, then in the neurology clinic, and now had been referred to the orthopedic clinic. Palpating the area elicited no pain, neither did movement of his left arm and shoulder. There was no history of an injury and nothing to see on the surface. I, like the others who had examined him, was baffled. But he begged for relief.

In those days patients suffering from bursitis in the shoulder region were often injected with a solution of Novocain (local anesthetic). It provided relief and sometimes led to a cure of the problem. Since I could think of nothing else, I decided to infiltrate the painful area with the local anesthetic. Believe it or not, it worked like a charm! The young man went on his way rejoicing.

But he was back the next Thursday afternoon. Same problem but this time begging for an injection of that wonderful medicine. "Please doctor, give me a shot." And we did and it again relieved his pain. On this, his second visit, I learned that he had tuberculosis with a large cavity in his left lung. Once a week (on Thursday morning) his left lung was being collapsed by the injection of air into his left pleural space (the space between the lung and the rib cage). Since antibiotics had not at that time been discovered, this was the treatment of choice.

What we concluded was that whenever his lung was collapsed adhesions between his lung and the rib-cage were stretched causing the pain. Over the months I became well acquainted with the lad. One afternoon as I was preparing to give him his weekly injection I noticed a band aide on the back of his right shoulder and another on the left front, lower neck. I asked him why he had the band aides and who had put them on. This is what had happened.

He had just had his injection of air and had crossed the street. While waiting for the tram that would take him to the White Memorial Clinic, a fight broke out between two rival gangs. Eventually shots were fired and a bullet had hit him on his upper back just below his right shoulder. It then had passed through the base of his neck on the right side and had exited on the left side of his neck just above his right collarbone (clavicle). Other than the two visible wounds, which had been dressed in the tuberculosis clinic, he had suffered not the slightest injury. The slug had missed the large nerves in his right lower neck, his right and left carotid arteries, the right and left jugular veins, not to mention his trachea and thyroid gland! The wounds healed without any infection and when I saw him again, his band aides were missing.

Truth sometimes is stranger than fiction!

A Crucial Test

Things were going as well as I could hope for. My teaching in Anatomy, my course in Medical Evangelism, and my research projects all were moving in the right direction. Then one morning there was a knock on my door. On my "come in," who must walk in but the President of the University, the Dean of the Medical School, the Chairman of the CME Board, and two other board members! I had but a single chair in my office so scurried around to borrow additional chairs. Then the President spoke, "Dr. Hardinge, Dr. Alfred Shryock, the Chairman of the Department of Microscopic Anatomy is getting old and is already well beyond retirement years. We have been watching you in your professional work and like what we see. We are here to ask you to consider transferring to the Department of Microscopic Anatomy where you will be the Chairman. We do not expect you to make a decision this morning, but ask you to give it very serious consideration. And do please pray about it. We do not wish to rush you in any way, but let us know as soon as you decide."

With that they all knelt and offered a prayer that God would guide me in my choice.

At lunch that noon I told Margaret of the request. To my surprise she burst into tears saying, "I don't want you to go into microscopic anatomy, and I don't feel you should give it any consideration!"

Periodically, over the next three months, by ones or twos, members of the Board and the Administration stopped by asking if I had made a decision on the matter. Each time they would have a prayer before they left.

At the same time, I was having a battle of my life. Constantly the request would fill my thoughts. The words of God's promise, "Commit your way unto the Lord, . . . and He will direct your paths," were ringing in my ears. "Could God really be leading in this request? But it didn't make sense. Why don't they find someone else? Why me?"

I didn't sleep well at nights. I lost my appetite and lost weight that I could ill afford at the time. Anyone of whom I sought counsel told me to forget it, which didn't help a bit! "What was I to do?"

About three months had passed. It was a Thursday afternoon, 5:00 PM, and all the workers in the department had left. I closed my office door and knelt down. I opened my heart to the Lord and told Him I was not interested in microscopic anatomy. "But, Lord, if this is what You want me to do, I will do it. And, Lord, I'll do it as if it was the only thing in life I ever wanted to do." When I got home that evening, I told my wife of my decision. This time her response was quite different. "If that is what you feel the Lord wants you to do, I'll support you."

It was seven o'clock the next morning as I was headed down the hall to my office. I heard footsteps following me so I stopped and looked back. It was the Dean of the School of Medicine and he was all out of breath. "My," he said, "you do walk fast!" And then he came to the point.

"Yesterday, I was in a committee meeting in San Diego when the topic of the Chairmanship of Microscopic Anatomy came up. The consensus of the group was that we should know your decision. We don't want to rush you, but Dr. Alfred wants to terminate his responsibilities. I hope you can make a positive decision, for if you don't, we don't know where to turn."

"I have made my decision."

"You have! I hope you have accepted the request. What is it?" He could hardly contain himself.

And then to my own surprise, I replied, "I will give my decision in writing. When do need to know?"

"So you won't tell me now? I need it by 10:00 AM, Sunday morning."

"You'll have it then," and we both went our separate ways.

Now why I had said what I did, I don't know. That afternoon I wrote the letter that said in essence: "I do not have a desire to enter the field of microscopic anatomy. However, I have prayed earnestly about the matter, and feel that if this is what the Lord wants me to do, I am prepared to accept the proposal." I showed the letter to Dr. Crooks, the Chairman of my department, Gross Anatomy. He read it through and then burst into tears. "Mervyn," he said, "you are making a grave mistake, but if this is what the Lord wants you do, the Lord bless you."

At ten o'clock I placed the letter on the Dean's desk. He opened the letter and read it through. In fact he read it through several times. Then looking up at me he spoke these words: "Mervyn, we appreciate very much your willingness to transfer to microscopic anatomy, but we couldn't possibly ask you to do so." He then slowly folded the letter and put it back in the envelope.

Meanwhile, I sat there in stunned silence "Did I hear right? Was I in a dream? Have they found someone else?" These and similar thoughts were racing through my head. I stood up, thanked him, and walked back to my office.

The first one I met was Dr. Crooks. "When do they want you begin your work in micro?" he inquired.

"They don't want me," I replied.

"Now this is too important an issue for you to kid around."

"I'm not kidding. It's true."

I had the same difficulty convincing my wife when I called her on the phone. But it was true. The administration had not found anyone else. Six months later one of my classmates was on the campus. He had just gotten out of the armed forces. He was offered the position and accepted it. He remained in the department until his retirement! God guides in strange and wondrous ways.

Visiting Medical Schools

The following year I was asked to visit the Anatomy Departments of twenty-two medical schools in the northeast corner of the United States. This was so I could learn firsthand how other departments of anatomy were conducted. While visiting the various medical schools I arranged to take the qualifying examinations to practice in Canada, which in turn had reciprocity in Great Britain and the British Commonwealth.

As we were driving through New Mexico (plane travel was still to come) my wife read me an article on "minimum protein requirements." At the time the intake of protein dominated nutrition research. I was revising the chapter in my syllabus ("Health Talks") on protein so the subject was on our minds (my wife was helping me).

"Who wrote the article?" I inquired.

"Doctors Stare and Hegsted," was her reply.

""Which University are they at?" was my next question.

"They are at Harvard," was her response.

"Then while we are visiting the Anatomy Department at Harvard, we can also visit the Department of Nutrition, and perhaps get to meet these men." And this is what we did. Dr. Fred Stare was Chairman of the department and met us most cordially. We were impressed with the type of research they were doing, and on the way back to Loma Linda I decided I would apply for admission to their program.

The Canadian Medical Board Examinations

The Canadian Board examinations were offered several times a year. Since the Friday afternoon exam alternated with the Saturday morning exam it was necessary to take four exams one session and then wait for the next session to take the fifth exam. While I was visiting the anatomy departments I arranged that I take the first four examinations at the University of London, Ontario, in the city of London, Ontario, and the fifth examination about a month later at the University of Toronto, in Toronto.

I had heard that a Dr. Fenton Argue, Secretary of the Canadian Board of Medical Examiners, was very hostile towards Seventh-day Adventists, and that his headquarters was in Toronto. I doubted that he would be at the exams held in London, Ontario, but did have the premonition that he would be present during the examination in Toronto. My wife and I arrived in the Toronto area on Wednesday and stayed at Oshawa Missionary College, about twenty miles east of Toronto. On Thursday I drove into the city to make sure I knew where the examination would be held, where I could park, etc. I did not want to be late for the exam.

Doctor Fenton Argue!

Friday afternoon I entered the examination room at two in the afternoon with my enabling certificate in hand. A tall, gaunt man was searching the students' faces as they came by him for a seat assignment. He looked at my enabling certificate and recognized my name. In a rage he shouted at me, "Come with me." He led the way to a desk right in front of where he was to sit as he presided over the exam. "Sit here," he yelled, "You Adventists make a convenience of us. Tell the men at Loma Linda that you are the last of their graduates to take the exams in Canada."

I sat down and waited for the examination paper. It was ten minutes after he gave out the exam papers to the others that I received mine. Off and on during the three-hour exam he hovered over me glowering at my answers. I prayed to the Lord to give me peace of mind as I answered the questions. And the Lord answered my prayer. I felt sure he would pick up my paper the moment the exam ended. And this he did. "Time up," he spoke in a loud voice, and my paper was gone! Ten minutes later there were others still writing on their exams. As I left the room he again angrily shouted at me, "Tell your men in Loma Linda that you're the last of their graduates to take these exams in Canada!"

On Monday of the following week I took the oral examination which covered the same subject matter as the written exam I had taken on Friday. It was late afternoon by now and as I was walking towards where my car was parked, who must I see coming up the road but Dr. Fenton Argue! He was on the opposite side of the street so I thought I might pass unnoticed. But this was not to be.

He recognized me and walked diagonally across the street and stopped by the curb adjacent to the sidewalk on which I was walking. In a loud and angry voice he reiterated, "Tell your Loma Linda administrators that you are the last of their graduates to take the Canadian examinations; that you Adventists are just making a convenience of the Canadian examinations, and that their graduates should go to Edinburgh and get British qualifications." All the while I was praying that God would help me to say the right thing. Then I spoke.

"Dr. Argue, it is a great convenience for us graduates to obtain our British qualifications here in Canada. We are a church organization and it is much more costly to send our missionary doctors to Edinburgh to obtain their British qualifications. That is the reason I am taking these exams so that if I should receive a call to serve in one of our mission hospitals, I would be ready to go without the additional cost of transporting my family to Edinburgh and supporting them there while I took their examinations."

Dr. Argue was strangely quiet and a wistful look crossed his face. He was no longer angry and spoke in a soft voice. "There was a day when I planned to be a foreign missionary doctor. I understand what you are saying for I was a member of our church's foreign mission board for a number of years. I am aware of the scarcity of funds that seems always to exist." Then he made the most astounding claim: "In fact, Doctor Hardinge, this is the reason we have begun to alternate the exam given on Friday with that given Saturday morning! It was I who worked out this arrangement so you men could take the examinations!"

I thanked him repeatedly for what he had done and requested his home address which he was happy to give me. We left on the most cordial terms. Seventh-day Adventist physicians never again have had any trouble taking their examinations in Canada. My wife and I sent him an annual subscription for the *Signs of the Times* for the next fourteen years, and we exchanged Christmas cards for each of those years. He retired in Tennessee. When he died his daughter informed us of his death.

A Different Story

Things are not always what one person tells you. The evening of the day I had had this visit with Dr. Argue, a totally different story unfolded. As the reader compares the two accounts of how the arrangement was made for Adventists to take the Canadian Board exams, I believe it will become crystal clear which one to believe!

Divine Providence

That evening my wife and I were invited to have supper with the Educational Secretary of the local Conference. During the meal I mentioned the events of the day. And this is the account he related to us, a story which reveals how God works in wonderful ways in behalf of His people and His cause. The five written examinations for the Canadian Board, as mentioned briefly above, were scheduled two on Thursday, two on Friday and the fifth on Saturday. Through the years the Board was unwilling to make any arrangements so that Seventh-day Adventist physicians could take the Saturday's examination at some other time. The principal opponent to making any accommodation for Adventists was the Secretary of the Board, Dr. Fenton Argue.

Two of Loma Linda's graduates, both Canadians, were interning in one of the hospitals in Vancouver, British Columbia. They were extremely well liked by the attending physicians. Both were invited to join practices of physicians practicing in the area.

"Why are you unwilling to practice in Canada?" they were asked."

"There is no way we can take the Canadian Board Examinations because one consistently falls on Saturdays," was their reply.

"This should be changed," was the response. One of the physicians was on the Medical Board (Canada) and, with the encouragement of several other physicians, made a request to the Board to work out some form of accommodation for Seventh-day Adventist physicians. Dr. Argue vigorously opposed any such idea. However, unknown to the supporters in the west, a delegation from the General Conference, the Canadian Union, and the Quebec Conference approached the Board. They got nowhere with Dr. Argue, so requested an interview with the Chairman of the Medical Board.

The Chairman, Monsignor Blank, was director of the teaching hospital of the medical school at the University of Montreal. When the delegation entered his room he was as cold as ice. They then made their request to which he replied, "You Adventists do nothing for Catholics. All you do is criticize us. Why should we do anything for you?"

"To the contrary," replied the Religious Liberty Secretary of the Quebec Conference, "We have been of great service to the Catholic Church."

"Tell me when and how," was his rejoinder.

"You will recall," the Secretary responded, "that after World War II the Greek government was planning to withdraw all religious freedoms for church entities other than the Greek Orthodox Church. The Seventh-day Adventist Church was appealing such legislation and was sending Dr. Nussbaum, a well known French physician active in government circles, to request the Greek government to give the Seventh-day Adventist Church freedom to practice their religion. Cardinal Pacelli (who later became Pope Pius XII) called Dr. Nussbaum asking that he please include the Catholic Church in his appeal. This he did with the result that not only Seventh-day Adventists but all religious bodies, including the Catholic Church, have freedom of worship in Greece today."

Monsignor Blank listened in silence and then spoke, "How can we help you?" He sat in silence for a while and then brightened up. "What would you think if we alternated the exams given on Friday afternoon and Saturday morning? This would allow you Adventists to take all the examinations without infringing on your Sabbath. It would, however, require your men to take four examinations on one occasion and subsequently take the fifth exam, when the examinations are offered again." And this was the decision the Board took. I was one of the early graduates of Loma Linda to take advantage of this provision.

Lincoln, Nebraska

On the way back to Loma Linda we decided to stop at Union College, Lincoln, Nebraska where Leslie, my brother, was teaching in the Bible Department. It was a Friday evening when we drove up their driveway. The mid-west was enduring a heat wave with temperatures and humidity in the high nineties. To say the least, it was hot!

Despite the weather conditions we enjoyed supper and the evening, and thanks to fans, had a good night's sleep. Sabbath morning we went to Sabbath School and Church. The afternoon was oppressively hot and around four in the afternoon, Les suggested we visit the zoo, the idea to which we all enthusiastically agreed.

My Brother and the Moose

The zoo was in its infancy located on the outskirts of Lincoln. High chain-linked fences enclosed cattle of various hues, sheep, goats, deer, and a moose. As we were strolling past the enclosure with the moose we paused to look in its direction. It immediately turned its attention to us and ambled over to take a closer look. In fact it brought its nose right up to the fence, hoping I'm sure, for a handout of some kind. It had huge pulsating nostrils, larger than I had seen in any animal at such close range. As I was looking around for some grass to give the beast, an idea crossed from one of my over-heated neurons to another. What would happen, I pondered, if a long piece of grass was thrust up one of its nostrils?

I shared the idea with the others. I immediately knew, from the twinkle in my brother's eye, that his response was a positive one. It didn't take him long to find a straw about eight inches long. He picked it up and approached the expectant nostrils. The procedure of inserting the straw up the nostril was not difficult and proved highly successful. It went in at least six inches!

The adult male moose was a monstrous animal and had an enormous rack of horns. It drew its head slightly backwards, contracted its diaphragm so as to fill its lungs to the full, and raising its head a few inches gave the most horrendous sneeze I've ever heard! The result of that sneeze was more than any of us could imagine. Since it lacked the manners of holding a Kleenex to its nose, a cup-full of grayish white mucus shot towards my brother as if coming from a fire hose. Some hung from the chain-link fence in large droplets but most of it passed through the openings in the fence and found lodging on Les's face, shirt, and even his trousers! A shower and a dry cleaner were both immediately in demand.

My brother was transfixed. His face had a look of horror on it. We, on the other hand, could barely stand upright, the paroxysms of laughter all but causing us to literally roll on the ground. Our merriment did nothing to lift Les's spirits which were anything but pleasant for some time afterwards. He could see nothing funny in the whole episode!

To his dying day (sadly, he passed away a couple of years ago) he maintained that I was the one who stuck the straw up the animal's nose. I must admit that the idea originated with me, but the thrust of the straw was entirely his. So, may he and the moose rest in peace.

Back at Loma Linda

On my return to Loma Linda, there were two things that I emphasized in my report to the faculty. First, it was absolutely essential that a basic science teacher have specialty training in the area in which he taught; and secondly that each faculty member must carry forward some type of research in his specialty area. Up to that time any physician who showed an interest in a subject area might be offered a position in the department, should there be an opening. He would gain expertise in his field with on-the-job training. It was on this basis that I became a member of the faculty.

The trip east cemented my desire to take training in nutrition. This would enable me to manipulate the rate of bone growth as well as bone healing, and would be my specialty area of research.

I came home for supper and as we visited during the meal Margaret told me of an interesting story she overheard, as she was in the Department of Motor Vehicles in San Bernardino. It was a swelteringly hot afternoon. Margaret was standing in a long line of men and women who were impatiently waiting to receive their new registration plates for their automobiles. It was before the time when one could register by mail! The line was moving at a snail's pace when the DMV's two Testing Officers stopped close to where she stood. They were not speaking in subdued voices so she could easily hear what they were saying.

The Cop Who Compromised

"Hi, Don! Haven't seen you since you were transferred from the high desert to the valley. How are things going?" Don and Bill had worked closely together in the area of Mohave.

"Just fine, Bill, but I sure miss the desert. I love the wide-open spaces, the Joshua trees and the sagebrush. I didn't even mind the rattle snakes!" They laughed together, and chatted for a while.

"Bill," Don inquired, "how is Mary Woodbury doing? I've often wondered if things are well with her?"

There was a long silence. My wife looked at the men. Bill had a sad expression, Don an inquiring one. Then Bill spoke, "She was killed in an auto accident about three months ago. Happened where the road she lives on crosses the north and south highway. Ran a stop sign!"

Don then told this story. Mary Woodbury and her husband Tom lived away out near a small desert community some twenty-five miles from the City of Mohave. They had occupied the same house for at least the last 30 years and were well known in the small community. Their home was on the outskirts of town, about two miles from their nearest neighbor. Tom had worked for the electric company while Mary had taught the third grade children in the local school. They both had been retired for some ten years.

About three years before the relating of this story, Tom had suddenly died of a coronary attack. Mary had never driven a car in her life. Tom had always taken her wherever she needed to go. Now she was in a pickle. Neighbors were kind enough to drive her to town once in a while to do some shopping, but she felt imprisoned and yearned to drive herself. Finally one of her friends offered to teach her to drive. This was wonderful news.

Mary, with the help of her friend, was gradually learning to handle a moving vehicle, but the progress was slow. It was difficult for Mary to judge distances and to anticipate what might happen around her. Even when there was no traffic she would not brake until the stop sign was upon her! As a result, she would occasionally go right through, or not notice the sign until it was too late to stop. But her friend was patient and Mary was persistent. Finally the day came when she applied for a license.

She passed her written examination without any trouble. It was her driving test where her difficulties surfaced. Don was the officer who was responsible for giving driving tests in her district. Mary and the officer went out on the road but Mary was unable to handle stop signs and left turns. He had to fail her and told her to come back in three months. Three months later the same thing happened. Don could see no improvement in her driving skills. This went on for over a year.

Mary would plead with Don to give her a restricted license. All she asked was to drive to town, and where, she promised, she would park on the outskirts. After her shopping was done she would return home. She would only drive during the day light hours and she promised to be especially careful when approaching and crossing the single highway between the town and her house. But Don could not in clear conscience agree to this. Finally one day, after her test was over, Don, overriding his better judgment, and feeling that she had performed a little better than in the past, issued her a restricted license. Mary was overjoyed.

Mary kept her promise. She only drove to town and back to her home, and only in daylight hours. She was always very careful when crossing the highway. But then the day came when she failed to stop at the intersection and was struck and killed by a passing truck!

Sympathy can obscure the obvious and compromise is always a dangerous thing!

Chapter 6

MY HARVARD EXPERIENCE

It was difficult to believe that Margaret and I were both enrolled in graduate degree programs at a University with a stature like Harvard's, both working towards our Master's degree in nutrition. God had worked wondrously and there had not been the slightest hitch in our acceptance and enrollment. We were in the School of Public Health with a class of seventy-one students. Of these, 65 were physicians, the balance made up of dentists, veterinarians, and other health professionals. Of the physicians, seven were Chinese, three Philippine, three Japanese, seven from Inter- and South America, a few from Germany and other European countries and the rest were from North America.

Three Discouraged Physicians

It was the second day of school and I was walking down the center isle of the large classroom in which one of two required courses was being taught. I happened to notice three of the most discouraged individuals I had ever seen. They were the three Philippine physicians.

That evening I told my wife about my impression of how depressed these men had looked, and suggested we invite them to have dinner with us Friday evening, serving curry and rice which I felt sure they would enjoy. This is what we did even though our apartment consisted of a bedroom with kitchen privileges. We soon discovered that it was indeed a privilege for my wife to get into the kitchen!

The evening together proved to be a most delightful occasion as we got acquainted with these total strangers. They had left their wives and families behind and had not as yet adjusted to a life in the United States. One of the three, the friendliest, became a good friend during the ensuing months. His name was Doctor Gaitmaitan. Following our graduation we continued to keep in touch, exchanging Christmas cards and an occasional short note. Several years later he was appointed the Minister of Health for the Philippines, a cabinet position. I wrote congratulating him on his success.

Little did I know when we first met Dr. Gaitmaitan in our small apartment in Boston, and when a long term friendship was established, that after some twenty years God would use this friend to do great things for His work in the Philippines. God works in His own mysterious ways to accomplish His plans and purposes. (The experience will be related later.)

My studies towards the Master's Degree went well. It was a pleasure to be in this strong academic environment. The lectures were well prepared, the lecturers having had personal experience in the areas they were presenting. The quizzes and exams were meticulously graded, notations being made in the margins of the papers. Even spelling and grammar were checked! But interestingly, although no grades were issued, the performance of every student was kept in the Registrar's Office. The beauty of this system was that there was no competition between students. We were competing with ourselves, each doing his very best.

Competitive Studies and Sports

And here I might add a comment. On my return to Loma Linda I presented in a report to the faculty the system of no grades being issued to the students. The faculty of the Medical School was so impressed that they adopted the policy of the non-issuing of grades. The students, if anything, studied harder; there was no quibbling about one student obtaining one point more than another, even though they compared their papers with each other. The system worked well, but over the years first one faculty member and then another began sharing the grades with the students and the system broke down. At Harvard, if this had happened, the faculty member who gave out grades would have been fired.

In our schools there has been a condemnation of competition in sports. Students, in opposing this attitude, have pointed out the inconsistency of condemning competition on the field but allowing, and even encouraging it in the classroom! Why not try the system of not issuing grades?

A Course at MIT

Harvard University and the Massachusetts Institute of Technology (MIT) worked closely together. The two institutions had a mutual agreement that any full-time graduate student at Harvard could take any course at MIT without being charged tuition, and vice versa, any full-time student at MIT could in turn take any course offered at Harvard at no cost.

Along with a group of other students at the SPH, six of us in all, I registered to take a course entitled "Food Technology," in the Department of Food Technology at MIT. Food technology deals with the technical aspects of food; for example, its nutrient content and how various factors, such as storage, cooking, freezing, drying, environment and genetics might affect it. In our nutrition classes we dealt with such topics as to what were the nutritional needs of the body, and how these needs might be met in both sickness and health.

Graduate students tend to help each other. I have, on numerous occasions, given blood to fellow students so they could carry out some research project. A thirty-five year old employee of Cudahy Meat Packing Company, with head quarters in Chicago, was taking her Master's Degree in food technology. For her research project she was investigating what constitutes flavor?

What Constitutes Flavor?

The project was a relatively simple but clever one. She assembled about twelve fellow graduate students and conducted the following study. She obtained a room that had no outside windows and when the door was closed it was pitch dark inside. In the room she arranged a dozen chairs in a half circle in which the subjects sat. She turned the lights off and in the darkness handed each a bowl of food. They were forbidden to share information with one another, and then, at a given signal each participant was to taste and determine what the food was. The signal was given and everyone knew what it was. There was great smacking of lips and sounds of enjoyment. It was delicious lemon meringue pie! She then turned the lights on.

As they looked at their bowls they saw some pale green slimy looking frothy material. Two of the subjects vomited and several of the others were queasy in their stomachs. After things were cleaned up and every one had equilibrated, she repeated the first procedure. The lights were turned off and in the dark each was handed a bowl of food. This time no one was able to guess what was being eaten. Then the lights came on. There in each bowl was a beautiful looking piece of lemon pie! The color and the texture had been altered. Instead of being soft and creamy it was coarse and gritty.

The bowls were removed and a different set of bowls handed out. Again no one was able to guess what it was. When the lights came on it was, as you might guess, lemon meringue pie. This time the taste had been changed. Finally the last set of bowls was handed out and again, no one was able to determine what the food was. But you guessed it. It was lemon meringue pie with a different but distinct smell (odor).

Flavor is a combination of appearance, texture, taste and smell. Sometimes one dominates over another but usually we select the foods we like or dislike because of a combination of these factors. God did not make all foods look or taste alike. He concealed the delights of eating in different colors, shapes, and textures, and added to this mix awesome tastes and subtle fragrances!

It happened one afternoon. I have no recollection what subject was under discussion.

A Blunder of Blunders

This particular afternoon Dr. Robert Harris, professor and co-Chairman of the Department of Food Technology, was lecturing. I do not recall how he got onto the subject of vegetarians. (All my fellow students knew I was one, but Dr. Harris didn't!) He gave the most brilliant, but scathing, denunciation of a vegetarian, with the concluding remark that "you can always recognize a vegetarian because they are sallow skinned, bleary-eyed, and dull mentally."

One could have heard a pin-drop in the classroom. In a quiet but clear voice I said: "Dr. Harris, I am a life-time vegetarian!" This was followed by a stunned silence. Then Dr. Harris turned a crimson red, stood on one foot and then another, and broke out in a sweat. All the while the class members stamped their feet and roared with delight. I really felt sorry for the man.

Finally he regained his composure, and in a relatively soft voice addressed the class. "Gentlemen, we can all learn a lesson from this experience; keep your mouth shut!"

But that is not the end of the story. Some two years later I received a letter from Dr. Harris. After the usual greetings this is what he wrote, "I had looked forward to being present at your defense of your dissertation, but at the last minute something came up and I had to be elsewhere. However, Dr. Stare called me to say that you had done very well in your examination. Congratulations for your good work."

Acceptance at Harvard

My academic background prior to enrollment at Harvard had been in small virtually unknown academic institutions. Newbold Missionary College was not accredited to give any degrees, while Pacific Union College was a marginally accepted institution at the time of my studying there. For instance, Dr. Raymond Mortensen on graduation from PUC was denied admission by Stanford for the Master's degree program. So he obtained a master's degree at the University of Southern California and then was accepted into the doctorate program at Stanford! It amazed me that both Margaret and I were admitted to Harvard..

I will jump forward a few years. I was now dean of the School of Public Health at Loma Linda University and was attending the spring meeting of all the deans of the Schools of Public Health. It was coffee break time at around 10 AM when I found myself sitting by the side of the then associate dean of the Harvard School of Public Health, a Dr. Wittenburg. He had been the chairman of the Department of Environmental Physiology when I was a student at Harvard, and I had taken a course which he taught. We chatted for a while when I asked him:

"On what basis was I admitted to Harvard University?"

After a pause he gave this answer. "When a student applies for admission and presents a transcript from institutions like Berkeley, or Stanford, or the University of California at Los Angeles we accept their evaluation of the student at face value. If their grades reach our standard for admission they are accepted, if not their application is denied. However, when an applicant's academic background is from a college or university whose quality of education is not known, we ask ourselves, how did this student do in the academic environment in which he studied? If he did poorly he is rejected, but if he did well we say to ourselves, He did well among his peers, why not give him a chance. It was on this basis that you and your wife were admitted."

Sabbath Problems

I have often been asked if I encountered any problems with my observance of the Sabbath while studying at Harvard and Stanford? My answer is no. After being accepted at the each of these universities I wrote a letter to the Dean informing him of my beliefs. I made it clear that I do not attend classes or take examinations from Friday sunset to Saturday sunset, the Sabbath. I asked if this might pose any problem. Without exception the reply was that lecture attendance was not a requirement, and that they saw no difficulty in arranging for the exams to be taken at a time other than the Sabbath.

Dr. Malcolm Fair

Dr. Fair, an Englishman, taught the class in Environmental Health; he was also Dean of the School of Sanitary Engineering. He dressed in expensive clothes, looked the picture of a self-assured professional, and gave the best lectures I have ever listened to, bar none!

The classes were held on Tuesdays, Thursdays, and Saturdays. It was the policy of the School that the final examination of all classes was to be held at the time of the last class period scheduled for the particular course. Thus no examination schedule was issued. The final exam for Environmental Health would fall on Sabbath.

It was during the last week of the course when I approached Dr. Fair. I said to him, "Dr. Fair, I am a Seventh-day Adventist and do not take examinations on Saturday. Could the final be arranged for some other day?"

He looked me in the eye, and he could not have shown less willingness, in fact he seemed to exude hostility. "Dr. Hardinge," he responded, "I am a busy man and don't have time to prepare a second examination. The final will be held as scheduled."

We both had issued our ultimatums. As we stood looking at each other, like Nehemiah of old, I lifted up a silent prayer to the God of heaven, to bring about a solution. I did not know what to do or say. And then he spoke, "Whatever you can work out with Mrs. Barnaby, will be all right with me." Abruptly he turned and walked away.

"Thank you, Dr. Fair," I called after him.

I bounded down to Mrs. Barnaby's office, she was the registrar, and told her of Dr. Fair's request for her to arrange for the time of my final exam.

"That's right, you don't take examinations on Saturday. When would you like to take it, Friday afternoon or Monday morning?"

"Either day will be O.K. with me. Which will be most convenient for you?"

"Come in first thing Monday morning," she replied.

I thanked her, and as I walked away my heart was filled with gratitude to God, who once again had solved what had appeared to be an unsolvable problem.

Aiming at a Doctoral Degree

Each semester at Harvard was divided into first and second halves. Since I had virtually finished all my class work by the end of the first half of the second semester, I requested Dr. Stare if I could start work on my doctoral program, that is, in mid semester. To this he readily agreed. A committee of three professors was appointed. The committee's responsibility was to guide, oversee, and finally to be the initiators of two exams that I was to take. The first was the candidacy exam which is designed to evaluate the knowledge of the doctoral student in his chosen field (mine was nutrition) and to determine if the candidate's approach to the selected topic of research was reasonable. The second was to evaluate the research findings presented in the form of a dissertation. If found satisfactory, the committee was to schedule the time for the candidate to defend his/her dissertation.

The committee members were Dr. Stare, Chairman of the committee; Mrs. Bertha Burke, a professor in the Department of Maternal and Child Health; and Dr. George Reed, from the Department of Biostatistics.

I had prayed earnestly that God would guide me as to the subject I would investigate and that it would prove a blessing to His work and an honor to His name (See Appendix 2). Soon after I was impressed to study the nutritional adequacy of vegetarian diets, and compare these diets to those of non-vegetarians, who would act as controls. This I decided to do.

When I presented this topic to Dr. Stare, he asked, "Has anyone studied that question before?

"No, not to the best of my knowledge."

"Have you done a library search on that subject?"

"I have, and I find nothing like it in the literature."

"Then that's the topic for you to study."

Dr. Stare presented the topic to the committee, and obtained their approval. I also got the approval of the administration of the medical school at Loma Linda.

Now I should point out something of both interest and concern. Doctor Stare was not a vegetarian. In fact, he and others in the Nutrition Department ridiculed vegetarians. In public meetings it was Stare's habit to lampoon vegetarians. Yet he readily accepted the project I had suggested. Mrs. Burke, another member of my committee was well known as an avid meat eater, and it was reported that she even ate some liver every day!

By the end of the semester the committee approved my taking the candidacy exam. Graduation was on Thursday; my candidacy exam was scheduled for the following Tuesday. The Lord blessed and I was approved as a candidate to work towards my doctoral degree. Because I was a vegetarian I was required to spend a few weeks learning about the size of servings and the preparation and cooking of animal foods, poultry, and meats of all kinds, fish and other sea foods. I did this in the kitchen of the Peter Brent Brigham Hospital, a hospital associated with Harvard Medical School. It was a most interesting experience!

During this time I also practiced how to determine the food intake of people, both vegetarian and non-vegetarian. The procedure I used was called "The Method of Burke." It had been devised by Mrs. Burke, now a member of my doctoral committee. I believed and still do that it is the most accurate way of assessing how much food an individual eats. After establishing the fact that I was proficient in both these requirements, I was permitted to work in absentia since there are more vegetarians in the west than the east. This allowed me to do my research at Loma Linda. A further requirement was that I was to write a report every three months on the progress of my research.

With a happy heart, in late August, my wife and I drove back to Loma Linda, with our little boy who had been born in Boston a few months earlier.

Back in Anatomy

No sooner did we arrive in Loma Linda (August 1949) than I was asked to see the Dean. What he said astounded me. "The administration has asked me to ask you to change your research project!" I could not believe my ears.

"Did I hear you correctly?" I inquired in an incredulous voice.

"Yes you did, and I hope you understand."

"But did I not get your approval and that of the medical school's administration?"

"You did, but on further consideration we have changed our minds. I expect you to comply."

"May I ask the reason for this change of mind?"

"If your findings show that a vegetarian diet is unsatisfactory, it will bring disrepute to the School and to the Church," was his reply.

"If the diet recommended by the Church is inadequate then we should be the ones to find it out, not some other group," was my response.

I attempted to explain to him that should I now change my subject I would be washed out for all further studies at Harvard. This I could not do and would continue my research as planned.

My Project

Between teaching Anatomy and miscellaneous work assignments, I organized my research project. The first step was to get subjects for the study. I needed Complete Vegetarians, Lacto-ovo-vegetarians, and Non-vegetarians. My aim was to find lifetime adherents in each of the categories! In the first group I needed adult men and women between the ages of 40 to 65. The second group was pregnant women, early in their pregnancies, so I could follow them until delivery. The third and last group was adolescent boys and girls, who were going through puberty.

To obtain subjects for my study I prepared a questionnaire asking vegetarians both lacto-ovo and pure, to volunteer for the project. Three organizations were a great help to me: *The Vegetarian Digest*, a magazine published in Los Angeles and patterned after the *Readers Digest*; *The Vegetarian World*, a newspaper published in Santa Barbara; and Worthington Foods. All three organizations placed, free of charge, questionnaires in their publications requesting all those who qualified to fill out the forms and return them to me. Worthington Foods printed and distributed 20,000 questionnaires to all their customers. But the one publication that I could not get a questionnaire into was *The Recorder*, the Pacific Union Conference monthly paper. *The Recorder* had a policy that any employee of any church organization could not use the magazine without a signed approval of the head of the institution. The Dean at Loma Linda refused to do so.

It was about this time that I wrote my first report and sent it to Dr. Stare. In a few days I received a letter from the Nutrition Department. On opening it I found it contained a short letter addressed to Dr. Stare from Bertha Burke. This is what she had to say: "I have read Dr. Hardinge's report. It is obvious he does not know what he is doing, and should, immediately, be dropped from the program." Written in the margin of the letter I read: "You're doing fine; keep up the good work," signed Fred. It seemed clear that Mrs. Burke was after my skin! I submitted no further reports!

I also prepared various forms in which to record the medical and nutritional data obtained from evaluating each subject. Tables for the analysis of the diets were also prepared. I traveled to all the SDA churches I could reach, asking for subjects. Progress was good but not what I had hoped for. The questionnaires sent out by the three organizations found subjects who were mainly complete vegetarians. What I lacked were lacto-ovo-vegetarians.

Betrayed!

And then the world fell apart! On August 31, 1950, the night before the beginning of the school year, Dr. Crooks died. I gave his lecture the following morning, Sunday. The Dean called me later that morning asking that I prepare for a committee meeting in my office at nine o'clock Monday morning. The entire personnel of the department were there when he arrived.

After a few comments regarding the loss of Dr. Crooks, he said, "We must carry on. The department needs another Chairman and I would like to introduce him at this time, Doctor Chuck Bowmen (a pseudonym)! I'm sure you will find him an excellent leader." The news was greeted by a stunned silence. I could not believe what I had heard; neither could the other members of the department. No one had expected this. And why had the committee been called in my office? Chuck's office was the exact size of mine! Was it to further humiliate me?

Chuck stood to his feet and expressed his desire to work with all present. He then shook hands with each of the staff, welcoming them into his department, but he skipped me! And I knew why. His office was adjacent to mine and for the three pervious years he had spent 99% of his work time remodeling a house he had bought! He did not want me around.

Perhaps it is here that I should make something very plain. It was and has remained a conviction of mine never to ask for a position, a promotion, or a pay raise. I believed and still do that God calls us to work where He wants us to work. Then as He sees best he will advance us. The Scriptures promise that, "promotion cometh from the Lord." I had not asked to be the future Chairman of the Department. The administration had come to me and had encouraged me to get training for this position. And this is what I had done. I would have been happy working under any reasonable chairman. But Chuck was of a different cut.

When I fully realized what had happened I was angry, very angry! It wasn't that I had lost the chairmanship but because Chuck was one with whom no one could work. If someone else had been made Chairman I would have been disappointed but that is all. I had forfeited my surgical residency and my opportunity to be Chairman of the Department of Surgical Anatomy. And what is more I was now out of a job! And where could I continue my research towards my doctoral program? I felt like Joseph must have felt when betrayed by his brothers. My future was dark and uncertain. The world in which I lived had vanished. I was not concerned about making a living, for I could go into the practice of medicine any time. But something quite unexpected had happened!

I went to see the Dean. He was aware of what Chuck had been doing for the last three years. I asked him if this is how he rewarded unfaithfulness? I reminded him of the commitment of the school to me. His response was that it was too late to make any changes. At last I said to him, "I predict that in five years from today Chuck will be the only member left in the department." His reply, "We'll see." But it took only three years. Chuck was one, as I mentioned above, with whom no one could work. The department was decimated. Secretaries, technicians, and professional staff all left. Anatomy had been a strong department but it was gone. The administration had to start from scratch and it took several years before there was any real recovery.

Starting a New Career

But although I had been treated like Joseph, I'm afraid I did not act like him for I failed to put my trust in God. Bitterness filled my heart. But my merciful God had not forgotten me. The arrangement was that I was to teach anatomy till the end of the semester. Unexpectedly a professor who taught nutrition in the Department of Therapeutics left for another position, and I was invited to fill the vacancy. In January I moved into my new office. The department had two technicians, a secretary that the other members of the staff rarely used, and a fine chemistry laboratory with a stockroom of chemicals! Anatomy had none of these facilities. It gradually began to dawn on me that God might have other plans for my life.

The Department of Therapeutics was a conglomeration of disciplines: Physical Medicine, Pharmacology, and Nutrition. The Chairman of the Department, a Dr. Moore, was Board Certified in Physical Medicine, as was an associate of his, Dr. Clarence Dale. Dr. Bill Maddox (a pseudonym) was preparing to take his Board examinations in Physical Medicine. Dr. Lester Lonergan taught Pharmacology, and a Dr. Gant had taught Nutrition. Lonergan's responsibilities were heavy as he taught Pharmacology to both the medical and nursing students! Drs. Moore and Maddox were scheduled to give a few of the lectures in pharmacology, the latter being placed in charge of the laboratory teaching in pharmacology. I had been hired to replace Dr. Gant and to teach a short course in Nutrition.

My Introduction to Pharmacology

Two or three weeks following my arrival in the Department of Therapeutics I was approached by the Dean and requested to help assist in the Pharmacology Laboratory sessions. To this I agreed. The laboratory sessions for the medical students were scheduled for Tuesdays and Thursday, morning and afternoon. The medical class was divided into two groups; each group had one lab session on each of the days.

Now I had had no exposure to pharmacology since completing my class during my sophomore year in medicine! Pharmacology is a changing subject with new drugs reaching the market almost every day. So I had a lot to learn! I arrived at the laboratory Tuesday, at seven o'clock planning to go over the experiment scheduled to begin at nine.

After greeting the two technicians who were chatting in the preparation room, I asked,

"What is the experiment for today's lab?"

"I wish we knew," they chorused!

"Isn't there a lab scheduled for this morning?" My voice betrayed my surprise.

"Oh, yes, but we haven't been told what it is," was their reply.

"Don't you have a schedule?" was my next question.

"A schedule! We've been trying to get one for the past two years!" They spoke in unison.

"Who is responsible for the lab?" I inquired with increasing amazement.

"Dr. Maddox."

"Then why don't you call him?"

"We have but no one answers." The tone of their voices showed their frustration.

"Then have you called Dr. Lonergan?"

"Yes we have. But there is no answer there, either." I stood looking at them. Was this real or a bad dream?

At nine minutes past eight Dr. Lonergan came flying through the room. "What's the experiment for today," I asked as he hurried past. "Ask Bill," he said, and was already in his office picking up his notes for the lecture that began in a minute.

At 20 minutes to nine Dr. Bill casually came in. What's the experiment for today?" was my immediate question.

"Oh, that's right. There is a lab this morning, isn't there." Dr. Bill was not the least ruffled.

In a minute or so, with a technician on either side, Dr. Bill sat at a table with the laboratory manual before him. "What about this experiment?" he asked.

"We did that one last week."

"Oh! And this?" pointing at another.

"We did that one two weeks ago."

"Oh! Let's do this one." Dr. Bill spoke with assurance.

"But we have no rabbits," was the technicians reply.

"Oh! And this one?"

"We have no frogs." I listened and watched the pantomime unfolding.

Then Dr. Bill said with finality, "Let's have a demonstration."

He scribbled something on a slip of paper and handed it to one of the technicians, " "Please give this to Dr. Lonergan."

I followed the technician out of the room and waited for him to return from the lecture hall. "What did the note say?" I was curious.

"Review the students," he answered with a slight chuckle in his voice.

And now I was beginning to understand why the students were so frustrated with the constant reviews that they had to endure time after time, and with demonstrations (which rarely worked) in lieu of laboratory assignments.

I returned to the preparation room and watched one technician hurry to get a dog from the animal quarters, while the other was trying to prepare solutions of the various drugs, the actions of which were to be observed during the demonstration. By the time everything was ready and the table with the anesthetized dog was wheeled into the lecture amphitheater, it was 20 minutes after ten! The results of the first drug that was injected were equivocal. The second injection of another drug promptly killed the animal! The students were excused. That was their laboratory exercise for the day!

The afternoon demonstration worked slightly better but apparently it had been presented to the students on two previous occasions! The following Thursday was a repeat of Tuesday, and the Tuesday of next week showed no change of menu. As we were leaving the amphitheater I turned to Dr. Lonergan. "Dr. Lonergan, we must have a schedule for the laboratory sessions."

"Yes, yes. We will have to work one out."

"Dr. Lonergan," and I spoke with determination, "we're all here, so why don't we do it now. If I don't get a schedule I'm going to tell the Dean that I can no longer assist in the laboratory."

We went into his office where he had a large table and in less than an hour worked up a schedule. The secretary made a copy for every member of the department. Then I spoke with the technicians. "I want to do the experiment for Tuesday on Monday afternoon, and the one for Thursday on Wednesday afternoon. In that way we can work out any bugs so that the sessions will run smoothly for the students. And by the way, order the appropriate animals for the various experiments so they are available on time."

"That will be wonderful." Their response was gratifying. And this is what we did for the rest of the course. Things ran smoothly and there were no more reviews and no more demonstrations!

It was about four years ago, while a medical colleague of mine and a good friend was visiting me that he revealed something I had never thought of. "Did you know why you were asked to be Chair of the Department of Pharmacology?" he inquired.

"Not a clue," I replied.

"I was a member of the class that was taking Pharmacology when you were asked to help out in the laboratory sessions. We were disgusted with the way things were run. Then suddenly we noticed a dramatic change. The lab sessions were on time, the experiments ran smoothly, and there were no more reviews and demonstrations that did not work. We spoke to the technicians and they gave you the credit. So the officers of the class, of which

I was one, went to the Dean recommending that you be asked to Chair the department!"

A Sad Note

Here I might explain something. During the War Dr. Lonergan and I had organized a Foreign Missionary Society. We met Friday evenings for 30 minutes and only during the winter months when the evenings were long. We had two or three sessions to go before ending the meetings for that year. World War II had ended a few months earlier. Dr. Lonergan announced that the following Tuesday at Norton Air Force Base, a few miles north of Loma Linda, a sale of portable x-ray machines was to be held. There were six in all. Only veteran physicians were eligible to purchase them, and names of those desiring one were to be drawn from a hat.

Dr. Lonergan had requested a number of Adventist veteran physicians to put their names into the pot. He then asked that the group pray that we would get at least one of the six. Tuesday arrived and the first six names that were drawn were Adventists! The next Friday he gave us the above report and all joined in thanks to the Lord.

Dr. Longeran became obsessed with the desire to supply our mission hospitals around the world with valuable equipment that was constantly being sold by the armed forces as War Surplus. A very noble task, but unfortunately he did it at the expense of his work. Pharmacology was neglected and the rapidly changing discipline passed him by.

My Project Again

But let's return to my project. I had obtained the needed number of subjects who were pure vegetarians and was looking for as many lacto-ovo-vegetarians as I could find by word of mouth. Things were progressing slowly. I had just completed the evaluation of a Pastor Breitigam, the Sabbath School Director of the Pacific Union, a lifetime lacto-ovo-vegetarian. As I was leaving his office I asked him if he knew of any other lifetime vegetarians.

"Oh," he replied, "there must be many out there among our members. Why not put a questionnaire in *The Recorder*."

"I would love to, but I can't get the Dean's approval," was my response.

He was aware of the policy and pondered for a moment. "Send me the questionnaire and I will see to it that it is published." There was hint of anger in his voice.

The returns from the questionnaire poured into my office! But I still did not have enough pregnant mothers. Then two schoolmates, who had a large obstetrical practice in Los Angeles, suggested I come to their office, and they would instruct their receptionists to direct the appropriate mothers to me. What a break! Soon thereafter, for reasons I do not know God worked in my behalf and I received the full support of the medical school administration. I was offered the services of two, trained laboratory technicians to assist in the blood analyses I was doing. My good wife, who is a trained laboratory technologist, and who had been helping me was near term with our second child and could no longer give me help. And believe it or not, the two professors in the School of Nutrition and Dietetics volunteered to analyze the dietary histories I had obtained, saving me much time and effort.

Everything in the project moved to completion by the end of August 1951, and I had all the data necessary to write my dissertation.

A Turning Point in My Life

One morning, a month or so before I returned to Harvard, I needed to obtain something from the Department of Pathology. The medical school campus at Loma Linda was made up of five buildings placed in the form of a rectangle. The men's dormitory was at the west end of this rectangle, the anatomy and microbiology/pathology buildings were on the north side, while the pharmacology/physiology/biochemistry and library/assembly hall buildings were on the south side. The buildings housing pharmacology and anatomy faced each other. It was my plan to walk towards anatomy and then turn right till I reached pathology. But who must I see coming down the sidewalk towards anatomy but my "Enemy number one, the Dean!" I was not going to pass him! So I turned towards the library and planned to cross directly across to pathology.

I had walked part of the way when, I believe, the Holy Spirit placed a thought in my mind. "If you have done nothing wrong, then why are you unwilling to pass the Dean and say "Good morning" to him? I stopped dead in my tracks and said to myself, "That's right." So I turned around and walked as fast as I could so I would meet the Dean. As I passed him I said the best "Good morning" I could muster! And that was a turning point in my life. I prayed for God to forgive my past attitude and decided to talk with the Dean face to face.

So I made an appointment to see the Dean at 10:00 o'clock one morning. As I walked into this office I could feel the tension in the room. He asked me to sit down in a chair on the opposite side of his desk. Then I spoke, "Dean, you have been instrumental in giving me a dirty underhanded deal. You know this, as well as I do. But that is not what I came here to talk about. I am here to tell you that, through the grace of God, I have completely forgiven you for what you did, and will try to treat you in the future as if you had never done it to me in the first place." I stood up and extended my hand to shake his. The giant red wood log of bitterness that had weighed down my shoulders rolled off, and I pursued my work with renewed energy.

As I turned to leave his office he was all choked up. We became good friends, and he is a friend of mine to this day. I have never spoken of the problem again but he, on a number of occasions, has said, "Mervyn, we made a mistake, but God worked it out by allowing you to do for His cause much more than if you had just headed anatomy."

I was now ready to return to Harvard and to write my dissertation.

My Final Return to Harvard

The writing went well. I got permission to work in the statistics lab in the evenings because they had an electric adding machine. Electric calculators had not yet been invented. Each student was lent a hand "calculator." To multiply one turned the handle clockwise; to divide you rotated it in the opposite direction.

During the day I wrote. I refused all invitations for supper or dinner by my numerous friends whom I had made two years earlier. "Thank you, I'll see you after my dissertation is complete," was my standard reply. I made it a point to exercise daily, eat frugally, and get my full quota of sleep.

"Mister, It's My Dog Not Yours"

It was a Sabbath afternoon and I was walking along a path in the Fen way. There was snow on the ground but only enough to make things look beautiful in the sunlight. I'm not sure how far I had walked, for I was deep in thought. Then in the distance ahead I heard periodic sounds of laughter, along with shouting and yelling. As I rounded a curve in the walk I looked with astonishment at the scene before me.

A group of about a dozen to fifteen children, probably between the ages of ten to twelve, was in a rather tight circle. Within the circle was a scared puppy. One of the boys would rush at the little dog that would try to run out of the ring. As the puppy got close to one or other of the boys, it would be kicked towards the center of the ring. As it rolled over and over, yelping as it tried its best to escape it would be kicked again and again towards the center. The boys would shout, laugh, and clap their hands.

Righteous indignation filled my soul! I strode towards the circle of boys and in a commanding voice shouted, "Let that little puppy alone." For a moment there was dead silence, and then a short little fellow looked at me and said, "Mind your own business, Mister. It's my dog not yours."

For a second I was taken aback. Then my unrighteous indignation was aroused! I was ready to pick the tike up by his collar and whack the daylights out of his sit-me-down. Instead I stood there not saying a word. Slowly I faced each kid and looked him straight in his eyes. One by one they sheepishly turned away, and in twos and threes, slowly walked towards some houses bordering the Fen way.

This experience has taught me a great lesson. When the Scriptures admonish us, "Be ye angry and sin not," they are speaking of anger that has no selfishness in it. The anger or indignation is directed towards the injustice that is occurring. This is the anger that Christ exhibited in the Temple while He drove out the merchants and moneylenders. But as soon as the boy challenged my authority, a different kind of anger filled me. This type of anger is sinful. The follower of Christ must, through the grace of God, not allow it to arise.

Efforts to Derail My Program

The first draft of my dissertation was completed by mid November. I gave it to Dr. Stare, who read and returned it in a couple of days with only a few comments. "When you get it through the rest of the committee, have the final draft typed up. " These were indeed welcome words.

"Do you want to see it again," I asked.

"No, when they're satisfied, have it typed and then bound."

I next gave the thesis to Mrs. Bertha Burke. Two days later her secretary called for me to see her. "You've done a fine job in presenting your findings. However, there are a couple of paragraphs which I think need redoing." The two paragraphs were in the chapter describing the "Method of Burke." So I rewrote them, and returned the re-write to her. The next day I was in her office again.

"You did a fine job in rewriting them (referring to the two paragraphs mentioned above), but on rereading this chapter I think these two paragraphs (which were previously acceptable) need clarification. Bring them to me when ready."

I smelt a rat. I had learned that Mrs. Burke was an avid meat eater. Ate some form of flesh food three times a day, and liver at least once a day! I rewrote and rewrote and rewrote every paragraph in this chapter but she would not approve it or the thesis.

It was now early December, and I was stalled, and time was running out for me to finish by January 10, when the semester ended. Then I happened to run into Dr. Stare.

"How is it going?" he inquired.

"It's not going," was my response.

"What's the problem?" His voice had a tinge of irritation.

I told him of the problem I was having with Mrs. Burke.

"This is all I have been doing since I saw you last," and took out of my brief case a good half inch of rewrites.

"Please give them to me." I handed him the papers. He turned and walked down the hall to his office.

I had nothing to do so I headed for my apartment about a third of a mile away. As I entered the door, the phone was ringing. It was Mrs. Burke's secretary. "Mrs. Burke asked me to tell you the thesis is all right and you can pick it up at your convenience." Delightful words to hear. What Dr. Stare said or did I will never know. But whatever it was it had worked wonders!

I immediately went back to Burke's office and picked up the thesis. Then I went to Dr. Reed's office. He, the statistician, was the last member of the committee required to clear my dissertation. An appointment was made to see him the next morning at nine.

He and I went over the conclusions I had drawn and the statistical support I had presented to support these conclusions. The morning went well and we broke for lunch. We met again at one.

Dr. Reed seemed to have lost interest in what we had been doing. He was lackadaisical and unwilling to proceed. Finally I turned to him.

"What's the problem, Dr Reed?"

"Well," he replied, "While I was having lunch with Mrs. Burke she happened to remark that your data regarding the food intake of your subjects was completely unrealistic. That it bore no resemblance to what the average American actually consumed." Then he added, "If your basic data is invalid, then any and all conclusions drawn from such data, are invalid."

The dagger had been thrust into my back, and now it was being twisted. For a moment I was taken aback. Such a criticism would completely ruin my dissertation. Then I replied, "That is a most interesting conclusion Mrs. Burke has reached. It is especially interesting because in the past three weeks, three papers have been published in noteworthy journals dealing with surveys of food intake of three population groups, in the eastern, central, and western United States. The findings of all three studies support the figures which I have presented in my thesis."

"Do you have these articles?" he inquired.

"I surely do," was my answer.

"Then you better give them to Mrs. Burke, and do it right away," was his advice.

I went to my apartment, pulled out the articles from my files and wrote Mrs. Burke a letter, sending a copy to Dr. Stare. In it I presented the data presented in these three papers and concluded my letter in this fashion:

"Mrs. Burke, you will see from the above papers that my data is well supported by the findings of these other investigators. Besides, I would like to point out, that the method used to derive my figures was obtained by using "The Method of Burke," which I still believe is the most valid procedure to obtain dietary intakes of food eaten. If my data is unrealistic, then I would call in question numerous papers which you and others have published, using this same method."

Fifteen minutes after I delivered this letter, I was informed, via her secretary, that my data was fine. Dr. Reed and I completed the evaluation of my findings without any further problems. On January 10, 1951 I satisfactorily defended my dissertation, and in spring of the year the doctoral degree was conferred on me.

God's hand is ever over His children and His wisdom guides and directs in all the affairs of those who serve Him.

Finished at last!

Back to Loma Linda

I returned to Loma Linda in time to teach the course in pharmacology to the medical students. I had not anticipated that the course would be thrust upon me so quickly, but with the Lord's help, the lectures and laboratories went well. Before the semester was over I was called to the Dean's office again. I wondered what I would encounter this time.

During my absence the School of Medicine had been accredited. Because the Departments of Anatomy, Physiology, and Pharmacology had no teachers with specialty training in the disciplines they taught, the entire medical school had been put on probation. This was a serious matter.

Five years earlier, after my visit to twenty-two university medical schools in the eastern United States (mentioned earlier), I reported to the medical faculty that the teachers in the basic science departments would soon be required to have specialty degrees in the disciplines they were teaching. A few years earlier the clinical departments had been required to do the same. However, the idea at that time was received with hilarity!

Asked to Join Pharmacology

The Dean greeted me cordially. "The Department of Therapeutics needs overhauling. The medical school administration has decided to split it up. Physical Medicine and Pharmacology will be independent departments, and Nutrition will be part of the responsibility of Pharmacology. We want to urge you to consider specialty training in pharmacology, and you are to be appointed Chairman of that Department!"

At the time only one Seventh-day Adventist had a Ph.D., in pharmacology and he was not interested in teaching. I enjoyed teaching. Anatomy had been taken from me. Once again I was faced with a major decision. But this time it was not as difficult as it had been previously. So after much prayer, I placed my future in God's hands and ask that He make my way plain. I agreed to the proposition that I would select a medical school pharmacology department in which to train at least to the master's degree level.

Soon thereafter, my wife and I drove to the medical schools of five western universities, namely, Utah, Berkeley, Stanford, and in Los Angeles the University of Southern California, and the University of California. Of these Berkeley and Stanford appealed to me. The Chairmen of both the Departments in these two universities had been most cordial and both had fine graduate degree programs. Since a state university was cheaper than a private school, I chose Berkeley.

Chapter 7

AT BERKELEY AND STANFORD

When I first visited Berkeley the Chairman of the Department of Pharmacology, Dr. Anderson, was very understanding of my academic background, and suggested, that if I decided to study in his department, a research project would be selected that would complement this background. I applied to Berkeley and was accepted.

When I arrived in the department, Dr. Anderson, known in the lab as "The Chief," was anything but friendly. He was abrupt, cold, and very domineering. I was assigned a project that was really in the field of microbiology! Although greatly surprised I decided I could learn to work in that area. He then left for a trip to the eastern part of the United States.

He was back in a week. Each morning he made rounds checking on all the graduate students. He usually arrived in my lab at about nine-thirty. As he walked into the lab he asked, "Hardinge, what are you doing?" I told him the steps I had taken on the project.

"Why are you doing that?" he demanded in a voice that betrayed his irritation.

"Because from the library research I have done, it seems a reasonable approach to the problem."

He then made several suggestions. "Why don't you do this, and this, and this?" and walked out.

I put my ideas aside and started working on his. He was back next morning, "Hardinge, what are you doing?" He seemed to be restraining his anger. I told him that yesterday he had made several suggestions and that I was trying them out.

"Are you a baby? Don't you have any ideas of your own? Can't you stand on your own two feet? Am I to tell you what to do?" And away he went.

Thereupon I put his suggestions aside and started to work on my own.

I began to dread his visits but they continued. The following morning he was again in my lab. "Well Hardinge, what are you doing today?" The tone of his voice was anything but pleasant. I tried to explain that I was trying out some of the ideas I had gleaned from reading the literature on the subject.

"Don't you understand simple English. I go out of my way to make suggestions as to how to proceed with your research, and you ignore them," he almost shouted, and walked out as abruptly as he had entered.

Once again I put my ideas aside and again began working on his. Each morning he asked the same question, "Well, Hardinge, what are you doing?" No matter how I replied I could not please him. It was hopeless. He glowered at me. "You're impossible. You don't listen to the one who is trying to help you. Why did you come here in the first place if you can't follow simple suggestions?"

This went on every day, sometimes twice a day, and occasionally three times a day for eight consecutive weeks! And the Lord gave me grace! However, by then I had had it up to the brim. I decided I would talk with Dr. Taylor, his associate. I told him I needed his advice. He was busy at the time and suggested I come to his house at eight that evening, handing me his card. When I arrived at his home he invited me in and I explained my problem. He shook is head. "I don't know what to say. I really can't help you. I'm biding my time." Then he asked, "Are you obligated to the Chief financially?" Often graduates get stipends through departmental funds.

No," I replied. "Then why don't you go some place else? If you do you will be the fifth graduate student to leave in the last three months. I don't understand what's got into the Chief."

I thanked him for his time and counsel. As I was bidding him goodbye he came to the door with me. "I have one word of advice for you. Remember, no matter what anybody says to you, it cannot affect you unless you allow it too. Good bye and good luck."

Dr. Entner's Appeal

I had been working with Dr. Entner, a microbiologist. A most congenial individual, very knowledgeable, and an excellent researcher. Next morning I told him of my decision to leave. He thought for a moment and then suggested, "If the Chief would allow you to work under me, would you be willing to stay?" His voice carried a deep concern as to my intended departure.

"I believe I would," I replied. "At least I am willing to give it a try."

He talked with the Chief that morning and an appointment was made for the three of us to meet at four o'clock the following afternoon. The next morning when the Chief made his usual rounds, he asked that I culture certain organisms. I worked all day to accomplish this task and had autoclaved (sterilized) the test tubes and Petri dishes filled with media (in those days no ready-to-use media was available). I had removed them from the autoclave and was allowing them to cool, planning to culture them when the meeting with the Chief was over. At four Dr. Entner and I entered the Chief's office.

We had hardly been seated when the Chief turned to me, "Have you cultured the organisms?"

"Not as yet," I replied, "I'm waiting for the tubes and plates to cool. They have just been sterilized and it is my plan to culture them following this meeting."

"So you didn't do what I asked you," he almost shouted. "Isn't that true?"

"I've done exactly what you asked me to do," I replied.

"So you haven't done what I asked you." He glowered at me.

"I've done exactly what you asked me to do," I answered the second time.

For the next minute or two he asked the same question over and over again, and each time I gave him the same reply! Finally he broke away from this foolishness. "If we have nothing else to talk about, let's end the meeting."

"Let's end the meeting," I said, and Entner and I walked out.

Dr. Entner stopped in the hall and shook his head. "I can now understand why you are leaving. I wish you every success. Goodbye."

My decision to transfer to Stanford or some other university was now irreversible. A year later I heard that Dr. Anderson, "The Chief," had suffered a nervous breakdown. He took a year's leave of absence but never returned as Chair of the Department.

The parting advice that Dr. Taylor gave me was well worth the emotional trauma of the preceding eight weeks. "Remember, no matter what anybody says to you it cannot affect you, unless you allow it to." How many problems at home or at work would be solved if we would but heed this counsel?

Off to Stanford

A couple of days later I drove over to the Department of Pharmacology of the Stanford University Medical School. At that time part of the medical school was in San Francisco. The entire medical school had not as yet moved to the University campus near Palo Alto, California. Dr. Cutting, the Chairman of the Pharmacology Department, was most cordial. I had decided to be frank with him, and tell him all that had happened at Berkeley, even though he and Dr. Anderson might be friends. I felt I had nothing to lose.

He listened quietly and then asked with a twinkle in his eye, "So you want your second choice to become your first choice?"

"That's exactly right, if you'll let it," I smiled.

He leaned back in his chair, and using my first name, replied, "Mervyn, we'll be happy to have you."

He then suggested that I talk with Jim Elliot, a young man who had obtained a master's degree in his department the year before. At the time Jim was working part time in the Department of Pharmacology at Berkeley while working towards his medical degree. "See what he has to say," were Dr. Cutting's final words.

I obtained an appointment with Jim the following day. I explained the reasons why I wished to transfer to Stanford, and that Dr. Cutting had suggested that I get his opinion. "I surely don't want to go from the frying pan into the fire," I said.

Without a moment's hesitation (with a curse word thrown in) he emphatically replied, "You won't go from the frying pan into the fire, you'll be going from hell to heaven!" That's all I needed to hear, and I soon learned that Elliot was absolutely right.

God Knows Our Needs in Advance

Margaret and I had found a very pleasant apartment on the second floor of a building overlooking the Golden Gate Park. It was easy for her to take the children for a walk when the weather was pleasant. At the time, it was a very safe neighborhood. When we rented it we didn't know that it was exactly the same distance from the Berkeley Medical School as it was from the Stanford Medical School! But the Lord did.

While I enjoyed my year at Harvard, I enjoyed my time at Stanford even more. I had been assured by the Dean of the Medical School at Loma Linda that I could remain at Stanford until I had completed my studies there, but this was not to be. During my early months at Stanford the administration of the Medical School at Loma Linda hired three retiring University professors, all Chairmen of their respective Departments, each on a four year contract: one for Anatomy, another for Physiology, and the third for Pharmacology. They were to hold office while men in each Department obtained their specialty training.

Doctor Gruber, who had been educated at Harvard, had spent his life teaching pharmacology at Jefferson Medical School and knew "his stuff." Although on a four year contract he made it clear that he planned to work at Loma Linda for only one, or at most two years. He insisted that I be with him for the duration of his stay so he could "show me the ropes." I learned a lot from his tutoring. Fortunately, before reluctantly leaving Stanford, I obtained my master's degree and was given permission to do my thesis research for my doctorate in absentia, that is, at Loma Linda.

Return to Loma Linda

On returning to Loma Linda we decided to build a home of our own. In 1949 we had purchased a lot in a newly developed subdivision. It was a former orange grove that had been divided into building lots. It was covered with beautiful orange trees, some of which we retained. The remainder of the trees were removed to allow us to have a home built. At this time we had two small children and were anxious to move from an apartment to a house of our own. We were able to obtain a loan to have it built, and it was a real pleasure to move in. And then the trouble began.

It seemed that every other home in the small subdivision had children about the age of ours. My wife had given up her job to raise our family so was a stay-at-home mom. Both parents of many of the children worked. Some left their children with baby-sitters. A number, however, decided to allow Margaret to take care of their children. When I would get home for lunch there would often be fifteen to twenty children playing in our front yard! Some had been fed breakfast and told to go play with the Hardinge children until lunch. Others who had not been fed were told to play with our children until they were picked up at five-thirty in the evening! They would plead for something to eat, "I'm hungry; I haven't had anything to eat; can't you give me a sandwich?" It was driving my dear wife out of her mind.

I fenced the yard but this did little good. Some would hang on the fence asking to play with Fred and Jeanne, while others would climb over. "Build a ten foot wall around the place," my wife urged.

"But what good will that do," I replied. "They'll find a 12 foot ladder."

"Then why don't we move away." This was not easily done. Property we could afford did not exist within miles of the school. But we prayed, and prayed. We asked God to lead us to where He wanted us to live. And God worked a miracle. We found a dilapidated grove slightly over a mile from the school with water rights for one house, and were able to obtain a loan for the total cost of the property! We in turn had to build a home on it for the lender's security. So we sold our house in the subdivision, and had one built behind the grove we had acquired. Again, it was like going from hell to heaven!

Fred's First Tooth Lost!

While the house was being built we lived in a dilapidated shed bout 20 feet square over looking our future home. Fred was ready to lose his first baby tooth. It hung by a tissue no thicker than a thread, but he did not want it to be pulled out. So I suggested we tie one end of a thread around it and the other end to the handle of a door. He could then swing the door shut and his tooth would be out! To this he agreed, but in attempting to tie the thread to his tooth, the tooth came out! We found an empty matchbox and, for safe keeping, placed his new treasure in it.

We had just finished breakfast the next morning when Mr. Moses, the contractor, and his men drove up. Now Mr. Moses was a kindly gentleman whom the children loved. "I want to show Mr. Moses my tooth," Fred shouted with delight.

"Better keep it in the box," I suggested. "You may lose it."

"No Dad," Fred replied, "I'll be careful." And with that he put the tiny pearl colored tooth in the palm of his hand, and off he sped.

He had barely reached the other side of the building when we heard a shriek and a wail such as only someone who is being tortured to death could utter. Mother, Jeanne, and I dashed toward the source of the sounds. "I've lost my tooth! It's gone. It's gone," he sobbed.

"I warned you not to take it out of the box," I reminded him, "But you were too smart, weren't you? Now you see what has happened."

This did nothing to console him. And then little Jeanne spoke up in a confident tone, "Daddy, why don't we ask Jesus? He knows where it is. He'll help us find it."

My heart sank. The ground around the half-built house was covered with sand and saw- dust. It was a mess. To find a large object like a half-dollar would have been difficult enough. But to locate a tooth the size of a brown lentil, and that looked like a large grain of sand—impossible. My faith failed me. I looked at my wife and she at me. And then the confident little voice interrupted our thoughts. "Why don't we pray to Jesus? He'll help to find it." So behind the half erected garage we knelt down on the litter-covered ground, and I prayed.

I asked my Lord to help us find the tooth. But my prayer gave God a loophole if we were unable to locate it. I sort of covered for the Lord. "Heavenly Father," I prayed, "Fred has lost his tooth and we do not know where it is. If You can forgive him for not taking advice, please help us."

We got up off our knees and began looking, but deep down in my heart I had a hopeless feeling. We all four spread out and began searching the ground. And in less than a minute Margaret picked it up. "Here it is," she called with a happy lilt in her voice. "It was away over here," some 10 feet from where he had been running. "He must have been swinging his hands and the tooth flew out." We all gathered around and there she had it in her hand, a miracle of miracles! We then went back to where we had prayed, to thank God for rewarding the faith of a little child. And in my heart I apologized to God for not trusting Him.

Then I spoke to Fred. "Fred," I said, "don't you think you should put the tooth in the match box to keep it safe?"

We all walked over to our makeshift home. Mother opened the box and Fred dropped the tooth into it. With a happy smile he ran off to show it to Mr. Moses. "Be careful," I called.

But on the way he took the tooth out of the box and again put into the palm of his hand! Within a few seconds we heard a mighty wail. "I've lost it again! Boo, hoo, hoo." We ran over to him.

"How did you lose it this time?" I asked.

He looked at me through his tears. "I took it out of the box; I shouldn't have. Boo, hoo, hoo."

Then the little confident voice spoke up. "Don't cry, Fred. We'll pray to Jesus again. He knows where it is. He'll help us find it."

Again we knelt together, and again I made a way of escape for God. "Lord," I prayed, "Thank you for answering our prayer and helping to find Fred's tooth. He's lost it again. Maybe this time You want him to learn a lesson to be more careful. But if You will, please help us find it." Again we arose from our knees and spread out looking for it.

It was not more than 30 seconds later when there, in the sand washed in a circle from turning on and off a faucet, was the little tooth. How I recognized it I do not know. We put it into the matchbox and knelt where we had knelt twice before. "Thank you Lord for answering the pray of faith of a little four year old, and for the lesson you have taught a faithless father." Fred showed the tooth to Mr. Moses and his helpers and I told them of my lack of faith and how God had rebuked me.

Fred still has the matchbox and the little tooth in it. What a God! And what a lesson!

Dr. Gruber Becomes Unhappy

For the first two years things went very well. I did my research whenever I wasn't teaching. Towards the end of Dr. Gruber's second year however, he decided he was not only going to stay for the full four years of his contract, he was going to stay on indefinitely! And suddenly I became "the David," and he became "the Saul." Working in the department became increasingly difficult.

It was Dr. Gruber's habit to sit through all the lectures that I, as well as the other faculty members in the department, gave. He had done this ever since he came. Now, however, during my lectures, he began to interject comments such as: "Hardinge, you don't know what you are talking about." Or, "Hardinge, what you just said was pure rubbish." Fortunately, the students recognized what was happening and I had their sympathy. It was certainly disconcerting to say the least!

My dissertation research was progressing nicely. Since some other research projects occupied my labs in the basement, I did my "Stanford" research in the main student laboratory when not being used for teaching purposes. Dr. Gruber loved to be involved in research. While I was researching some aspect of my study he would enter the laboratory and come over to where I was working. "Well, Hardinge, what are you working on today?" was his usual inquiry. So I would explain what I was doing. "Let me give you a hand," and he was into the project up to his elbows! From then on he would work with me for hours.

I did not object to this because he taught me many things. The problem was that starting in his third year, he began making comments around the campus that I did not know how to do my research, and that he was doing it for me! My only recourse was to do my investigations in the evenings and on holidays when he wasn't around. And this is what I did. He never learned when and where I did my research! The department kept the secret with me.

Stanford had an interesting provision regarding graduate studies. If a student had completed his thesis research and had the approval of his guiding committee, he could request the Dean of the Graduate School to allow him to take his final examination and defend his dissertation even before he had written it. Dr. Cutting, newly appointed Dean of the Medical School, was the chairman of my dissertation committee. A search committee was seeking a new chairman for his department. I felt it would be wise to take my final examinations before a new head of the department arrived.

My guiding committee agreed that the research for my dissertation was adequate. So I requested the Graduate Dean to schedule the defense of my thesis. The exams were scheduled for 10:00 AM, on a Friday. The entire department at Loma Linda knew I was leaving for a long weekend during which I planned to take my finals. No one broke the news to Dr. Gruber. For this I should congratulate my colleagues. God blessed and I passed without a problem. This was in June 1956.

Dr. Gruber was in his fourth and final year of his contract. He spent his summers in the east. During the summer I tied up the loose ends of my research, organized my data, completed my graphs and charts, and registered for the fall quarter at Stanford, at which time I planned to write my dissertation.

When a new chairman is appointed to a department, he often dismisses all the previous members of that department. This is what I feared might happen. A new Pharaoh would arise who knew not Joseph. And this is exactly what did happen! In August Dr. Avram Goldstein, from Harvard, was appointed the new

Chairman of the Pharmacology Department at Stanford, with tenure. He promptly quarreled with Dr. Cutting, the Dean, and dropped five graduate students and dismissed the entire faculty, except for one. I was the only surviving graduate student.

Writing My Dissertation

On arriving on the Stanford campus in late September I immediately called Dr. Cutting and Dr. Driesback, Chairman and co-Chairman of my thesis committee, to tell them I had arrived. Both men told me I should talk to Dr. Goldstein, the new Chairman of the Department. I immediately realized there must be a problem. I scheduled an appointment with Dr. Goldstein on the 28th.

When I walked into his office, he was as cold as an iceberg. He offered me a chair across the desk from where he sat. I told him that I had completed my research, had successfully defended my dissertation, and now planned to write my thesis. He immediately took over the conversation, and spoke in no uncertain terms: "Hardinge, I want to tell you something. I am a young man and am extremely ambitious. If your dissertation fails to reach the quality that will enhance my stature, you're out. And I don't care what your committee thinks. And by the way, don't give me your dissertation one day and expect it back the next; I want it on my desk one month before it is due in the Registrar's Office." With that he indicated the interview was over.

I told him that I believed my dissertation would reach his standard of excellence, and started towards the door. I then turned and came back to his desk.

"Dr. Goldstein, I believe I can fulfill all you have asked of me, except one thing."

"What is that?" He looked surprised.

"To place my dissertation on your desk one month before it is required in the Registrar's Office."

"When is it due?" he queried.

"November one!"

A faint smile crossed his face that he immediately wiped off. Looking at me, he inquired, "How many chapters have your written?"

"None," I replied with a smile. "But I have all my data ready and well organized."

"Then give it to me as soon as you can." Those words were music to my ears.

I went to the secretary of the department and asked if she would type my thesis. "I'm sorry but I do not type dissertations anymore. They were too much for me. However," she added, "Marge, a friend of mine, who is working on a research project in an adjoining lab, and who also holds a master's degree in pharmacology, might be willing to type it."

"Please call her and see," I asked.

The answer was, yes. Marge came over in a few minutes and we agreed on a price. "Now," I told her, "if I give you a new chapter every day at 5 PM, could you have it typed for me by 8 AM next morning?" Her reply, "No problem."

I put myself on a rigid schedule – worship, writing, breakfast, writing, exercise, writing, dinner, writing, exercise, writing, supper, worship, writing, exercise, sleep. The Lord blessed and by October 15 I had the preliminary draft ready to submit to Dr. Goldstein.

Although the Department was in San Francisco, he lived in Palo Alto, near the main campus of Stanford. He usually left the office at around 3.30 PM. I got him just as he was leaving. It was Friday.

"Here's my dissertation," I said, handing him the preliminary draft. He took it and slowly leafed through its pages.

"There goes my weekend."

"Please may I have it back?" and I reached for the dissertation.

"Why do you want it back?" he asked in surprise.

"Dr. Goldstein, I was thinking only of myself. I had no intention of ruining your weekend. Please give it me and I will bring it to your office Monday morning."

"Oh, no, you won't. I'll have more time to read it over the weekend than I will during the week. Come to my office at nine o'clock Monday morning." And with that he turned and walked to his car in the parking lot. I was overjoyed and had a most wonderful Sabbath. I began slowly to unwind!

With a prayer in my heart I went to see him Monday. He could have torn the thesis apart, demanding major changes that would take days or weeks to make. The format might not be to his liking. All sorts of criticisms could be leveled towards it. I entered his office and could hardly contain myself when he informed me that he wanted me to make two changes, neither of them major. "Have the other members of the committee clear it."

"Do you wish to see it again?" I asked.

"No, after they approve it you can have the final draft typed."

I thanked him and walked out of his office on air!

An Unbelievable Miracle

The next stop was to see Dr. Diesback. He was in his lab. "Bob," I said, "here is my dissertation. Will you please read it?"

"Have you shown it to Goldstein?" was his immediate question.

"Yes, and he's approved it!"

"He has?" Bob exclaimed in amazement! Phew! He whistled softly. "I'll have it for you on Friday."

I must have looked disappointed for he questioned, "Is that too late?"

"Not really, Bob. However, I was hoping to turn it in November one, so I would not have to register for another quarter."

He thought for a moment; then responded, "How would Wednesday be?"

"So much better. I sure appreciate it."

There was nothing more to do but to relax. I went for a long walk and tried to read something light. Next morning I leisurely walked to the Department. As I entered the office the secretary greeted me, "The Dean's secretary just called to say Dr. Cutting had asked that you pick up your dissertation; it's in her office."

"How did he get it?" I exclaimed in disbelief. I bounded up the stairs where his office was located. As I entered, the secretary picked up my dissertation and, as she handed it to me remarked, "Dr. Cutting has read and has approved it." I was stunned!

"Can you tell me how he got it?"

"Well," she replied, "I don't know all the details but this is what he told me. Last evening Dr. Driesback studied your dissertation and completed reading it at two this morning. He then drove over to Dr. Cutting's home, woke him up, and told him that Dr. Hardinge needed it right away, so would he please read it. Dr. Cutting has read it and both men have approved it." The Lord had worked a most remarkable miracle.

"May I see Dr. Cutting to thank him personally?" I inquired.

"I'm sorry," she replied, "he just left for the airport. He won't be back for two weeks!"

I thanked her and walked out of her office. I decided to go to the restroom just down the hallway. As I was opening the door, I bumped into Dr. Cutting. He greeted me warmly, "You did a fine job on your dissertation and I enjoyed reading it. I have made a few suggestions that you'll find in the margins. Congratulations."

"Dr. Cutting, I don't know how to thank you, not only for your reading my thesis this morning, but for all the things you taught me while working in your Department."

"No, Mervyn, we did not teach you very much, you taught us a lot more." With that we shook hands, and with a parting smile he added, "Goodbye and good luck."

The dissertation was completed on time and I returned to Loma Linda to enjoy a deserved vacation. God guides in His own mysterious ways. "Thank You Lord for Your wondrous blessings."

And the Miracles Continue

But the story does not end there. A day or so after Dr. Goldstein had approved my thesis, he invited me to have dinner in his home, Saturday night. He must have noticed a slight hesitation on my part. "It is all right, I've checked the time of sunset, and it is after your Sabbath closes." I immediately accepted his invitation. Dr. Goldstein's father was a prominent rabbi in New York City and it surely was nice of him to respect my beliefs.

A couple of days later I stopped by at his lab. He was studying something under a microscope. "Can I help you?" he asked.

"Dr. Goldstein," I replied, "I don't know if you have ever met a vegetarian, but I would like to introduce myself." He smiled, "No problem, my wife will fix something."

"Please, Dr. Goldstein, I don't want your wife to go to any trouble. The reason I mentioned it is that I didn't want to offend her by refusing some special dish she might have gone out of her way to prepare. There will be plenty of dishes from which I can select a lovely dinner."

"No, no. She'll fix something acceptable, and she'll enjoy doing it."

Friday morning (the day before the dinner), I met him in the hall. "Hi, Mervyn, my wife has it all taken care of. We're having salmon roast!"

"Dr. Goldstein, when you go home tonight, please thank her for her thoughtfulness, and when I see her I'll thank her myself. And, by the way, did you know there are two kinds of vegetarians? Some who eat fish and fowl, and some who do not!"

He looked at me with a twinkle in his eyes, "And you're one that does not?"

"I surely am. But please do not worry. There will be plenty to eat."

We both laughed, and then he added, "It will need to be like you first suggested."

When I arrived for dinner he introduced me to his wife. She was a most charming woman. "What would you like to drink?" she immediately inquired.

"Just a glass of water, thank you."

"Water," she exclaimed! And then quickly added, "Would you like a coke or a cup of coffee?"

"You'll think me strange but I don't drink any caffeinated beverages. Just give me a glass of water!" The Chairman of the Biology Department, his wife, and Dr. Goldstein's research associate were also guests. The next twenty minutes they discussed the impossibility of really relaxing and having a good time without a drink of alcohol to depress their inhibitions!

The dinner was delightful. There was an abundance of foods other than the large salmon roast that was the centerpiece of the table. After dinner we all returned to the front room. Every one present was well-educated and had traveled the world. The conversation settled down to giving personal experiences of travels abroad. I was able to hold up my end of it. We really had a delightful evening. All were relaxed and enjoyed themselves.

The following Monday morning I met Dr. Goldstein in the Department. "Mervyn," he said, "my wife and I are amazed and cannot get over the fact. You are the first person we've ever met who appeared completely relaxed and enjoyed himself who hadn't had a drink of alcohol!"

I looked at him with a smile. "Dr. Goldstein, I had a most pleasant evening and thoroughly enjoyed myself." When the day finally came to wish him goodbye, I invited him, if he ever was near Loma Linda, to come visit our Department of Pharmacology. This he promised to do.

A Friendship Established

About two years later I received a call from him. It was a Tuesday. He was in Pomona, a city about 30 miles west of Loma Linda. He had time and would like to accept my long-standing invitation to visit my department. It was arranged that he come out on Thursday, have lunch with the faculty members in my department, look around the department and campus, and be the speaker at our weekly research seminar at 4:00 PM, and finally, to have dinner that evening in our home. To this he readily agreed.

He had no interest in the buildings on the campus until he saw the University Church. "What building is that?" he inquired.

"That is the University Church. Would you care to see inside?"

"I surely would." I was surprised at his interest.

As we were getting out of the car to walk over to look at the church, I turned to him. "Dr. Goldstein, I hate to suggest you do something that I do not believe is good for you, but you have been here since noon and have not smoked a cigarette since your arrival." He was a chain smoker, and he loved his cigarettes. "Mervyn," and his reply astounded me, "Since you last saw me I have decided to give up smoking, and I decided this morning to use this opportunity of being with you to strengthen my resolve." Wow, I thought, but I said, "I'm happy to hear that."

The seminar went well and so did the evening. I had invited Dr. and Mrs. Mortenson (he was Chairman of the Department of Biochemistry) to have dinner with us and to meet Dr. Goldstein. At around 9:00 PM, Dr. and Mrs. Mortenson prepared to leave, saying that he had a lecture to give at seven AM the next morning. We all went to the door to wish them good night. I thought Dr. Goldstein would also be leaving. Instead, he returned with us to the front room.

My wife and I sat on the couch together. Dr. Goldstein picked up a chair, placed it in front of us and sat down. "Now that the children are in bed and your guests have left, I would like to ask you, what is a Seventh-day Adventist and what do they believe?" Then he added, "While I am not an orthodox Jew, my father is Rabbi Goldstein of New York. I have been thoroughly schooled in the Old Testament, but since I live in a Christian culture I have read the New Testament through twice." He had, indeed, and must have possessed a photographic memory for he could quote chapter and verse as we discussed the various questions he raised.

Starting with Genesis one and the Creation story, we talked and listened until one in the morning. It was a wonderful experience, for I was dealing with a sincere and brilliant mind. I was indeed grateful that the Holy Spirit brought to my memory those things that I needed to know.

Dr. Goldstein became my friend and a friend of the Department. Through the years he sponsored me to memberships in several prestigious, scientific societies. He did the same for others of my faculty. Based on a finding in my dissertation research Dr. Ian Fraser (my right hand man in the Department who later became Chairman when I moved to the School of Public Health), Dr. Goldstein and I published a paper in the *Journal of Molecular Pharmacology*. The paper described an enzyme not heretofore shown to be present in the capsule of red blood cells. Dr. Goldstein remained at Stanford until his retirement.

Chapter 8

TEN TRANQUIL YEARS

The pressure of work and study was over. Harvard, Berkeley, and Stanford experiences were now in the past, and were fast becoming memories. Dr. Gruber had retired and all in the Department, both faculty and support staff, were congenial and busy with their teaching and research activities. We enjoyed the whole-hearted support of the medical school administration, which makes a very real impact on the moral and productivity of a Department.

My responsibility, as Chairman, was to see that all the workers in the Department had the best facilities that could be provided so they could accomplish their own goals and those of the Department. Through the ensuing years the Lord greatly blessed the Department as a whole. Research money was made available to the faculty. This support allowed them to work productively in their chosen specialty areas within the framework of pharmacology. Articles were published in peer review journals, and papers presented at Society meetings. The Department prospered.

And then I received an incredible offer.

An Incredible Offer!

I was in my office working at my desk when the phone rang. My secretary informed me that a Mr. Hugh MacDonald from the Lederle Laboratories wanted to see me. I assumed he was one of their "detail men," representatives of the company who visited physicians, dentists, and veterinarians, that is, professionals who prescribe drugs.

"I am not a detail man," he said with a smile as he entered my office.

"Please do sit down," and I offered him a chair.

"Nice office you have. Do you enjoy your work?"

"I do indeed."

"Let me get to the point for my visit. Are you and your Dean getting along?"

"We are! Why do you ask?"

"Well, I was hoping you weren't! You see I am one of the officers of our company, and we are looking for someone to replace our Research Director, who is soon to retire. You have all the qualifications for which we are looking. You have an M.D., a Ph.D., in pharmacology from Stanford, and as a bonus, you have a doctorate in nutrition from Harvard. But let me tell you something about the position. You would be responsible to no one except the Chief Executive Officer of the company. You would be provided a travel budget that you alone would sign. You need get no one's permission and you may travel to any part of the world, to any convention or meeting, as long as it might be of some benefit to our company. On occasion you may take your wife along with you!

"The company will provide you a handsome life insurance policy to which you will pay nothing. You will have complete medical and dental coverage for your self, your wife, and your children up to the age of twenty-one. You will have four weeks vacation each year while your salary continues. And then, of course, you will receive a generous salary. And while we are talking about salary, I would like to emphasize that the terms are completely negotiable."

He leaned back in his chair, and the look on his face showed he was enjoying himself. "Now as I said, your salary is up to negotiation but we have to start some where. What would you think, since we are in the year 1957, of fifty-seven thousand dollars a year (my annual salary at the time was $8,000!)?" He waited for my response.

As you might imagine all kinds of thoughts were racing through my mind. What an incredible offer! I could take a leave of absence for a few years and then return with an enormous amount of experience in the field. It certainly would allow me to stabilize my finances and liquidate my indebtedness. But on the other hand, did I not take the training to enable me to better serve the cause of God? My thoughts went back to Moses and the even greater offer that he turned down. No, I must not play with temptation.

"I'm sorry but I cannot leave my current employment. I must say, however, your offer is most tempting…"

He interrupted me, "Perhaps you did not hear me right. Fifty-seven thousand dollars is only the starting point for our negotiations. I just threw that figure out as we have to start somewhere."

"No," Mr. MacDonald, "my decision is final, but I do appreciate your visit and I'm sure you will find someone to fill the position." We shook hands and wished each other goodbye.

In the late sixties or early seventies I was asked by Andrews University to teach two classes for their extension school to be held in Singapore. As I neared the end of this teaching assignment I received a request from the late Dr. Rhoda, the then president of Philippine Union College, to come to their campus to advise them on their health program, which I was able to do.

God Knew Beforehand

After a number of discussions with the President, the Graduate and Academic Deans, and the senior faculty involved, I recommended that the Academic Dean request the Ministry of Education of the Philippine Government to approve, on a five-year experimental basis, the offering of a Master of Science Degree. Rather than requiring as part of the program, a research topic and a dissertation (required at the time for all graduate degrees), the student would evaluate the health needs of a barrio and recommend ways in which these health needs might be met.

All members of the committee were in favor of such a program, but the Academic and Graduate Deans were adamantly opposed. This was especially true of the Academic Dean. He emphatically stated that no advanced degree had ever been granted in the Philippines without the requirement of research and a dissertation. Finally the recommendation was approved on the condition that I make the proposal to the Minister of Education, and talk in its favor. The Academic Dean was to make the appointment with the Minister.

The President, the Academic Dean, the Graduate Dean, a senior professor, and I were ushered into the Minister's office. We were seated around a rectangular table with the Minister of Education at one end. As I was making the proposal I noticed the Minister, a large broad-shouldered man, clench his right fist and slowly raise it to shoulder height. As I completed my presentation he brought his fist down onto the table top with a resounding bang, and in a loud voice, almost a shout, exclaimed: "That's just what we need; a dissertation might have some value in a classroom but sometimes I wonder!" From that moment on the graduate and academic deans were in complete favor of the proposition!

As the Minister of Health was an important member of the committee that must give final approval to the proposal, I requested that I be taken to his office that afternoon as I was scheduled to fly out of Manila the following morning. So to Dr. Gaitmaitan's office we went. I was able to pass the first and second secretaries without trouble. Finally I reached his personal secretary. When I asked her if I could see the Minister, she looked at me incredulously: "You have no appointment. There is no way you can see him and besides he is presently in an important committee."

"I know, I know," I replied. Then taking out my personal card from my pocket I placed it on her desk in front of her. "Just give him this card and tell him that an old friend from Harvard came by to say hello." At which she immediately said, "Just wait a minute," and jumping up, went into his office. And now it was my turn to be amazed, for as I watched, seventeen committee members came out of his office, Dr. Gaitmaitan being the eighteenth. He came over to where I was standing and we gave each other a big hug. "Come into my office. It is so wonderful to see you."

We chit chatted for a few minutes and then he asked, "What brings you here?"

I told him of my request to the Department of Education regarding an experimental Master's degree program and hoped that he would give it his support. He leaned back in his chair and with a smile responded: "Dr. Mervyn, any proposal you make is approved already in advance!"

We visited a little longer and then embraced each other again. I had a short prayer for him. He was a devout Catholic. In the ensuing years we met again twice. He not only supported the proposed Master's degree program, but a few years later gave his support for the accreditation of a School of Public Health at Philippine Union College, the second such school in the country.

Twenty plus years earlier while at Harvard, God impressed me to invite three discouraged Philippine physicians to have a rice and curry supper with Margaret and me. One became a friend and that friend was Dr. Gaitmaitan. God knew that one day this man would do great things for His work.

I enjoyed teaching, carrying a fair sized load of lectures in pharmacology for both the medical and dental students, plus the short course in personal health (formerly Medical Evangelism and later called A Philosophy of Health). Requests for special lectures on nutritional topics came periodically from the various schools of the University. Meanwhile the health lectures that I began giving during my student days had multiplied into a series presented at doctor-minister retreats, workers meetings, camp meetings, and talks given during evangelistic efforts. The inviting organizations paid my travel expenses. The administration was happy to allow me the time to make these contributions as the Medical School and University benefited from the goodwill engendered.

Our Medical School had two campuses, the first two years at Loma Linda studying the basic sciences, and then the last two years at the White Memorial Hospital in Los Angeles, where we obtained our clinical training. More or less on a weekly basis I traveled to the city to work at the White (as we called it), and on occasions to give lectures.

Two Flat Tires

It was a beautiful spring day and I was five miles away from the White Memorial Hospital, Los Angeles. I had been asked to give three lectures, one a week, to the senior medical students on "Pregnancy and Lactation." The lecture started at 8:00 AM. This was to be my third and last. The White was sixty miles from Loma Linda and the freeway between the two cities was almost complete.

So I decided to leave at six AM even though I might have to waste sometime at the White. Twenty miles from Los Angeles the traffic stopped. As far as I could see all four lanes were bumper to bumper. But I was not worried for I had plenty of time, or so I thought. Thirty minutes later I was on my way. I still had about thirty minutes to make the last five miles and then it happened. My right rear tire went flat. I pulled over onto the shoulder, got out leisurely and opened the trunk. I threw the spare tire on the pavement and removed the bumper jack, putting it on the pavement. Placing the bumper jack under the bumper, I started to raise the rear end of the car. Just as the flat tire was leaving the pavement I heard a snap and down went the wheel onto the blacktop. I tried several times to get the wheel off the pavement but to no avail. The jack had broken.

Now all I needed was to raise the tire an inch or so. What could I put under the jack? A board? I had none. I had just cleaned out the trunk. A book? I had brought none. I usually take along a book but not that day. I checked the freeway for anything. It had been cleaned recently. How to get another bumper jack? I stood at the side of the freeway waving my hand, hoping someone would stop. Have you ever tried to stop someone on a freeway at twenty minutes to eight in the morning? Everyone is rushing, trying to get to work on time. I finally gave up and stood wondering what I should do next. And then the thought struck me. Why not ask God to help?

So I walked over to the chain-link fence that bordered the freeway, closed my eyes, and offered up a petition for help. When I opened my eyes an old car was moving over onto the shoulder. I ran up to the driver, who asked, "Can I be of help?" "I need a bumper jack, mine has broken." He hopped out, opened up his trunk, and pulled out his jack. It fit my bumper (which itself is remarkable as bumpers and their jacks differ widely) and soon the flat tire was off. He was in a hurry so I only used three lugs to hold the spare on and let the wheel down. He was already on his way as I threw his jack into the trunk and slammed it shut.

As I turned toward my car, I discovered, to my horror, that the spare tire was as flat as a pancake! Now what was I to do? Two flat tires and time running out! This time it was my fault for I had not checked the spare for air for some time. Maybe the Lord was teaching me a lesson? But I was now in dire straits. Once more I walked over to the chain-link fence and closing my eyes asked the Lord for forgiveness for my negligence, and for help in my predicament.

When I opened my eyes, here came a highway patrolman with his car lights flashing. The officer pulled up behind me and got out. "Having trouble, young man?" he asked. I told him the sad story and he laughed. "You are in trouble, aren't you?"

"And what is worse," I said, "there are a hundred medical students waiting at the White to whom I am to give a lecture in ten minutes."

He thought for a moment and then he came up with this: "When does your lecture end?"

"At nine," I replied.

"I'll tell you what. Let's put the flat in my trunk. I'll take you to the lecture hall. While you are lecturing I'll get it fixed, and then pick you up at nine, and bring you back here."

And that is what he did. God has a thousand ways to answer prayer that we could never think of. And to this day I ask myself, "Was the one who helped me a patrolman or was he an angel in a patrolman's uniform?"

Consolidation of the Medical School

Through the nineteen fifties and early sixties the question of uniting the two campuses of the medical school was constantly discussed in faculty meetings and in special committees appointed by the dean.

Beginning a few years before World War II, the Council on Medical Education of the American Medical Association and the executive Council of the Association of American Medical Colleges began to urge medical schools which were on two campuses, to consolidate on a single campus. At the beginning of the 20th century, when medical education was in the process of overhauling itself, medical schools were requiring formal education in both the basic sciences and clinical areas. The majority of medical schools taught the basic science years on the main University campuses, which interestingly, were generally located in rural settings. To obtain sufficient patients for clinical training the majority of medical schools set up a clinical division (campus) adjacent to a large hospital in a convenient city.

Examples of this arrangement would include the University of California at Berkeley (rural) with their medical center in San Francisco. Stanford University taught the first two years at the University base in Stanford (rural), and used the San Francisco General Hospital for clinical instruction. Cornell University divided their medical school with the first two years at Cornell in upstate New York (rural) and the clinical years in the Bellevue Hospital in New York City. The college of Medical Evangelists followed the same prototype, the non-clinical instruction at Loma Linda (rural) and the last two years of clinical experience in Los Angeles.

A controversy developed between those who believed the entire medical school should be at Loma Linda and those who believed it should be in Los Angeles. The majority of the faculty at Loma Linda believed the counsels given by Ellen White were a mandate regarding the medical school being at Loma Linda and not in a city environment such as Los Angeles. On the other hand, the clinicians advocated, that from a practical standpoint, the entire medical school be adjacent to the White Memorial Hospital and clinic in Los Angeles. It appeared that all groups concerned—faculty, alumni, and church leaders, were all divided about fifty-fifty on the issue.

The dean of the Medical School, Dr. Walter Macpherson, and his associates, Dr. Varner Johns, associate dean, and Dr. Fredrick Norwood, the academic dean, were determined to consolidate in Los Angeles. A number of fact-finding committees appointed by the University Board recommended that the clinical facilities at Loma Linda be developed, but such recommendations, although approved by the Board, were never implemented. In the early sixties Dr. David Hinshaw was appointed dean. He was willing to consolidate in Los Angeles but favored the Loma Linda campus. With his encouragement the decision was finally reached and the clinical division was moved to Loma Linda.

During these years I had been placed on numerous committees and was deeply involved in preparing materials which showed that the trends in medical education supported Ellen White's counsels to consolidate the University campus. Dr. Bernard Briggs, chairman of the Department of Anesthesiology, who was also a member of the University Board, was also active in providing pertinent information to key members of the Board and to many of the Alumni. The wisdom of this move in subsequent years has been more than vindicated by the progress and contributions made by Loma Linda University's medical school.

Skill with Small Motors

We lived only a mile from the school, on the outskirts of Loma Linda, which in the earlier years was but a small town. With the establishment of a large Teaching Hospital, a Veterans Administration Hospital, and a Community Hospital, the one-time small town rapidly became a sizable city. Our children grew to young adults while my dear wife kept a wonderful home. She also periodically assisted one or another faculty member on some research project.

And while I am talking about my wife, Margaret, I should mention some of her many abilities. Others will be featured in due course. She possessed an uncanny knowledge of gasoline motors, especially small motors that powered lawn mowers, water pumps, and other equipment found around a home with a large garden or small farm. This knowledge she successfully passed on to her son but not to her husband!

The Stubborn Lawn Mower!

It was Friday, and, as so often happened, duties in the office prevented me from getting home until late in the afternoon. My children were away at school so it became my duty to keep the lawns mowed. I hauled the mower out of the garage and tried to start it. I pulled on the rope to activate the motor with no success. So I choked the engine. Again, I pulled without success. I waited for a few minutes so the engine could dry out, as I thought I might have over choked it. Pull as I would the stubborn motor remained silent. My right arm became tired so I pulled with my left arm! Do you think it would start? Frustration began to build.

Just then the back door opened and Margaret emerged. "Having trouble?" she called in a cheerful voice. That in itself is enough to give one trouble!

"I can't get this thing started," my voice betrayed my frustration.

"Maybe you should choke it." Her voice was as calm as a lily pond.

"I tried choking it."

"Then maybe you over choked it." Self-control was reaching its limits!

"I've tried it with the choke on and with the choke off and it won't even give a splutter." All the while my wife is diddling with something on the motor.

"Give it a pull," she suggested.

So I gave it a pull. You've guessed it. It came to life with a pleasant purr! And so it always seemed to happen.

When we bought the property where we lived, it came with a large number of Valencia orange trees. While they make good eating they are especially known for their juice. Margaret grafted or budded over a number of these trees to navel, tangelo, tangerine, lemon, and grapefruit! We planted avocado and other fruit trees such as peaches, apricots, plums, and persimmons. With our vegetable garden we had quite a little farm! During the late winter it was sometimes necessary to heat some of the orange trees to keep the fruit from freezing. Smug pots were still in use.

The Pump on the Oil Truck

One day she reported that we were out of smudge oil, used to burn in the smudge pots. "Why don't you order some?" was my suggestion. So she did. Next day when I came home for lunch I asked if the smudge oil had been delivered. It had. As we were eating our meal she casually remarked that the men delivering the oil had trouble starting their pump.

"And you got it started?" I inquired with a little chuckle.

"Well, not exactly," she quietly replied.

"Then what happened?" I was curious.

"Well, I was working in the garden when they arrived. About an hour later I had not heard the motor start to pump the oil into our tanks. So I casually went to see what they were doing. They could not get the motor to start and were using a beaten-up pair of pliers and a screwdriver that was in no better shape, to adjust some part of the motor. So I offered to get them some wrenches and a good screwdriver. They were most grateful. A half-hour later there was still no sound of a motor. So I went to see what their problem was. One glance showed me that they had fouled up all the jet settings."

"So you fixed them." I was sure she had!

"You know how Spanish men do not like to be shown up by women, so I was diffident about doing anything. I finally suggested that they turn one jet one way, and a second jet another way. Finally I made the fine adjustments."

"And the thing started!"

"It did, and they were pleased and happy. They could not thank me enough. So I picked up the tools I had lent them and came back to the garage. The tanks were soon full and they waved and smiled as they drove away."

And before I leave the subject of my wife I must share with you one more experience. We lived against hills covered with sagebrush. This terrain provided habitat for an occasional deer but chiefly foxes, coyotes, possums, skunks, rabbits and rattlesnakes (we usually killed one or two in our yard every year). As I have already mentioned Margaret enjoyed gardening.

The Skunk and the Rose Bush

Margaret had transplanted some flowers towards evening, and had left the hose dripping to thoroughly soak the ground in the area of the transplants. I was awakened by my wife's sudden movement as she jumped out of bed. I glanced at the clock and it was a few minutes after 1:00 AM.

"Where are you going?" I asked sleepily.

"To turn the water off," was her reply as she left the room.

I decided to go to the bathroom. As I came out into the hall I found that Margaret had not yet returned. So I headed for the front door from which she had exited. Now the previous owner of our house had had it so wired, that a single switch by the front entrance turned on lights under the eves of the roof all around the house, lighting up the entire perimeter of our home. Since there was sufficient moonlight Margaret had not turned on these lights, but I did. I had walked through the porch and was standing on the sidewalk which led to the driveway.

At that moment Margaret came around the corner of the house to my right both laughing and crying. I thought she was hysterical! She was standing on the lawn about three feet from me, and between laughing and crying she told me what had happened.

"I had just turned off the water when you turned on the lights. There five feet in front of me was a skunk, his tail was up and he was thumping the ground with his front feet. So I slowly began to back away from him, and the next thing I knew, I had backed into that large rose bush. The skunk began coming towards me so I shrieked, pulled myself out of the rose bush, and here I am."

At that very moment I heard the automatic sprinklers for the lawn come on. So I reached out, grabbed her arm, and shouted,

"Look out!" At which Margaret let out a terrific scream and threw herself into my arms, sobbing. She was sure the skunk had got her! It took a little while to calm her down but gradually she saw the humor in the event, and my close proximity to her in bed gave her enough assurance that she slept through the rest of the night.

The moral of this story is: "Turn on the lights before you go out at night, or at least take a flashlight with you when the water is running at one o'clock in the morning!"

We were having breakfast and were discussing a distressing problem that had developed. We had been able to secure a "dilapidated" orange grove (it could not support itself) and had built a home on the upper end of the property.

Blackbirds!

A succulent weed had spread over the lower two acres and thousands of army caterpillars had developed to maturity on these plants. They were now on the march upward to where our house was built. On the way they left their droppings filled with the seeds of the succulent! This would spread the weed all over our grove including our flower and vegetable gardens, and the orchard.

Margaret and I had arisen early. The caterpillars were just below our home site and a few had already arrived at our home. What were we to do? We tried spraying the upper line of advancing creatures with smudge oil but to no effect. Just below our house there were three irrigation furrows that ran crosswise above the last of our trees. Ah! We thought we had the problem fixed. If we turned on the irrigation water full blast it would form a barrier to our home and gardens. At least that area would not be seeded with weeds by the advancing pest, but to no avail. The pesky creatures crawled into the water and although swept along with the current made it to the other side down stream! We were desperate but the children had to be fed before they left for school, so we went up to have breakfast.

As we were discussing the problem with the children, Jeanne, our little eight-year-old asked the question, "Why don't we ask Jesus to stop the caterpillars?" And why not? So we stopped eating and put the problem in the Lord's hands. We had no idea what the Lord might do. When we stood to our feet and looked over the grove, blackbirds were flying in from every quarter. They came in tens, in twenties, and in flocks of fifty; there were hundreds of them! Ten minutes or so later, they left as abruptly as they had arrived. Breakfast over, we went down and walked the length of the grove. Not a single caterpillar could we find anywhere!

Time was running out for the children to leave for school, so we all ran back to our home and knelt down again. We thanked the Lord for the wonderful miracle He had wrought right in front of our eyes! God has a thousand ways to accomplish His purposes and to answer the faith of a little child.

A Spiritual Atmosphere in Our Home

From the cradle till our children left home my wife, Margaret, and I did our best to instill into their minds spiritual things. We used all the books written for tiny tots and those prepared for the growing child. Since there was over two years difference in the ages of Fred and Jeanne, each took a different child for a month at a time for their evening worship. As they grew older this became unnecessary and our worship schedule settled down (with exceptions of course). Family worship and prayer, first thing in the morning, was directed towards the children. My wife would often read to them while they were having breakfast.

In the evening after supper and play (when small) we would have evening worship, again directed towards the children. Just before going to bed and after they were all ready, they would call out to us: "Come and kiss me good night." Whenever I was home this became an established routine for the children and me. My wife did the duty when I was away. After they left for college or boarding academy, whenever they were back, this custom was faithfully followed. It proved to be a wonderful blessing for if there had been any unpleasant feelings between the children or between the children with their parents, things could be talked over quietly in the dim glow of the night light. The Spirit of God would come into hearts, apologies made, forgiveness given and received, and prayers offered up to the God who knows, understands, and loves. At other times it would be just a few moments between the two of us.

My mind goes back to the first evening Fred brought back to our home his new wife. Fred has a slightly different version of the final events of that evening (which you can read in his autobiography if he ever writes one!). Their honeymoon was over and they were spending a few days with us prior to returning to college. All the events of the evening had ended, and Fred and I were visiting in our study. Everyone else in the home had one by one, with a yawn or two, said good night and gone to bed. I could see Fred was tired and so was I. But I did not want to be the first to cut short our visit. Things were dragging and I was wondering when it would end.

Suddenly light dawned! Turning towards Fred I said: "Fred, why don't you go to bed and I'll come and kiss April and you goodnight." He immediately stood to his feet and looking at me with a smile replied: "Thanks Dad." All of us were soon in our beds with hearts glowing with joy. Habits die slowly. May all of ours be good ones.

Whenever I was away from home, which was not infrequent, Mother would play and study with the children. We often went camping over the weekends or would go out with friends for Sabbath evening supper and worship. Campfires are wonderful for communing with one another and with God (in those days campfires were not prohibited). We made every effort to maintain childhood relationships. God has put into the heart of a child a loyalty and love for his/her parents that never should be broken. And this is only possible if parents are willing to put **time** and effort into maintaining this loving relationship. Play with them, read to them, study with them, holiday with them and above all, worship with them. Whatever activity you are involved in, if you can involve them in it, do so as friend with friend, not as some stern mentor to a student. They are the most precious things God has given you. Allow no generation gap to develop for Satan will make every effort to do just that.

And pray. Without the help of God the task is well nigh impossible. Parents, you must be willing to sacrifice time and money, and of these two, time is the more important. My good wife gave up much of her professional ambitions to be a stay-at-home mom. And only eternity will truly show how worth while it was. God has already rewarded us with two wonderful children and several grandchildren who carry on the tradition of their parents.

The Lord will surely reward this godly woman for her love, toil, sweat, and tears.

Research and Resignations

I had a large screening program in which we were testing extracts of plants indigenous to Southern California against a variety of cancers: breast cancer, leukemia, sarcomas and others. We had these tumors in what were called "donor mice," and these provided cancer tissue that was implanted in test animals. These animals were then injected with the various extracts derived from the plants. I hired my wife and Mrs. Crooks, both avid plant lovers, to collect and classify the plants we later extracted. They loved the work.

I paid the taxi driver and turned towards the motel where I was to spend the night. In the morning I was scheduled to visit a cancer-screening laboratory at the University of Alabama in Birmingham, Alabama. The motel had been arranged for by the head of the Cancer Screening Program and was located opposite one of the entrances to the campus. It had been a long wearying flight from Los Angeles. It was before the days of jets and the air in the plane had been heavy with a growing concentration of tobacco smoke. I had a dull headache.

A Run for My Life

I decided to go for a walk. Why I did not explore the campus I do not know. Instead I decided to walk in the opposite direction. Now I get easily lost in a city. I get turned all around. So emerging from the motel I decided I'd walk down the street to the right, and told myself that if I didn't turn on any side street, when I turned around and came directly back I should end up where I began!

It was a beautiful summer evening, the sun was still up, and the temperature was just right. So I set off striding down the road. I was absorbed in my thoughts and time must have slipped by, for I suddenly realized that the streetlights were coming on. I found myself in an industrial area of the city, and it came to me that I had not seen a soul for sometime. I turned around and headed back. I must have walked four or so miles and was halfway to my motel when I noticed in the block ahead of me two men lounging in front of a Chevron gas station. I recalled passing it, and it, like all the other businesses along the road, was closed.

An uneasy feeling swept over me. Should I turn left or right at the intersection I was approaching? Or should I try to go directly past the men? The blocks in this industrial area were long and the sidewalks wide. I crossed the intersection as one of the two men disappeared somewhere into the station. I decided to pass the man ahead of me and gradually moved towards the curb. I resolved that if he asked me for a match or some other handout, I would take this as a signal and run diagonally across the street and down the opposite sidewalk.

The distance between us was closing. When I got about 10 feet from him he took two big strides towards me and asked for a match. And I took off and he behind me, and the second man behind him! Now I am not a sprinter; I have never been able to run fast. But as I headed for the other side of the street no Olympian had ever run as fast and I'm sure I was easily breaking the world record for the hundred-yard dash! I could hear the man's breath just behind my shoulder. My legs were beginning to tire as my adrenaline was flowing freely. How much longer could I keep the pace up? What would they do if they caught me? These and other thoughts were racing from one neuron to another even faster than my legs were carrying me. And then to my great relief the breath sounds of my pursuer grew fainter. I was gaining on him but I could still hear his footsteps and those of his companion. And then there was silence except for the pounding of my heart and heaving of my chest. I had outrun them!

Then for the first time I looked behind me. The closer of the two was about fifteen feet from me and the other about five feet further back. I began to walk as rapidly as I could and kept watching them in case they decided to take up the pursuit again. But apparently they had had enough and turned and walked in the direction they had come.

The Lord had watched over me and had given me strength to outrun these men who, I am sure, had chased me for no good purpose. Thank You, Thank You Lord, for Your protection and care.

And as I write these words my memory takes me back to another occasion when I ran for my very life. I was about 13 or 14 at the time. I was returning from school where I had been playing soccer. The game had lasted longer than usual and it was already growing dark as I started for home. Now I could go one of two ways. The longer road wound through a forest reserve along which no one lived. The shorter path ran through the outskirts of town and then along a half-mile of pine forest to my left and dense lantana to the right. I decided to take the shorter route home.

Just in Time

I was nearing the last of the houses before the uninhabited stretch when I noticed two men standing in front of a village home. This house had a hedge on four sides—made of what, I don't know— but it was eight to ten feet high with a single opening onto the street. At the time there was considerable unrest among the hill tribesmen, as they were demanding of the British an independent state. They looked my way and almost immediately disappeared through the opening in the hedge. A feeling of unease came over me.

As I approached the spot where they had been standing I wondered if I was being foolish to worry about their behavior. Why would they do anything to me? I was just a boy. I was not involved in politics. But the unease I felt grew stronger. I moved over to the side of the road to be as far from the entrance to the house as possible. I was walking as fast as I could. About 50 yards from the gate the road turned left and I decided that once out of their sight, I would run. When I thought they had arrived at the turn I would start to walk again. Rounding a further curve in the road I would run again.

I had hardly passed the gate when they both emerged and began following me. I turned to the left and then sprinted. When they arrived at the turn of the road the distance between us had considerably increased. Walking around a curve in the road I again was out of sight and once more began to run. But the men had realized what I was doing and were in full pursuit. I passed the last house on the right and started down the half-mile stretch to our home. They were now not far behind and I realized I could not outrun them.

They were about 10 feet behind me when I literally ran into two men; one was carrying a lantern. "Baba, baba," (boy, boy) they shouted. They were two of our servants whom Mother had been impressed to send to meet me on my way home! I almost fell into their arms with relief. The pursuers were alongside me when one of the servants asked the men what they were up to. They mumbled something and then turned back the way they had come.

Before we ask the Lord knows our need and provides it in His own good way.

Note. Just before I left India I sold my double barrel, 12-gauge shotgun to a Khasi gentleman. After he had paid me and had the gun in his possession, he said, "One of these coming days I will use this gun against you!" Soon after India obtained independence the hill people of the five different tribes rebelled against the Indian Government. The real cause of the civil war was that the Government, the majority of whom were Hindus, had required textbooks in the schools filled with pictures of the pantheon of Hindu gods. The majority of the hill people had accepted Christianity and refused to expose their children to such books.

Back Again to Loma Linda and the Research Lab

The Five-day Plan for Stopping Smoking

In the fifties, scientific evidence regarding the harmful effects of smoking was mounting. Dr. Wayne McFarland developed the idea of a program to help smokers quit the tobacco habit. It was called "The Five-day Plan for Stopping Smoking," and proved to be highly successful. Pastor Elman Folkenburg teamed up with him and together they conducted many such programs on University campuses and in community halls. Dr. Wayne presented the scientific evidence regarding the harmful effects of smoking while Pastor Elman discussed the psychological and spiritual aspects of quitting.

There were, as one might expect, those who considered the program as some fad idea. I decided to run such a program on the Loma Linda campus. Dr. Wayne and Pastor Elman were happy to cooperate and were to conduct the actual program. The Loma Linda Medical staff was fully in cooperation and provided the names of those patients who wished to quit smoking. The sessions were to start Sunday evening and run through Thursday evening. Dr. Wayne arrived in Loma Linda on Wednesday and was in my office Thursday morning when the phone rang. My secretary informed me that it was the president of the University.

I picked the phone up and said, "Good morning, Mr. President, how may I be of help?"

"Are you planning to conduct one of those newfangled ideas of how to quit smoking? Now what do they call it, some Five-day...Plan?"

"Yes, I am, and Dr. McFarland has just arrived from Washington, and Pastor Elman Faulk..." and the president cut in, "I'm calling to inform you that you are to cancel the project. You are not to conduct such a program."

"But Dr. Anderson the subjects are..." and I was interrupted again. "I'm not here to argue with you. Do you understand? As I just told you, cancel the program!" and with that he banged his receiver down.

I turned to Wayne and told him what the president had said. We could not believe what had happened. So the project was cancelled.

The incident bothered me not a little. Then one afternoon about two months later the Lord put an idea in my head. Why not do a scientific study on the process of stopping smoking, —an investigation of the "Acute Withdrawal Symptoms from Nicotine Addiction?" I discussed it with my staff and they were all happy to cooperate. So I had it announced in the University magazine—*Scope*. The Medical staff was again most cooperative, and we studied three groups of 35 smokers in each group.

We used the Five-day Program to get subjects who were suffering from acute withdrawal, but never mentioned the plan by name! We also made the following evaluations: prior to the program we did on each subject a step test (now called a treadmill or physical fitness test), a respiratory function test, a taste test, and a skin temperature test. We did the same evaluations immediately after the five-day Program, and then at intervals of a month, three months, six months, and 12 months. The results were excellent and three papers were published in peer review journals. Two years after the sessions 26 per cent of the subjects were still ex-smokers! Few if any, quit smoking programs have been as successful as were these.

"The Five-day Program" almost became a symbol of the Seventh-day Adventist Church! Programs are still being conducted in various countries of the world either as "The Five-day

Plan" or a recently modified approach called "The Breath-free Program."

The Lord guides us even in the mundane activities of life.

The screening for anti-cancer agents was a relatively large one. We had a resident colony of some 10,000 mice! The National Cancer Institute provided the funds for the research.

The Head Technician

As one may surmise a project of this size required a large number of technicians, ten in all. Byron Fujikawa was an American born Japanese, and had fought valiantly in the United States Marines. He was a good organizer, a very hard worker, and fast in what he did. He was placed in charge of the day-to-day operation of the project.

One morning Byron burst into my office. He was beside himself with anger and was muttering something. As I listened to him it finally dawned on me that he believed one of his fellow technicians, Ernie Daniels by name, had called him a liar, and Byron was telling me all things he was going to do to Ernie.

I waited until he began to simmer down, and then asked him to sit down.

"Are you a liar," I inquired?

Byron jumped to his feet. "You are siding with him," he shouted! I wondered for a moment if he was going to attack me!

"Sit down and relax," I commanded him. I waited several minutes before asking him again, "Are you a liar?"

"Of course not," he yelled.

"Then why are you disturbed? If someone calls you a fool, it doesn't make you a fool. But if you respond like a fool, you are a fool."

Byron got the point. I encouraged him to forgive and forget and we had prayer together. As he was leaving, I asked if he would have Ernie come to my office.

The two men reconciled and remained good friends from then on.

Years later, just before I left Loma Linda to come to the Northwest, I ran into Ernie. As we were wishing each other goodbye, he said to me:

"Doctor Hardinge, do you remember the day when Byron and I had a quarrel and you asked that I come to your office? I was certain that I would be fired. Instead of firing me you gave me a Bible study! It changed my life."

I have no recollection of what I said that morning. But I praise the Lord that through His Spirit's guidance, I said the right thing, at the right time, in the right way.

Things went very well with the project for the first eighteen months. Then strange things began to happen. I would come to work, usually around seven, only to find that Byron had called the crew to work at 2:00 AM, and they had been working ever since! On another occasion the "crew" was informed at five in the evening that transplanting would start in half an hour, requiring them to work till twelve or one in the morning!

"What is going on?" I asked Byron.

His usual reply was that the tumors in the donor mice had come to maturity and had to be used. But the "crew" was increasingly unhappy. Why, after eighteen months had such problems developed? Tumors had not matured at odd hours prior to this time. So I decided to set the schedule for each day's work first thing in the morning. It worked for a few days and then reverted to an unpredictable schedule. Nothing I could say or do could change Byron's behavior. So I decided to let him go, though it was hard to make such a decision.

But Ralph, the department's general technician interceded. He informed me that Byron was having a hard time spiritually, and that I was his sole connection to God. "Don't fire him," was Ralph's advice. Ralph was a hard-working, faithful worker, and, although untrained in the sciences, was possessed with an unusual degree of wisdom. What was I to do? I was torn between getting someone else to head the screening program or going on with the chaos in the lab. And then into my mind came an idea, why not ask God to intervene and put it into the heart of Byron to resign?

I knelt in my office and appealed to Heaven that "if it was the right thing to do, I would dismiss Byron, for I was the director of the project, was using Government money, and therefore had the duty to see that things ran smoothly. But if it would be for Byron's best good, put it in his heart to resign. Lord, please make it plain."

Next morning, at the stroke of eight, there was a knock at my office door. "Come in," I called. The door opened and there was Byron, dressed in a suit with white shirt and tie. He came over and sat down in the proffered chair. "Dr. Hardinge," he spoke in a soft voice, "I don't know how to say it. I've enjoyed working with you and you have been tolerant of me. But I am here to resign so I can pursue advanced studies. I hope you will understand." And of course I did.

But then, you won't believe it, I talked him out of it! For the next twelve months I went through hell. The screening project was going nowhere and the lab was in constant turmoil. Now what was I to do? Then I made my decision. I again knelt down in my office and apologized to God. "Lord," I exclaimed, "you were gracious enough to answer my prayer a year ago, and what did I do? I slapped you in the face! Please forgive me. And, Lord, if I have to fire him I will, but if you believe it would be better for him to resign, please put it in his heart to do just that. Thank you, merciful Lord."

The next morning at exactly eight o'clock there was a knock at my office door. When I called "Come in," the door opened and Byron, in suit and tie came in and sat down in the same chair he had sat in a year ago. "This time, Dr. Hardinge," and his voice was firm, "I have come to tell you that I must resign. I am getting older and I must pursue my studies. Please understand." And understand I did! "Thank you, Lord, for your patience and mercy, and for solving my problem one more time.

Since that time I've made a lasting decision, and that is, that should any one come to me resigning, the resignation is immediately accepted! In the years to come, all workers in my Department, and in the school of which I was later Dean, knew of a certainty that if they resigned, at that moment their connection with the organization was severed.

May I add a word of encouragement to administrators who are faced with difficult decisions relating to problem workers? I have had to dismiss individuals on occasion but only after I have taken the matter to the Lord and allowed Him to show me what I should do. You do the same and He will make it clear, and when He does, don't slap Him in the face.

Note. Byron died some years ago of pancreatic cancer. A few days before his death he requested that I come to see him. I traveled to the Veteran's Hospital in which he lay. His faith was strong in the Lord and his friendship to me was as sound as it ever had been. We prayed together and I look forward to the day when we can give each other a big hug in the earth made new.

Some of the Side Benefits of Doing Research

Before I leave the subject of research, I would like to point out one of the benefits the investigator derives from his research. Over time he becomes cautious of accepting at face value the reports and conclusions derived from the investigations of others, and even those based on his own efforts. Perhaps the best way I can make my point is by discussing two of my personal experiences.

Toxins in Common Mushrooms

A paper appeared in *California Medicine*, a journal published by the State Medical Society, which concluded that the common mushrooms one regularly buys in the produce section of supermarkets, may at times, be poisonous. The author related the circumstances on which his conclusion was based.

A family of four, father, mother, and two children had had, among other dishes, mushrooms for dinner. The adults had taken a little wine with their meal but not so the children. A few hours after dinner both adults became desperately ill, with nausea, vomiting, abdominal cramps, profuse sweating, and diarrhea. They were treated at a local emergency room. By morning they were well over their frightening experience. The two children suffered no ill effects from the meal, but only those who drank the wine.

Many species of mushrooms are highly toxic but this was the first time that the common white mushroom appeared to be poisonous. The author felt it should be reported.

What the author did not know was that the common mushroom contains a substance called Antibuse that is often used by physicians to help alcoholics kick the habit. The way this agent works is that while it is non-toxic, in the presence of alcohol it breaks down into highly toxic substances causing severe symptoms as described above. An alcoholic is placed on the drug and advised not to take a drink. If he does so, he immediately reaps the unwelcome results!

I wrote a letter to the editor of the journal requesting that he share my letter with the readers. This he declined to do. I discovered he was both the author and the editor of the paper under question!

Another example of how observations may not always lead to the correct conclusion came home to me in an unexpected manner. In the *Journal of Pharmacology and Experimental Therapeutics* appeared an article that seemed quite clearly to demonstrate the effect of tranquilizers. So we used the data for an experiment the students performed in the laboratory (we placed it in the Laboratory Manual). We used the experiment for several years!

The Action of Amphetamine and Tranquilizers

The experiment was a straightforward, simple one. Three two quart juice cans and a mouse cage were supplied to each student group. Seven of ten mice were given a "lethal" dose of amphetamine. The three non-treated mice acted as controls. The three control mice were place in can number one, while three injected animals were placed in each of cans two and three. The one remaining injected mouse was put in the mouse cage by itself.

The amphetamine injected mice in can two were highly agitated and died within twenty minutes, while those in can three given amphetamine and the tranquilizer were no more active than the controls. The single amphetamine treated mouse placed alone in the cage, burrowed around in the wood shavings at the bottom of the cage, and showed no great agitation.

Conclusion: Amphetamine treated mice interact with one another causing extreme excitement resulting in death, whereas the control animals and those given a tranquilizer show no abnormal activity. The single amphetamine treated mouse had no other animal with which to interact, so it was able to handle the level of excitement produced by amphetamine.

A very neat experiment, or so we thought.

It was about three years after we first used this experiment that, one afternoon, a student remarked that the three highly agitated mice were wet with sweat. I looked at them and their hair was wet from nose to tail. It struck me to be an astute observation. On checking up in the literature I discovered that mice do not sweat, they lack sweat glands! The wet fur resulted from the profuse salivation of the mice. So I wondered, what would happen if we cooled the mice with air from a fan? When we did this, all the amphetamine treated animals lived whether they received a tranquilizer or not!

We applied for a research grant and a year later found that what the amphetamine treated mice were dying from was not extreme excitement, but hyperpyrexia (extreme elevation of body temperature) due to uncontrolled heating of the body resulting from their muscular activity.

We submitted a paper with our findings to the *Journal of Pharmacology and Experimental Therapeutics* only to have it rejected. The author of the original paper showing the presumed action of tranquilizers was the editor of JPET! Our article was subsequently published in another Journal. And so it goes!

Some Interesting Experiences During These Years

A Priceless Gift!

I had just completed a week long Health Evangelism workshop at a Mission Outpost in one of the Solomon Islands. The last meeting had been followed by a large number of questions by the more than the sixty attendees. After a quick lunch I was packing my few belongings when the captain of the Mission Launch blew the siren which meant he was anxious to leave. Almost at the same moment there was a knock at the front door. Mrs. Caldwell, my hostess, answered the knock. It was one of the ministers who wanted to give something to me. She explained that I was late for the departure of the launch and urged him to give it to her, and that she would see that I received it. But he was adamant that he be the one to give it to me directly. To save time I hastened to the door.

Now a throw back to one of the statements I had made during the morning. I had been urging the attendees to continue the aggressive evangelism they were already pursuing, and that their faithful witness would have a wide spread influence. I mentioned that one of their older kinsfolk, Brother Kata Rongoso, once a great warrior and cannibal, had visited the United States to tell of his marvelous conversion and the work that the Lord had called him to do. That he was attending a campmeeting in Southern California at which my wife, Margaret, had as a little girl sat in his lap, and the profound and lasting influence it had made in her life.

At the door I recognized one the ministers who had been at the meetings. In his hand in held an object crudely wrapped in newspaper. And then this is what he said:

"I am the brother of Kata Rongoso. He passed away a few years ago and that he would have been greatly pleased had he been at the workshop. What I am holding in my hand is an ebony carving of a kooro kooro bird* that he kept on a small bedside table. I have kept it on my bedside table ever since his death. Had he been alive and had heard what you said about his visit to California, he would have given this bird to your wife. Please accept it from "him," and present it to your wife in remembrance of my brother."

With a lump in my throat, I thanked him for his loving thoughtfulness, and while holding his hand, told him I looked forward to the day when my wife and I could together shake their hands in the earth made new. What a gift and what an example of true generosity!

These dear people have so little of this worlds goods, yet they are eager to share some of their treasures with those of us who have so much.

* A kooro kooro bird is a dove. The beautiful carving stands about six inches tall and has had an honored place in our front room.

Slim and Trim

My brother Leslie and I were both speakers at a camp meeting held by the Ohio Conference. I had just finished my morning talk and it was noon. My brother was waiting for me and broke the news that we were to have lunch (dinner) at the home of Mr. and Mrs. Baker together with their family of four. Les had his car and we drove over.

It was Les's custom to visit with them every year for the purpose of urging them to send their children to Washington Missionary College (now Columbia Union College) when they reached the proper age. My brother was head of the Religion Department. On the way he warned me that they were among the biggest eaters he had ever witnessed! He assured me that I would see more food disappear at the meal than I had every seen before. "They all look like it too," he added.

Dinner was ready when we arrived and we were promptly seated at the table, as Les had an appointment immediately after the meal. As the various dishes were passed around every one of the Bakers took small servings. The only two who had reasonable helpings were Les and myself. Not one of them accepted a second helping! This included desert.

As we drove way after thanking them for their having invited us, Les turned to me, "Merve, you sure inhibited them, (I had been speaking on nutrition in my series of health talks), and I've never seen anything like it in my life. I bet you if we were to drive back you would find them around the table having their usual meal!"

Years passed, I'm not sure how many. I was giving a series of health talks as part of an evangelistic meeting being held in one of the suburbs of south Los Angeles. As I was headed for the exit I was pushing my way through the lobby which was packed with attendees. Suddenly a woman blocked my progress and asked if I remembered her name. I searched her face but could not recognize her.

"You were a guest at my house and had a meal at my table, and you don't remember who I am?" She was giving me a hard time! Racking my brains I finally admitted that I had no recollection of her.

"Please," I begged, "do jog my memory."

With a broad smile she replied, "I'm Mrs. Baker, of Ohio!"

"No, you're not," was my immediate response.

"Oh yes, I am," and she turned and called her husband who was a few feet away. "Come meet, Dr. Hardinge; he didn't even recognize who I was after having a meal at our home!" Mr. Baker came over with a broad smile and we shook hands.

I looked at one and then the other. They were slim and trim! "And do meet our two children who are still with us," as she presented two teenage youngsters. Not one of them was an ounce over weight!

"We took your talks to heart. Remember speaking about overweight?" She had a real twinkle in her eyes.

I congratulated them on the decisions they had made, and was so glad to meet with them again, and see first hand their success.

If a reader is struggling with the problem of overweight, perhaps this little story with encourage you to not give up.

The Coat I Saved

Dr. Ian Fraser and I were returning from Atlantic City where we had attended the meetings of the Federated Societies of Biology and Experimental Therapeutics. We were in the Chicago Airport and we both wished to go to the restroom. It was winter time and the weather was quite cool. As we entered Ian went over to a clothes rack and hung his overcoat on an available hook. Having finished I decided to stay in the restroom as it was warmer than in the terminal.

As I was standing to one side watching people as they came and went, a man entered and walked directly towards the clothes rack. He checked several of the coats and then picked up my friend's coat, threw it over his arm, and headed for the door. I intercepted him, and with a fairly loud voice, said; "That's not your coat, it belongs to my friend." Whereupon he muttered something I could not understand, and returning to the rack hung the coat up and hurriedly left the room.

It was just then that Ian emerged from his cubicle, washed his hands, and picking up his coat came over to where I was standing. "You had better thank me, Ian, I just did you a good deed." My voice had a chuckle in it.

"What do I have to thank you for," he inquired?

I then told him of the man who had come into the room, had walked over to where the coats were hanging, had picked up his coat (pointing to the coat over Ian's arm) and was heading out, when I stopped him with, "That's not your coat." And added that the man had immediately returned it to the rack, and hurriedly headed out of the restroom!

Ian looked at the coat that he had hung over his arm. "Mervyn," he spoke in a strange voice, "But this isn't my coat!" We looked at each other in disbelief.

"But you hung it on that peg, I watched you, and that is the same coat you just picked up."

I reached for the coat as he handed it to me and looked on the inside of the rear collar, and there written in bold letters was "H A R D I N G E!" It was my coat.

As I was looking at the coat hanging over my arm, Ian spoke: "That's my coat, how did you get it?" And it was. We had picked up each other's coats that morning and the coat I had saved was my own!

Moral of the story: Watch out for your friend's coat, it might be your own!

One afternoon around four o'clock my secretary put a call through to me from a local dentist. He wondered if he could see me regarding his weight problem. "I'm not that much over weight but I am a bit paunchy," he said casually.

The Dentist Who Nibbled

"How about seven o'clock this evening at my office?" I responded.

"See you then," and he hung up.

He was there at seven when I arrived back from supper. We sat down across a table I had in my office. "Tell me your problem," I said. The dentist was in his early forties, solidly built and about 5' 10" tall. He was not bulging and carried his weight quite well. He could, however, lose a few pounds and look a lot better.

"There's nothing wrong with my diet," he answered. "My wife is a home economist and she sees to it that all our meals are balanced and wholesome."

"Do you help yourself to large servings of the food?" I inquired.

"No, I don't think so," he replied.

"Do you eat between meals, then?"

"Not quite. I never eat anything after we finish a meal until just before the next meal," was his response.

"Then what do you do?"

"I like to nibble a little while my wife is giving the finishing touches to the meal," was his answer.

And then I asked the obvious question. You guessed it, "What do you nibble?"

With a look of satisfaction on his face, he replied, "I love chocolate."

"What did you nibble this evening before your dinner?"

"Chocolate chips."

"How many?"

"A full package, a sack, the kind you buy in the store," he responded.

"You mean a full pound package?" My voice obviously carried a note of surprise.

"I surely did. Sometimes I'll eat two in a day! You think that's a lot too much?"

"Come to the board with me," I suggested, and picked up a piece of chalk. I opened a food composition book and looked under chocolate. On the board I wrote, one pound provides 3500 calories of food energy!

"That's probably more calories than I get from all the other food I eat in a day," he exclaimed.

"It probably is." I looked him in the eyes with a half smile.

"Thanks a lot for what you've told me. I won't take anymore of your time. I know what I must do." With that he walked to the door and waved goodbye.

I watched him off and on over the next several years. His paunchiness was soon gone. The last time I saw him he looked slim and trim. The topic of chocolate never came up again.

Nibblers, watch out!

The afternoon lab had just finished and I was headed for my office. A student stopped me. "Dr. Hardinge, I understand you know something about nutrition. Is that right?"

Too Much Margarine

"Yes, a little," I replied. "Can I help you in some way?"

"I was wondering, Doc, if you can eat too much margarine?" he questioned.

"That was a bad question; you can eat too much of anything," I replied with a smile.

"I know. I know. But seriously, can one really eat too much margarine?" He looked at me expectantly.

"How much do you eat each day?"

"Three or four pats. Is that too much?" His answer was given in all sincerity.

"You mean the little servings you get in a cafeteria on those small paper plates?"

"No, no, Doc. The pats I'm talking about are the four that come in a packet. Are three or four too much in a day?"

"You mean the four cubes you get when you buy a pound of margarine?" I asked in astonishment.

"That's it, that's it; are three or four too much?"

I could not believe my ears! Three quarters to a pound of margarine a day! "How on earth do you eat that much margarine?"

"Oh, that's easy. I use at least three pats with my baked potatoes. I love baked potatoes. Then, of course, I spread it on my bread. Goes real fast, you know!"

"Come with me to my office, I'd like to show you something." As I had done with the dentist I did with this student. I simply showed him in a food composition book that a pound of margarine provided 3500 calories in food energy! And on my query, he replied that his wife consumed about the same amount as he did!

I had to give him a short course in nutrition to show him his problem. He listened quietly as I spoke. "I gave up the use of margarine some twenty years ago. I haven't used any pure fatty spread since then. The savings I get from not eating plain fat calories (a highly refined and concentrated food) I put towards more wholesome and nutritious foods. And these unrefined foods provide me an abundance of fiber and are more filling."

He thanked me and left. It was about two months later when he stopped me again. "Doc, you know that advice you gave me. It surely worked. I went home and explained to my wife what you had told me. Between us we haven't eaten a pat of margarine since. I've lost 15 pounds and my wife has lost the same amount. We both feel so much better. I have more energy, sleep better, and my grades have really improved because I no longer fall asleep at my studies. We've resolved to keep the program up. We sure appreciate your advice. Thanks again!"

Three quarters to a pound of margarine a day! If I hadn't heard it with my own two ears I would find it hard to believe. But that's the fact.

During the summers I would accept speaking appointments at camp meetings, workers meetings, and doctor-minister retreats. I was a guest speaker at a campmeeting, in Ohio I believe. It was between nine and ten in the morning and about 400 people were present in the auditorium. It all happened unexpectedly and spontaneously.

"I'm not an Animal!"

I'm not sure precisely what I was talking about but in my presentation I used the phrase, "man and other animals." A dear brother in the audience rose to his feet and in a virtual shout, exclaimed, "I'm not an animal!"

"Biologically speaking, you are," was my response.

Again on his feet with arms waving in the air, he shouted, "You may be but I'm not."

I should have let the matter rest at that, but at that moment the synapses between my neurons were firing too rapidly, and I spoke without giving what I said any thought. "Brother," I replied, "You are not only an animal but you are an unclean animal!"

Beside himself, he yelled, "I'm not unclean!"

And then it came, the clincher. "I've never seen a human being who chews the cud and has cloven hooves!"

At that the audience fell apart! Later, when my gray matter had cooled down, I realized I had made a fool of the dear man. I sought him out but could not find him. I have, however, promised the Lord that should we meet in His kingdom I will apologize to him for what I said and the way in which I said it.

Friends, a warning. Be careful what you say!

I had just completed a series of talks at a campmeeting in Oshawa, Canada, and was returning to Loma Linda via Highway US 70. My plan was to spend that night in my sister's home in Lincoln, Nebraska. It was late afternoon and the shadows were beginning to lengthen over the rolling hills of western Iowa. Coming over the brow of a hill I looked upon an oft-repeated scene. There before me was a gently sloping downgrade, at the bottom a bridge crossing a little winding stream fringed irregularly with scattered clumps of trees, and a slightly curving road on the opposite side of the valley climbing up to the top of the next hill.

A Kid's Life or Corn?

I had just reached the top of a hill and had started my descent to the bridge below when, glancing ahead, my eye caught sight of a large, slowly moving truck lumbering up the hill ahead. The bed of the truck consisted of an iron-sided bin formed from about four foot high metal plates. The bin was filled to the brim with shelled dry corn. A pickup truck was following the larger vehicle and was obviously anxious to pass. Halfway up the hill the pickup swung to the left and started to pass. Then a strange thing happened. For reasons I cannot explain, the pickup made a 90-degree turn to the right and ran straight into the side of the large truck. The large truck veered to the right, crossed the shoulder, and ran partly up the sloping bank. Then everything disappeared in a cloud of dust!

Driving to the scene of the accident, I jumped out and ran to see if I could be of help. As the dust cleared it showed that the pickup had run head-on into the side of the big truck, the impact throwing the occupants out. The corn-filled truck had run its outside wheels part way up the bank and was tilted precariously. The side of the bin on the downside had buckled and the shelled corn was pouring through this "lip."

As I came up I found that the driver of the large truck and his helper were urging an older man, the driver of the pickup, to get to his feet. His face and hands were cut by splintered glass. Blood seemed to be flowing everywhere. "Lay him down and make him comfortable," I told the men. They looked at me as if to say, "Who are you to tell us?" Then I spoke again, "I'm a physician." Immediately they gently laid him down and placed a folded jacket under his head. It was then that I heard ear-piercing screams for help coming from the opposite side of the pickup. Turning away from the three men I ran around the back of the pickup in the direction of the screams.

Then I saw a scene that chilled my blood. In the angle between the truck and pickup was an ever widening and deepening sea of corn. The screams were coming from a lad, about 12 years old, who, under the lea of the larger truck, was completely covered with corn except for his left arm, which he was wildly waving. His face, upturned towards the sky, was all but covered with corn. His eyes were bulging with terror, for the corn was already above his chin and lapping at his lips. Wading knee deep through the corn I reached his side and began, with frantic efforts, to scoop the corn away so it would not fill his mouth. But no matter how hard and fast I worked, the corn kept gaining on me. It was then that I shouted for help, and almost immediately there was a helper by my side. Together we scooped away the corn from the boy's face, but as hard as we both tried it was a losing battle. Our arms were caked with perspiration and corn husks and our faces were no different. Sweat was dripping off our chins. Our strength had all but run out. Were we going to lose the fight?

It was then that a farmer with a broad corn shovel stepped up. Soon another joined him. Together they heaved away the onrushing tide of corn. We both relaxed and tried to catch our breaths. But the lad, who had grabbed my arm when I first arrived at his side, would not let me go. With fingers like steel he held on and with a pleading voice begged that I not leave him. I gently patted him on his head and assured him that I would stay. But frightening thoughts were racing through my mind. What if the truck would tip over onto its lower side? All the boy's would-be saviors would be killed, some crushed under the truck itself and others buried under an avalanche of corn. Who would take care of my wife and children? And then foolish thoughts would intrude. How will the papers report the accident? Professor saves boy's life? Passing physician risks his life to save a 12-year old? But then I was jerked back to reality.

From the belly of the truck an endless torrent of corn continued, like a cataract, to gush forth, and little progress was being made to uncover the boy's body so he could be pulled free. Just then two farmers climbed into the bin, and, thigh deep in corn, began to shovel it out throwing it over the back gate of the big truck. Suddenly a voice was heard: "Take it easy guys, that corn ain't insured!" The owner had said the wrong thing. A moment of silence swept over the crowd that had gathered and the mounting tension could be felt. There was a slowly increasing murmur of anger and resentment. Then a rage-filled onlooker raised his clenched fist in the air and shouted: "What's worth more, a kid's life or corn? Throw the whole damn load out. We'll take care of him!" The angry voices were stilled and now a murmur of approval could be heard.

And all the while the crunch and shush of working shovels were the only sounds that could be heard. I looked up and saw that the corn bin was full of farmers and corn was flying through the air both front and back. Finally, the flow of corn slowed and then abruptly stopped. A shout of joy now filled the air. The men on the ground who were shoveling were also making progress. The corn surrounding the boy was lessening. First his neck, then his shoulders, and finally his whole body were released from the enveloping grain. Now it was easy to see what had trapped the boy.

When the boy was thrown out of the pickup cab he had landed on the lower slope of the bank just as the big truck with its load of corn keeled over on its left side and the side buckled. Both ankles were crushed between the left diesel tank (just behind and below the driver's door) and the ground. He was lying sideways, his right hand and arm holding him off the ground as far as he could stretch. And that is why he was waving only his left arm.

The police and ambulance had arrived, but the medics could not pull him loose. Each time they tried the boy would shriek with pain. They then shoveled under his ankles, but as the earth was removed the truck would settle just that much. The boy would cry out in pain and his grip on my arm would tighten.

The pickup had been pushed out of the way so the wrecker could, hopefully, lift the truck's body off the boy's ankles. Unfortunately the wrecker was only large enough to handle cars, not huge trucks. When the wrecker attempted to raise the corn truck its front wheels would rise up into the air! Finally someone suggested that as many men as possible get under the leaning body of the truck, and that the wrecker, with men standing on its front bumper to weight it down, would all try at a given signal, to lift the truck body. When all was ready, a voice called out, "One, two, three lift." At the same moment the medics pulled the boy free. A shout of triumph went up. Men and women began to laugh and pat each other on the back.

The boy was whisked away by the medics into the waiting ambulance, and with wailing sirens it was off to the nearest hospital. An audible sigh of relief broke from the crowd. By ones and twos they headed for their automobiles, leaving behind a scene of utter desolation. The driver/owner of the corn and his helper were surveying the scattered piles of corn, much of it trampled by the feet of men and women who had only stopped to whet their curiosity. No reporter, if any were there, had even approached me, let alone asked my role in the saving of the boy's life. I felt a little let down. The adrenaline high of the moment had ended.

The shadows were a little longer as once again I headed west. Material things had lost their value for a brief moment of time. In my ears I could still hear the words of an angry man demanding of the crowd, "What's worth more, a kid's life or corn?"

Epilogue. Some forty or more years have passed since this episode occurred. During that time some details have faded from my memory. I'm not sure whether the highway was US 70 or US 80? There were, of course, no freeways then. I remember, as I drove west, entering a little town. Its name I've forgotten. At one of its streets there was an obvious sign with an arrow under the word "HOSPITAL." Was it there that the young lad was taken? How did his ankles heal? I would love to hear from him. If any reader should remember the experience, it would be a delight to hear from you. And more, what a pleasure it would be to shake the hand of the boy, who now, of course, is a grown man.

Chapter 9

MY SABBATICAL YEAR

I had received a travel grant to take me to the University of Glasgow in Scotland, and to the University of South Africa in Cape Town, South Africa. I wished to study with men who were working in a field of research in which I was also involved. The grant provided funds for a round trip ticket from Los Angeles to Cape Town. Since I was to be away for a year the air-travel expenses for my wife and two teenagers were also included. It proved to be an extraordinary trip.

After receiving the funds I discovered it was cheaper to travel around the world than just to Cape Town and back! So this is what we did. Shortly before leaving Loma Linda in September 1965 I was informed that the researcher in Glasgow with whom I was to work had died, so I decided on an alternate plan. It was to spend the fall at McKerrie University in Kampala, Uganda and then on to Cape Town in January.

We flew from Los Angeles to Brussels, Belgium, where we picked up a Volkswagen, and toured Europe for the next ten days. We then spent a week in England and Scotland. The things we saw were both inspirational and educational. From London we flew to Venice, Rome, Athens, Jerusalem, Cairo, Addis Ababa, and on to Kampala, Uganda. At each stop (except Venice) we were met by an Adventist "guide" as prearranged who took us in charge and showed us the worthwhile sights and institutions of the area. Unfortunately, the equipment in the laboratory in which I was to work at McKerrie was broken down and my wife became seriously ill during our stay in Uganda. So the academic experience there was not as profitable as I had hoped.

A Short Sojourn in Rwanda

While in Kampala I was requested by the Mission to visit one of our hospitals in Rwanda. I spent a weekend at the institution. There I met former colleagues and students, and held a series of meetings beginning Friday evening and ending Sunday morning. It was surely an inspiration to us, and I believe, a blessing to the staff. It was necessary to spend one night at Ronkerrie, the headquarters of our mission work in Rwanda, both going and coming. This was because it was a day's journey by car, on dirt roads, from Ronkerrie to the hospital. Dr. Bert Whiting, one of the medical staff at the hospital, drove us back on Sunday. The trip was a delightful one, and one of the highlights was that we met along the way some of the pigmies who are forest dwellers. They had come out on the road to sell some of their wares. We bought a primitive bow and some arrows!

My Last Delivery

We arrived at Ronkerri a short time before dusk, tired and hungry. Dr. Whiting had to return immediately so, as soon as we were unloaded, he said goodbye and was on his way. He had hardly driven out of sight when there was a knock at the door. I went to see who was there and was introduced to a Norwegian nurse who ran the clinic at the station.

"Oh, doctor, I have been praying for your return all day and am so relieved that you are back. I have a young mother who has been in labor for fifty-four hours and is making no progress! Will you come right away and help the poor woman?" Of course I had to agree. What else could I do?

As we walked the eighth of a mile to the clinic I was racking my brain as to what I should do. I had not delivered a baby since I finished my internship 23 years earlier! The nurse was chattering away but I heard none of it. My prayers for help were ascending as I tried to remember the various maneuvers I had once known when encountering difficult deliveries.

"Do you have forceps?" I inquired.

"Yes, but I have never used them," she replied. "I never learnt how," she continued, "as we nurses were not permitted to do deliveries. They were kept for the midwives."

"Where is the nearest hospital?" I asked.

"About 70 miles from here. But they have a resident physician who only comes in once a week. It is run by a hospital assistant."

"Do you have rubber gloves?" was my next question.

"I only have one pair that has no holes in them, and they are size four and a half. I have small hands. What size do you wear?"

"Six and a half is the smallest size I can get into and that is with difficulty!" My few options were running out.

As we approached the clinic, a small frame building, I saw along the footpath leading to the side door somber-looking men and women, doubtless next of kin of the patient. We entered a small room that was moist with heated air. On a kerosene burner, in a chipped, enamel pan two rubber gloves were boiling away.

"I'll have them out in a jiffy and dry them off," she said cheerfully. All her anxiety had left her since my arrival. It had shifted from her shoulders to mine!

"You had better put them on for they are way too small for me," I told her.

As she was busying herself with the gloves, I looked at the young woman lying on a high bed and covered with a sheet. Seated on a stool at the head of the bed was a young, perhaps 20-year old, African girl, doubtless the nurse's helper. As I watched the young mother she had a very strong contraction. About 15 seconds later she had another. My, I thought, such strong contractions and no progress, there must be something seriously wrong. But soon she had a third and even stronger contraction.

I uncovered the woman so I could see her perineum (the opening of her birth canal). With the next contraction I watched her perineum bulge. Was the baby coming, I wondered in unbelief? But my wonderment didn't last long. With her next contraction the vulva opened and I saw some black hair appear.

"You had better come right away and get the baby, or I'll have to take it in my bare hands," I excitedly called to the nurse. She was there in a moment and we had the pleasure of seeing a beautiful healthy baby boy born into this world! It was a wonderful sight and what an answer to prayer.

The young helper, I noticed, left the room but was back in a minute. Later I discovered she had gone to tip the relatives off as to the baby's birth. The nurse and I examined the lustily crying boy. He was in fine shape, not a thing wrong with him. As the nurse cut the cord I said to her, "You don't need me any more. I'm sure everything is all right." She thanked me profusely as I left.

As I exited the same door I had entered a few minutes earlier, on both sides of the walkway were smiling men and women bowing low to the ground giving me the most undeserved honor I have ever received. Think of it. Fifty-four hours and the nurse could not deliver the baby. The American doctor arrives and in less than five minutes a healthy baby is born, and what is more, it is a boy!

The Lord surely answers prayer.

A Simple Lesson

Dr. Lugunda, Minister of Health for Uganda, was a member of the Seventh-day Adventist Church in Kampala. He wanted me to visit a project in a village called Empiggi, some fifty miles away, and arranged for my transportation there and back. Now some of the villages in Africa have large populations. They are not laid out with regular streets and roads as are cities, each village being a cluster of homes and gardens more or less in a haphazard arrangement. Empiggi comprised seven such contiguous villages.

The Empiggi Project

The British, who had ceded independence to Uganda two years earlier, had employed a hospital assistant (physician's assistant) and sent him to the Philippines in order to obtain some public health training. On his return he was assigned to Empiggi to carry out an experimental program. He was to do three things; clean up the water supplies, teach the villagers to build and use slit latrines, and to encourage the women to cook their food on raised hearths. Sounds simple enough!

Cleaning up the water supply meant fencing off the area surrounding a spring to keep out live stock, directing the water to a single source, and having it flow from a pipe onto a cement slab. A slit latrine is a hole in the ground some two feet wide, six feet long, and six to eight feet deep, with a slit four by six inches placed in the middle of a platform covering the hole. Human waste was to be discharged via the slit. Interestingly, such a hole is dark, has no flies, no smell, and is an efficient way of disposing of human waste. A raised hearth is pounded dirt six feet square and two feet high, the fire being placed in the middle of the raised area. The purpose is to prevent a crawling baby from getting burned while the mother is attending another child or carrying out some other household chore.

The hospital assistant with his family moved into one of the villages. The village chiefs called their people together and warned them to have nothing to do with this government stooge. If you do, they prophesied, your property will be taxed, the government will confiscate our water supply, and bring hardship on you and our villages. No one would listen to the hospital assistant or cooperate in any way. But after two years during which he lived among them, they began to accept him as one of their own.

By the time I arrived to evaluate the program, he had cleaned up all but one of the 13 springs. In what he termed "good villages" eighty to ninety per cent of the homes had met all three requirements. A "poor village" was one in which only thirty-five per cent of the homes had made the three changes. The slit latrine project had had a setback. Termites had weakened some of the wooden platforms covering the holes and two adults and three children had fallen in! The government had come to the rescue and agreed to provide a cement platform for every home that prepared a suitable ditch.

On arriving back at the hospital that he now ran, he showed me on a large chart the patient load the hospital had carried before and since the project started. There had been a dramatic decrease in the number of patients seen in the clinic and a still greater decrease in the number admitted into the hospital. "Dr. Hardinge," and although he spoke with enthusiasm there was a tinge of sadness in his voice, "see those two empty wards, they used to be full with patients from the "good" villages but now they are empty. If only the government would allow me to continue the project, I could close down this hospital!" The project had been abandoned two years earlier after Uganda had gained its independence from the British.

Three rather simple goals but what enormous results!

Note. All societies suffer from lifestyle diseases. Should Americans adopt the habits of the Africans we would suffer from the same diseases from which they suffer, and vice versa, when they come to America and adopt our way of life they get the same diseases which plague us.

At the University of Cape Town

From Kampala we flew to Johannesburg, South Africa, stopping briefly in Malawi and Zimbabwe where we had missionary friends. From Johannesburg we went by train to Cape Town and miraculously found very suitable lodging not too far from the Grotsburg Hospital where I was to work in the Department of Internal Medicine, Nutrition Section, of the Medical School of the University of Cape Town. It proved a most rewarding experience attending conferences, clinics, and making ward rounds.

While our children, Fred and Jeanne, were doing home study, they spent considerable time in the dormitories of Helderberg College where they were warmly welcomed. Fred spent the next year at the school that proved to be a wonderful experience for him.

The Nutrition Section was studying the nutritional deficiency diseases of kwashiorkor and marasmus, commonly seen in infants and young children among the poor of the large cities and in many of the villages of rural Africa. Kwashiorkor occurs when mothers cannot breast-feed their newborns and the infants are fed refined carbohydrates (starches and sugar) in its place. Growth is stunted and generally the young are bloated and edematous. Marasmus occurs when an infant is fed reasonably good food but an amount insufficient to meet its needs, in other words, starvation in the very young. One of my patients weighed three and one half pounds and was twenty-three months old!

My project was to determine if the fat digesting enzymes were still functioning in the intestines of advanced cases of kwashiorkor and marasmus. While my children were at Helderberg College my wife assisted me in my research. Blood specimens, taken by Dr. Welsh, a pediatrician working at the Children's Hospital, were the samples that we studied. One afternoon he told of an experience he had had the previous day.

A Sad Story

A mother brought her infant to the clinic at which Dr. Welsh was the attending physician. The baby was wizened and shriveled, weighing only five pounds although sixteen months of age! After examining the infant he inquired, "What are you feeding your baby?"

"Black tea," was the mother's prompt reply.

"Black tea! What other foods are you giving the child?" was his next question.

"I no feed the baby no other food," was her confident reply.

"But," Dr. Welsh advised, "black tea by itself will kill your baby."

The mother angrily arose and picking up her baby walked out of the clinic room. At the door she paused and looking at Dr. Welsh, asked: "How many children do you have?"

"None," was his answer.

"Well then, you don't know nothing about raising children. Black tea may not be good for white babies but black tea is good for black babies!" And, as she was exiting the door spat out the words, "I have fourteen children!"

The results of ignorance are tragic and widespread.

A Health Workshop

On leaving South Africa we stopped in Malawi to conduct a one-week workshop for the ministers and teachers of that Mission. The meeting place was a small village called Martendarni where we had a fairly large boarding academy. The meetings went very well and the time spent at the Mission was a most enjoyable one. We stayed in the home of a Pastor and Mrs. Green, who were then retired, but were giving volunteer service to the school program.

Pastor Green was a very capable gentleman. In his earlier years he had been sent to Martendani to establish the school and a mission in that area. The country around the village was hilly and a small waterfall could be seen from across the campus. He had made an artificial dam above the waterfall using the water to operate a hydro-electric generator. This provided electric lights and power, not only to the mission, but to the school as well. And then the Greens told us of an interesting development.

The Milling of Corn

Corn meal is a staple of the region and was used in both the Mission and the school. After electric power was available, the Greens installed an electric mill to grind the dried corn into meal. In the villages at large, the making of corn meal was the responsibility of the women. After they had removed the dry kernels from the cob they would soak the corn for a certain length of time so that the kernels, when struck by a pestle (in a wooden mortar) would not shatter nor squash but would split. Then kernel by kernel the women and children would remove the germ (fed to the chickens), and the sticky de-germinated corn was molded into large "cakes" about 12 inches in diameter and a third of an inch thick. These are then dried in the sun and keep well. When meal is needed pieces of a cake are broken off and pounded into meal in a mortar. A lot of work indeed!

The Africans employed to run the mill saw how simple it was to make corn meal. After some time a delegation of village women approached the Greens and asked if he would grind their corn for them. A certain allotment of the cornmeal was given the mission in return for doing the grinding. Both parties were happy with the arrangement, although the husbands of the villagers objected to the taste of the whole corn meal (it tastes different from the refined cornmeal). But the women would hear none of it. They were not going to make corn meal the old way, and if the men wanted it the old way they would have to grind it themselves!

Some nine months later several government officials arrived at the mission. They wanted to see for themselves how the corn was being ground. The reason for this was the decline in the number of mothers bringing their babies to the well baby clinics, and the drop of patients being admitted to the village hospitals. Beriberi and pellagra had all but disappeared from the villagers using the whole corn meal! The incident of these diseases had remained the same in clinics and hospitals where corn meal was made the old fashioned way. So impressed were the visiting officials that they reported the matter to Dr. Banda (a physician), the president of Malawi. As a result the government set up mills all over the country and encouraged the use of milled ground cornmeal!

Each morning women and their children filled the lawn outside the milling area. Their sacks of corn were arranged in order of first come first served. While the corn was being ground the women and children enjoyed the time as a festive occasion!

Simple changes in lifestyle can bring about vast changes in the health of a population.

I should add that we took time to visit the game parks in Uganda, Zimbabwe, and South Africa. Time, unfortunately, did not allow us to see the Serengeti game reserves in Kenya nor to climb the heights of Kilimanjaro. So we ended our sojourn in Africa. As we flew eastward towards home we stopped in India, Singapore, Japan and Honolulu. It was a wonderful experience for all.

Chapter 10

A SCHOOL OF PUBLIC HEALTH

Conflict Between Public Health and Preventive Medicine

It was now 1962 and things in Pharmacology were running as smoothly as one could wish. One morning the President of the University, Dr. Godfrey Anderson, called me personally asking that I be a member of a committee to meet the following morning. The agenda dealt with a problem that had developed between the Department of Preventive Medicine of the Medical School and the Division of Public Health, a part of the Graduate School. Hostile feelings between the two groups, which had been smoldering for several years, had eventually burst into flames. The Chairman of each group had written to the President demanding that he step in and do something, even if some heads should roll!

The committee was a small one made up of Dr. Anderson, the Vice President of Academic Affairs, the Associate Dean of the Medical School, the Chairman of the Microbiology Department, one other whose name has left me, and myself. The consensus of the committee was that a czar be appointed over both groups, who would then knock heads together to obtain peace. I disagreed strongly saying that I knew the men in both groups and that such a plan was doomed to failure.

"Then what do you suggest?" was their obvious question.

"Both groups should," I suggested, "be brought together in a common goal under the umbrella of a School of Public Health. To form such a school, the Departments of Epidemiology of the Medical School, the faculty of the Division of Public Health, the School of Nutrition and Dietetics (a small struggling school which trained a handful of dietitians), would respectively form the Departments of Epidemiology, Health Education, and Nutrition. Such an arrangement would go a long way towards the development of a full-fledged School of Public Health. This would form a common goal and would, if anything could, bring the warring groups together."

The idea was scoffed at as being too ambitious, especially since the University Administration was struggling with the financial burdens arising from the Medical School's two campuses, Loma Linda and The White Memorial, in Los Angeles, being recently united at Loma Linda. The suggestion was made that I become the czar over the two groups. This idea I immediately rejected, assuring the committee members that under no circumstances would I even consider such a proposal. The meeting was then adjourned.

A School of Public Health Approved

Over the next two years the conflict between the two groups continued. The committee met on several occasions without making any progress. Then in May of 1964 Dr. Anderson, the President, called me at my home at 4:00 PM, one Sunday evening, asking that I present to the Board of Trustees of the University a proposal to organize a School of Public Health. The Board was to meet the next morning (Monday) at 9:00 AM.

"You haven't given me much time," was my response, "but I will do what I can."

I had been working in the yard, so I went in, showered, and went to my office. I soon realized that to prepare an outline of a proposal was the best I could do. And this is what I did. It was well accepted next morning with such remarks as, "I wish all proposals were presented in outline form. You can see at a glance what is required." Or "The points made are so clear, it is unnecessary to read through a lot of material." With very little discussion the formation of a School of Public Health was voted in principle. The administration was advised to bring, at the time of the

August meeting, a detailed report as to precisely what would be required, with a five-year projected budget.

The next morning the President called to inform me that he wanted me to find out precisely what would be required to develop an accredited School of Public Health. So I traveled to the headquarters of the Accrediting Commission in Washington D.C. The secretary, a Dr. Troupin, was most helpful and I came away with a number of documents. I also visited the Schools of Public Health at Columbia University and the University of California at Los Angeles. The Deans were cordial and answered the many questions that I raised. On my return to Loma Linda, I worked with the Vice President of Finance and together we developed a five-year projected budget. The proposal was submitted to the Board during their August meeting.

As the proposal was being presented, one of the board members interrupted with the question, "What is it going to cost?" I replied, "It will cost a lot more than any one imagines," but that, "the Vice President of Finance will present in detail the five-year projected budget." As Mr. Cone, the financial officer of the University, rose to his feet he said, "It's going to cost a whale of a lot of money!" He had hardly begun his report when he was interrupted by a member of the Board who interjected, "I move that we establish a School of Public Health." This was immediately followed by, "I second the motion." And then, believe it or not, a third voice spoke, "Question on the motion." The motion was unanimously passed without any real discussion!

Subversion

The two professors who had led out in the Division of Public Health proffered their resignations on hearing of the positive vote. On their departure a few days later they left behind "a scorched earth." Every document and file that had been kept of the operation of the Division since its inception had been destroyed. The only files inadvertently left behind were found in a cardboard box in the stockroom. These files contained all the correspondence of the past three to four months, directed to all who might be in favor of a School of Public Health, urging them not to cooperate with the proposed school. A letter was also found addressed to the Chairman of the Accrediting Committee giving more than a dozen reasons why a School of Public Health should never be allowed at Loma Linda University!

It was then that I was asked by the Board and University Administration to become the dean of the proposed school. What should I do? I had already made many major changes in my professional career, from Ministerial, to Medicine, to Anatomy, to Pharmacology. I had some administrative skills but no practical experience in Public Health. God had greatly blessed the department of Pharmacology, surely He didn't want me to shift gears again? But as my wife and I prayed for guidance, His voice came through to me: "Commit your ways unto the Lord...and He will direct your paths."

I decided, against the advice of my colleagues and friends, to make the shift. "Lord, if this is what You want me to do, I'll do it. Give me the wisdom I need and bless the undertaking."

The School Develops

And the Lord did just that. He gave me a wonderful helper in Dr. Bill Dysinger, a young physician who had trained in Public Health at Harvard, and had experience in the foreign diplomatic service. He had joined the Division of Public Health a year or two earlier, and was strongly in favor of working towards establishing a School of Public Health. He was gifted in the area of administration, and to him I gave the responsibility of organizing the academic program of the school. I devoted my efforts towards the general organization of the school, the budget, and the recruitment of faculty. Our working relationship for the next twelve plus years, until I gave up the deanship, could not have been better.

It was my plan to leave for a sabbatical in the fall of 1964. However, the President urged me to postpone my sabbatical until the following year so as to get things going towards the formation of the School of Public Health. To this I agreed. As I was leaving his office he asked, "Do you really think you can find a faculty for the School?"

"If the Lord wants a School of Public Health," I replied, "He has a faculty out there, and it is my responsibility to find them." And this is what I set out to do. The Lord in His foresight had prepared the minds of men and women, and made others willing, to prepare for essential positions in the school which He had envisioned. When asked, they accepted, many at considerable sacrifice to themselves and their families.

The following year was a busy one as the details as to how the Department of Preventive Medicine and the School of Nutrition and Dietetics should be merged into the framework of a School of Public Health. Faculty members were being sought, a few of whom were already trained, while the majority were sent to various universities to study in their specialty areas. We believed we would be ready for accreditation in 1969 when we expected to have a reasonably competent staff.

However plans changed drastically in the summer of 1966. On my way back from Africa I spent a month in Japan during which I held a health workshop for the ministers, teachers and other workers. Towards the end of this period I received a letter from Dr. Dysinger informing me that the School of Public Health in Hawaii had just been accredited, and suggesting I visit the school to find out just how they had gone about obtaining their accreditation. I had no time to make arrangements before leaving Japan and so on arrival in Honolulu went directly to the school.

I found the secretary to the Dean very accommodating. "May I see the Dean?" I asked.

"I'm sorry," she replied, "he is in Indonesia."

"How about the Associate Dean?" was my next inquiry.

"He is in the United Sates on vacation," she replied.

"Then may I speak with a senior faculty member?" I was running out of options.

"We don't have any," was her surprising reply!

She then asked, "Just what did you have in mind? Maybe I can help you."

I told her that Loma Linda University was establishing a School of Public Health, and that I wanted to find out just what they had done to obtain their accreditation. "Oh," and she brightened up, "Mrs. Tabochi can help you. She knows all about what they did because she worked closely with the Dean. I'll call her and see if she can talk with you."

Mrs. Tabochi was an extremely gracious person and proved to be most helpful. She gave me the details of their proposal including their budgetary projections, probably more than the Dean himself would have disclosed! It turned out that they had but one faculty member (the one in the United States) at that time, and yet they were accredited on the basis of their long-term plan of recruiting their full faculty. I suddenly realized that we at Loma Linda already had significantly more of an organization than they had, and that we should immediately apply for accreditation. Accredited Schools of Public Health were eligible for funds not available to unaccredited institutions.

It was with a joyous heart that I flew out of Honolulu thanking the Lord for the foresight of Dr. Dysinger, and for the information I had received. As soon as I was back on the campus of Loma Linda, I spoke with the Academic Vice President, Dr. Bob Cleveland, suggesting that we immediately apply for accreditation on the basis of our current staff and our future plans. To this he readily consented. "Give it a try, we have nothing to lose," were his parting words.

I called the Secretary of the Association of Schools of Public Health, Dr. Troupin, requesting that we would like to apply for accreditation as soon as he could arrange for a sight visit. The committee on accreditation met on the occasion of the fall meeting of the Public Health Association in early November. The sight visiting team arrived on our campus in the middle of October, and was made up of Dr. Troupin and two deans of other Schools of Public Health. The visit went well and the three unanimously recommended that we be accredited.

Accreditation

I arrived in San Francisco the evening of the day the Committee on Accreditation had met. The team was furious! Never in the history of accrediting schools had a unanimous recommendation of a sight visiting team been rejected. I learned that the chairman of the committee, Dr. Chuck Smith, Dean of the School of Public Health at Berkeley, had dragged his feet and that the decision was postponed until the spring meeting of the Public Health Association! It was to Dr. Chuck Smith that a letter had been written, giving twelve or more reasons why a School of Public Health should never be establish within Loma Linda University. What a disappointment for we lost a grant of over eight hundred thousand dollars that had already been approved had we received accreditation before November fifteen!

Prior to Christmas, Chuck Smith died of a heart attack. I visited the new Chairman in early January. He was most pleasant and assured me that there would be no problem in our receiving accreditation at the time of the spring meeting. He paused for a moment, and then spoke, "Chuck had a conflict of interest. He did not want another School of Public Health in California which would compete with his school!" We received accreditation for a two-year period in April 1967, at which time I relinquished my Chairmanship of Pharmacology to become the first Dean of the School of Public Health at Loma Linda.

Years of Growth and Frustration

I remained Dean of the School for the next ten years. The first two of these years were most pleasant. Dr. Godfrey Anderson, the President of the University took a personal interest in the school. He would come up periodically to inquire how things were going, look over the student roster, and ask whether additional faculty were needed. The student enrollment skyrocketed and the School prospered. He then resigned for political reasons and another "Pharaoh" arose who knew not Joseph!

For the next eight years, under the next two presidents, four years under Dr. Baker and another four years under Dr. Hanson, I was constantly harassed. Repeatedly, the cost of operating the school was brought up at board meetings despite the fact that each of the ten years the school was in the black at the end of the fiscal year. In fact, one year we were able to persuade the Board to put a hundred thousand dollars into a contingency fund because of surplus income! This came about in an unexpected manner. Our annual budget was based on the running average of full time students attending during the previous three years. We had prepared a budget for 143 full time students. The day following registration we were delighted to learn that 181 students had registered!

Examples of Harassment

It seemed that Presidents Baker (a pseudonym) and Hanson (a pseudonym) had in mind the dissolution of the School of Public Health. For example, President Hanson obtained the approval from the Board that an architect be hired to prepare a five year projected plan for the development of the campus, what new buildings would be erected and which would be replaced or destroyed. When the plan was presented to the Board nine months or so later, all the Schools of the University were assigned locations except for the School of Public Health; it was not even mentioned! When I raised the question as to why the School of Public Health had been left off the plan, I was curtly told that "we'll find some place for the school at the appropriate time!" It was never included or mentioned again.

This did nothing for the moral of the faculty of the School of Public Health. Rumors were constantly circulated that the school was to be closed.

It was budget time. The budget for each school was prepared each spring and presented, for final approval, to the Board at its May meeting. I had prepared the budget for the up-coming year and the time for its consideration by University officials was set for 7:00 AM, Friday. I arrived at Mr. Cone's office (he was the

Vice President for Finance at the time) at 6:55 AM. The door to his office was open so I walked in and wished him "Good morning." I then began to place, on a large rectangular table he had in his office, a copy of the proposed budget for each of the members of the committee.

Mr. Cone, who had been sitting at this desk, arose and walked over to the end of the table where he was accustomed to sit. Picking up his copy of the budget he slowly flicked through it. He then slung it down on the table (I was then standing at the opposite end) saying, "This isn't a budget, it's a want list!" One by one I picked up the copies of the budget I had been distributing and inquired when he would like to see me again. "Next week, same time." I wished him goodbye and left.

Next Friday I was there five minutes early. Again I began placing a copy of the budget in each appropriate place. Again Mr. Cone came over and picked up his copy. Again he slowly flicked through it. "You haven't made many changes," he remarked.

"I haven't made any," I replied. He looked at me in utter surprise. I then walked over and facing him said, "Bob, I want to tell you something. I have been assigned the responsibility to run the School of Public Health and I assume you and the Administration want me to do a good job. This is what I believe it will cost to operate it this coming year." And looking him full in the face continued, "I never pad a budget because I believe it would be dishonest to request more than I really need, but I never sell one short."

Seven o'clock arrived and all were present except President Baker. He always came late and everyone believed he did it on purpose. Fifteen minutes after seven he walked into the room and half-way to his seat at the head of the table said, "Hardinge, we're going to have to cut your budget $200,000 from what you had last year." He then sat down. A few moments later he spoke again. "I didn't hear your comment."

"I didn't make any, yours was not worth a response!" He had not as yet even looked at the budget.

As each category of the budget was presented he raised some question or made some critical comment. And then Mr. Cone spoke up. "Mr. President, you and I know nothing about running a School of Public Health. Dr. Hardinge has been asked by the Board to run the School and I'm sure they expect him to do a good job. This is his area of expertise, and if he thinks it is going to cost this much, then it's our responsibility to see if we can find it!" I could not believe my ears. From that day until Mr. Cone retired, I had a friend at court.

On another occasion President Baker was presenting some item relating to the School of Public Health. He had the ability to confuse the issue by speaking out of both sides of his mouth at the same time. And this is what he did with the item at hand. One of the Board members requested that he hear from the Dean, as to what he had to say. The Chairman turned to me and inquired, "Would you like to comment on the item?"

"Yes, I would," I replied. I then gave utterance to something that had been racing from one neuron to another. "Members of the Board, as a teacher I spend my life trying to make difficult things simple. But I have a hobby, and that is to make some simple things difficult. Let me try one on for you. There are individuals in this world who have the ability to phonate out of their oral cavities simultaneously and bilaterally!" There was a roar of laughter from about half the members. I watched as the other half asked those seated next to them what I had said, and this was followed by a second peal of laughter.

I then sat down. Enough had been said.

Health Productions

The graduates of the School increased steadily in numbers but many of those in the area of Health Education lacked the tools to effectively carry out the responsibilities expected of them. The Lord impressed me to prepare health lectures on the topics included in the course Philosophy of Health. These were made in the slide-tape format, then the cutting edge of communication technology, and could be used in presentations to the public, either to small or large audiences.

The Lord in His wisdom had allowed me to become a friend of a wealthy businessman, Mr. Rex Callicot of Baton Rouge, Louisiana. He saw the usefulness of the project and gave it liberal financial support. Support also came from friends of the School of Public Health so an up-to-date facility was established.

Where would I get the personnel to carry out the project? The Lord knew and brought together a team of four essential men to do the work. One came from our hospital in Denver, Colorado, an electrical and electronic engineer (Martin Knopper). Another came from being a principal of one our schools in Michigan (David Young), a gifted narrator. Still another was a recent graduate from Pacific Union College, a talented graphic artist (Sherwin Goerlitz); and finally a master photographer (Elwyn Spaulding) from the Loma Linda area, who gave up a lucrative business to join the group.

The work progressed harmoniously and twelve programs were prepared. They were well received and used worldwide. As technology changed, they were transferred to video offset. While many were updated in the late eighties some are still in use.

An Offer of a Conditioning Center Twice Ignored!

Two objectives which I sought were never achieved, namely, the building of a Conditioning Center and the establishment of an Endowment Fund for the School. Brother Rex (as he was commonly called by friends) along with Dr. Dysinger and Elder J. Lee Neil held a 10 day Physical Fitness Institute (October-November, 1965) at Fountainebleu State Park near New Orleans, LA. Brother Rex was desirous of building a Conditioning Center for the School. He, together with Dr. Dick Walden, my wife and I visited eight of the most successful Conditioning Centers in Europe. On his return to the States he came to Loma Linda to speak with the President of the University.

Sitting across the desk from President Baker, Mr. Rex made an uncommon offer: "Mr. President, I have been desirous for sometime to provide a Conditioning Center for the School of Public Health. I will build it, equip it, and endow it." To which the President never said a word, not even a word of thanks for the offer! A similar event transpired some four years later. Once again Rex sat in the same chair in the same office but this time President Hanson sat across the desk from him. "Mr. President," and he spoke with some conviction, "I have for many years wanted to give a Conditioning Center to the School of Public Health. I have already given away large sums of money that I had planned for this project. But I am still interested and will see it through." Again, no acknowledgment of the proffered gift and no word of thanks! Unbelievable! Sometime later Rex and I were visiting when he said to me, "Mervyn, it is seldom that a man comes hat in hand and offers a University a sizable gift, and the gift is not even acknowledged nor appreciated!" Some three years later President Hanson showed some interest in a Conditioning Center but the day of opportunity had passed.

The interest in different professions varies from time to time. When there is a dearth, for example, of physicians the applications to medical schools increase. When there is a glut of engineers, schools of engineering suffer. For this reason an endowment fund for a school is of great value to tide it over times when tuition income is at a low. Every effort on my part to get approval to establish an endowment fund for the School of Public Health was blocked by the University administration. Eventually, while I was working at the General Conference, permission was obtained to set up an endowment fund for the School. Millions of dollars over the years had been lost to the University, as some donors are interested in supporting one school but not another.

But despite the harassment, the school grew and prospered. We had a wonderful faculty and staff all working on a denominational salary (the only School of the University to do so). A spiritual atmosphere pervaded the classrooms. The faculty was encouraged to pray before lectures and, when appropriate, draw a spiritual lesson from some area of the study. We were ridiculed by some on the campus for this. The School shared half of the old hospital on the hill (Loma Linda is Spanish for "hill beautiful"). Remarks were made that the School was the "New Jerusalem," and that "Hardinge did not hand out diplomas, but haloes." Be that as it may, the School grew to an enrollment of over six hundred students both on and off campus, for we had an off campus program in full swing.

Boards of Institutions

Deans of the various Schools of the University were "invite-members" of the Board of Trustees of Loma Linda University. An "invite-member" can speak to a motion but cannot make a motion or vote on any action. Periodically my frustration with the Board would rise to the point at which it had to be released! Let me share with you one such occasion.

The Loma Linda Board

The then Treasurer of the General Conference never lost an occasion to criticize the School of Public Health. The usual attack was directed towards the cost of operating the School, which as I pointed out earlier, was ill founded. However that may be, he had just ended one of his expected tirades when another member of the Board suggested to the Chairperson that he would like to hear from the Dean. To this request I responded.

"Members of the Board, I must speak frankly to you this morning. Not one of you knows anything first hand about the School of Public Health, and that includes the President of the University, who is the sole person who presents to the members of the Board the issues related to the various schools. Not one of you has ever set foot in the School, spoken to any of the administration, or talked with a single member of the faculty, and that includes the President and the Treasurer!

"You come to meetings with other agenda items on your minds. Take for example the Treasurer of the GC. His usual procedure, following his tirade against the School of Public

Health, is to walk out to an adjoining room, and with him go five or six Union Presidents, to have a sub-committee meeting. He and the others returned not having heard a word of the discussion. On seating themselves they lean over to their nearest companion to inquire what the current motion is all about. They and you then vote!

"You, Ladies and Gentlemen, make literally life and death decisions regarding the operation of programs you know absolutely nothing about. And you do this time after time and meeting after meeting. Let me tell you an experience I had at Harvard.

Harvard's Board of Overseers

"One morning as I was working at my bench in the Nutrition Laboratory in walked Dr. Connant, President of Harvard University, the Dean of the School of Public Health, the Chairman of the Department of Nutrition, and two very distinguished looking gentlemen. The Chairman, Dr. Stare, introduced me to Dr. Connant, who then spoke, 'You are of course acquainted with the Dean. Let me introduce you to Mr. K., president of the Bank of Boston, and Mr. W., who is the CEO of Banding Corporation (a large manufacturing firm in the city). These gentlemen are members of the Board of Overseers of our University, and would like to ask you certain questions. Please answer all questions frankly and completely. Tell them what's on your heart. The rest of us will step out and wait in the hall. When they are through questioning you please bring them to the door.' With that the three walked out of the lab and closed the door into the hall.

"For the next ten to fifteen minutes these gentlemen plied me with questions. Why did you choose Harvard in which to take your post-graduate work? Are there not other Departments of Nutrition in other Universities? Are you satisfied that you made this choice? Is your laboratory work supervised? If you have any questions are they promptly answered? If you run out of a chemical how long is it before you can obtain it?

"Are the lectures you attend well prepared? Are assignments you are given promptly returned and have they been examined thoroughly? Are you satisfied with the library, and should you be unable to find something is a librarian available to help you? If you had to make your choice of coming to this Department over again, would your choice be the same?"

"When they had finished the questioning I led them to the door where the other gentlemen were waiting!

"They not only questioned graduate students but employees, faculty, anyone who worked or studied in the institution. In the spring, the same thing happened again at which time a different pair of trustees did the questioning. I had the same experience at Stanford. Members of the Board, some of you have been on this Board for twenty years and not once have you taken time to obtain a first hand knowledge of the institution you govern. And we have to live with your ill conceived decisions!"

Interestingly, at the next Board meeting it was announced that five members of the Board had been appointed to each of the schools to get an in-depth knowledge of the operation and needs of their particular school, so they could speak to the needs of that institution. Of the five appointed to the School of Public Health only one actually worked with the School. Of the remaining four two stopped by once to say they were too busy at the time to talk with me. The remaining two never once spoke. Neither did they speak to any other member of the school!

Reader, if you accept the responsibility of being a member of a Board of any institution please take your responsibility seriously. The God of Heaven expects you to do no less.

Chapter 11

AT THE WORLD HEADQUARTERS OF SEVENTH-DAY ADVENTISTS

I retired from Loma Linda University on January 31, 1980. It was strange suddenly to have no precise schedule, no lecture schedule or committee meetings to attend. It was a feeling of both regret and of relief. I had never experienced it before!

In early November I received a call from Elder Neal Wilson, the then President of the General Conference, asking if I would consider coming out of retirement and heading the Department of Health and Temperance at the World Headquarters. I went to Washington, D.C., and talked the situation over with the President. I mentioned to him that I had never rejected any invitation to labor in any area of God's work to which I received an official call.

Early January found me at the General Conference. I discussed with the President that Hospital Administration was not where I could serve best but rather in the area of Health and Health Evangelism. To this he readily agreed. At the time of the meeting of the General Conference Session in 1980, the leaders had decided that certain departments of the Church, including those at the Headquarters should be united. Examples would be Sabbath School and Lay Activities, Religious Liberty and Public Relations, and, among others, Health and Temperance. One of the responsibilities placed on me was to meld these two areas that had had independent department status into a single department.

This proved to become a bone of contention. The staff in the former Health Department were ready to cooperate in this endeavor, that is, to unite the two former independent departments into a single entity, but not so with those in the

Temperance area. They made it plain that they would remain separate and resist any and all attempts to amalgamate health and temperance. They openly expressed the idea that if they did so, that at the next General Conference Session the decision to unite the two entities would be reversed!

Their open defiance of the recommendation of the Church body led to virtually the disintegration of the Temperance area as two of their men were discharged because of their continued resistance to the plan. This resulted in ill feelings between those who remained and the others in the area of health. It was a most unfortunate situation.

My burden was to encourage health workers around the world to use their knowledge and skills to educate the church members and the communities in which they lived regarding the advantages of the healthful way of life. Healthful living as a way of life was something that the Lord had graciously revealed to His people. In the time that was available to me I was able to accept many invitations to speak to our members in various continents of the world. I also helped Elder Neal Wilson in his evangelistic meetings that he held in Manila, Philippines, and in Panama City, Panama. Let me share with you my experience on one such trip.

My Trip to India and Pakistan

I had been invited to visit the hospitals in India and Pakistan. Pastor Baird, a man from Australia and at the time Health and Temperance Director of the Southern Asia Division accompanied me. He was a delightful person with whom to travel. He left me at the India-Pakistan border from where I entered Pakistan alone. My visits complete, I found myself at the Karachi airport. I was headed for Singapore and the Philippines. I laid my passport and tickets on the airline counter, requesting as I did so, a seat in a non-smoking section. To my dismay the agent said it was "open seating!" Horror of horrors.

My daughter Jeanne, and Merlin, her husband, a dentist, were working in the Adventist Hospital in Taipei, Taiwan. They had a family of three children. My son Fred and his wife April with their two children were living at Philippine Union College where Fred was a teacher. The plan was that we would all spend Christmas together.

The Karachi Airport

The plane was delayed because of some mechanical problem. It was a 747 and all the passengers had been required to exit the plane on arrival. We were all in one large room anxiously waiting to embark. I then realized that my neuritis would not allow me to go very fast over the tarmac to the waiting plane once boarding was announced. I would be competing with hundreds of Filipinos returning for Christmas from Saudi Arabia and the Emirates. Each traveler hand-carried all that arms would hold or legs would support!

I believe I was the only new passenger boarding at Karachi. I walked to the very front of the waiting room and sat down on my brief bag, there were no seats available. As the time for boarding the plane drew near passengers crowded in ahead of me. There was nothing I could do so I resigned myself to having to sit in a smoking section with smokers behind, in front, and beside me! I lifted up my petition to the Lord that somehow I would find a seat in a non-smoking section.

The ticket agents arrived at the gate and every waiting passenger was on his or her feet, pushing and shoving towards the closed door. And then a wondrous thing happened. One of the agents by the door looked in my direction and beckoned with his finger that I come forward. I was the first passenger to exit the waiting room! I hurried towards the plane that seemed a long way off. But my efforts to get there early were futile. A sea of racing, pushing passengers soon engulfed me. By the time I arrived near the boarding ramp there must have been a hundred or more people ahead of me.

And then the host who had been standing at the foot of the ramp climbed up three or four steps and surveyed the crowd. His eyes met mine and, raising his hand he beckoned with his finger that I should come forward. I was the first passenger to re-board the plane! As I made myself comfortable in a seat in a non-smoking section, I raised my silent prayer of thanks to a God who, while ruler of His vast Universe, is interested in the seating arrangements of a tired passenger.

Again in India

While in India in 1984, Elder Christo, the President of the Southern Asia Division, invited me to return the following year to speak in several of the large cities of India. Elder Christo had in mind that in each city invitations would be sent to all those who made large contributions to the Ingathering fund. These were businessmen, lawyers, physicians, and other wealthy donors. The dinners were to be held in upper class hotels. There were to be no solicitations. After dinner I was to tell them of the health and medical work of the Seventh-day Adventist World Church. The schedule called for my starting in Calcutta, then speaking in Madras, Bangalore, Poona, and New Delhi. From New Delhi I was scheduled to fly to Shillong, in Assam, where I was to conduct a health workshop that would last a week.

On the way to India I had visited our University of Central Africa in Rwanda. I was traveling Air India and was scheduled to leave Nairobi, Kenya, at 9:00 PM, Saturday night. I arrived in Nairobi Thursday evening and notified the airline office that I was indeed in Nairobi, and confirmed my flight plans to fly out Saturday evening on Flight 29.

Dr. Louis Hart and his good wife entertained me during my stay in Nairobi. I visited our Clinic in the city, spoke to the nursing students Friday morning, and held the Friday evening and Sabbath morning services in the church. After thanking them for their kindness, Louis left me at the airport at 8:45 PM in the evening. My check-in time on Air India, Flight 29 was in fifteen minutes. The passengers planning to board the plane were gradually increasing.

The Angel of the Lord

Exactly at nine o'clock the ticket agent came to the gate. Only one passenger was ahead of me. The agent held a long list of names on a sheet of paper. When my turn came I stepped up and placed my ticket and passport on the counter. The agent noted my name and searched the list to see if it was on it. It wasn't!

"I'm sorry, sir. Your name is not on the list. Come back Tuesday!"

"But I must be in Calcutta tomorrow evening. I have an important speaking appointment. I have to fly out tonight." My voice was both firm and pleading.

"I told you, sir, you are not listed on tonight's flight. There is nothing I can do. Come back Tuesday evening." There was finality in what he said.

"Where is the manager's office?" I inquired.

If I had to wait until Tuesday, which was the next scheduled flight, the whole plan for my trip to India would be ruined.

I put my ticket and passport in my pocket, picked up my brief bag and suitcase, and headed for the manager's office. The door to his office was open. In fact, it had no door! Nairobi is close enough to the equator so that many hotels and airports tend to have no doors or windows to their rooms on the first floor. Things were wide open in Nairobi. The temperature is ever cool and balmy. As I arrived at the manager's office he looked up.
"Can I be of assistance to you?" He spoke in perfect English, but with a tinge of an Indian accent.

"I have a problem," I replied. "I have just been denied a seat on your Flight 29 to India, leaving later this evening."

"I'm sorry sir, but your flight is overbooked. I have no seats to offer you."

I thought for a moment and then asked, "Don't you fly to India via Saudi Arabia and the Emirates?"

"We do, but we do not go to Bombay."

"I do not need to go to Bombay. My final destination tomorrow is Calcutta. Can you get me there?"

"I believe we can. Come over to my desk and let's see what we can do." Fifteen minutes later a flight program had been worked out.

"I don't wish to disturb you further, so I'll wait outside your office till your secretary confirms the flights." I thanked him and left the office. Seated in one of the chairs provided for that purpose, I felt relieved and thanked God for his intervention.

Meanwhile the flight to Bombay had been delayed. It had been scheduled to leave at ten. Then the departure was postponed to eleven. The most recent announcement put it at one AM! As I sat in the semi-darkness my prayers ascended to the One who guides and directs in our lives. I reminded the Lord that I was His ambassador to these men of influence to whom I was to speak. Please work it all out.

I'm not sure how long I sat waiting for the confirmation of my new flight plan; possibly half an hour; maybe an hour.

And then from the gloom in front of me a tall Indian gentleman dressed in a white shirt and trousers, black tie, black leather belt, and black shoes approached me. When he was about ten feet away he paused and with his finger beckoned me to follow him. I got up immediately, collected my bags, and followed him to the front of the airport.

"I will have you checked in," he informed me.

By that time we had reached the agent who had the long list of names and had told me to come back Tuesday. The tall Indian gentleman spoke to him, "Please check this passenger in." I thanked him for his help and walked to the check-in counter.

"Once again I put my ticket and passport on the counter. "A seat in a non-smoking section," I said.

"I'm sorry, sir, we have only one seat and it's in the smoking section. Do you wish to take it or do you want to come back Tuesday?" He waited for my reply.

"I'll take it," I quickly responded. He handed me my boarding pass and took my suitcase. I was walking on air as I strolled in the garden surrounding the airport. What a relief! My heart was full of gratitude for God's intervention.

A little before one in the morning a call came over the loud speaker that all passengers for Flight 29 to Bombay must board immediately. Since I was to be in the smoking section I was directed to the rear ramp. I mounted the steps only to discover an African occupying my seat! Now what? As I looked around there was not a single vacant seat. Three rows forward and to my left a commotion was going on. An American lady, I'd guess around thirty-five years of age, had her two teenage girls with her. She was standing in front of the middle seat in her row and was demanding that the African gentleman occupying the window seat show his seat assignment. This he emphatically refused to do.

The hostess then requested him to show her his seat assignment. In a loud voice, almost shouting, he replied: "I told this white lady I was not going to trouble myself to show her my seat assignment, and I am not going to show it to you either. I have it somewhere among my papers but I am not going to bother to find it." With that he slouched down in his seat and put his legs up on the back of the seat in front of him.

The hostess called a male attendant who demanded he produce his assignment card. To this he responded, "I came in this seat from Lagos and I am going to sit here till I reach my destination. And as I have been saying, and no one seems to be listening, I'm not going to be bothered to find my assignment card."

The male attendant bristled. "If you don't show me your seat assignment card I will be forced to call Security." To which he responded: "Get all the Security Guards you want but I'm staying here." With that he began looking out of the window. There was a moment of calm; then the hostess turned towards me and inquired, "Can I help you, sir?"

"Yes, this is my seat assignment but there is someone occupying it," and I showed her my assignment card.

She was an Indian lady and if she could turn pale she did. Just then down the isle came two security guards dressed in white shirts, white trousers with black ties, black leather belts, black shoes, and each carried a black ebony cudgel (baton). Behind the guards came the male attendant, and behind him was the tall Indian gentleman who had had me checked in. As they drew nearer I noticed the African man, who had refused to show his assignment card, getting out of his seat! And then my eye caught the eye of the tall Indian gentleman. He raised his hand and beckoned with his finger that I should follow him.

I pushed my way past the two teenage girls as they were now standing in the isle, past the security guards, past the male attendant and followed the tall Indian gentleman down the right side of the plane. He led me almost to the front of the plane and then stopped and pointing in the direction of two seats he said, "Here is an isle seat and it's in a non-smoking section." I put my brief bag onto the seat. That took but a second and I turned to thank the man. But there was no one there! He could not have passed me and there wasn't a soul in sight!

With a chill running up and down my spine, I put my brief bag in the overhead rack and sat down. Thank you, Lord, for sending your angel to solve an impossible problem. The Lord is good! It is my plan, some day soon, to say a sincere thank you to and to shake hands with that heavenly angel, who came in the form of a tall Indian gentleman, clothed in the humble garb of a lowly servant, to solve the problem of a weary traveler.

The trip to Calcutta was without incident and the speaking tour of India was a joy. My week in Shillong, the city in which I spent 17 years growing up, was a wonderful place to hold the health workshop. At the time of my visit I learned that our membership among the hill people was over 10,000! I returned to the US with renewed faith in the God who guides and directs our paths.

Towards the end of one such trip, I had arrived at the Baltimore airport and had secured a seat in a limousine headed for Takoma Park where my wife and I had an apartment. I found myself between two gentlemen. Since the trip was going to last over an hour I thought I would get acquainted with my seat mates. The man on my right indicated he wished to be left in silence so I turned to the gentleman to my left. He was a very affable individual and turned out to be an engineer. He was working with a large number of fellow engineers in a facility located near the airport. Their assignment was to use the knowledge gained in the Vietnam War for the civilian population. His project was to design a human hand for any who had lost a hand, forearm, or arm.

I inquired as to how the project was going. He replied that it was going very well, and then told me of an experiment conducted a few days earlier.

The Great Designer

"An amputee had an artificial hand fitted to his forearm. He was then asked to make a fist followed by opening his hand as wide as possible. These movements he did without any trouble. He was then asked to pick up a styrofoam cup which he did without crushing it in the least. Then as he held it out, the cup was gradually filled with BB shot poured from a bottle. As the weight of the cup increased his fingers would automatically tightened so that the cup did not slip. After the cup was full a hole in the bottom was made with a knife to allow the BB shot to flow back into the bottle. Now as the cup became lighter and lighter the fingers would relax in proportion to the weight of the cup. When the last BB shot had fallen into the bottle he placed the cup back on the table. During the entire operation the cup had never slipped nor had the cup been crushed in any way!"

He went on to say "that minute electrical motors control the various movements of the hand. When these motors are correctly attached to electrodes placed on the muscles that normally performed these tasks, the currents sent by the brain to these muscles are picked up and activate the appropriate motors turning them either on or off. Should the amputee lack any of these muscles, any muscle or muscles of the body can be trained to accomplish the desired tasks."

A marvelous accomplishment, indeed! But did you realize your hands are performing these and even more difficult tasks all the time. For instance, when you pick up a glass and fill it with water from the faucet your hand does all the automatic hand did. And as you hold it to your lips and drink, your fingers relax in proportion to the decreasing weight of water in the cup!

Our Creator deigned this human frame, and as he reviewed His work declared it to be "very good!."

Encouraging Health Evangelism

I had accepted the call to the General Conference with the understanding that my term of service there would be approximately two years. However, once there, the President urged me to stay on until the time of the next General Conference Session. During the last two years of my service, cost-cutting plans were being drawn up to reduce the number of staff at the General Conference as a whole. The number of elected staff of the Health and Temperance Department was reduced more than was that of any other department! When I arrived at the General Conference, the total number of budgets available for staffing the Departments of Health and Temperance were fourteen. When I left the General Conference the elected staff, for the now combined Departments had been reduced to four!

And here I might introduce a sad note. God has given to His Church a wonderful message of health and healing, not only of the body but also of the mind. Looking back over the years, two periods of the history of our Church stand out. Beginning in the 1880s a small medical institution was started, teaching a new way of life and using principles of healing not common in the medical institutions of the day. Within twenty years it had grown to be one of the most famous medical institutions in the world, Battle Creek Sanitarium. This institution attracted the elite of the world. But the Church as a body rejected the God-given message of health and healing, supposedly because of the apostasy of the medical leader. What unfortunately happened was that the baby was thrown out with the bath water!

But the Lord is merciful and patient. Beginning in the early fifties research done by Adventist investigators at Loma Linda University led to a revolution in the field of nutrition and health. This revolution of thought in this area did not occur in the United States alone but in most of the major countries of the world. The Adventist Health Study is one major demonstration that the Adventist Lifestyle is the most healthful lifestyle to adopt.

Then beginning in the early sixties, God raised up another institution at Loma Linda, the School of Public Health. Within a few years its student enrollment made it one of the largest Schools of Public Health in the world. A spiritual atmosphere pervaded the halls and classrooms. Students came from all parts of the world to learn something not taught in any other educational institution. And then, after their graduation, returned to their homelands, advocating the advantages of a healthful lifestyle.

Health education within the church body in North America grew rapidly. Nine of the ten Union Conferences forming the North American Division had full time trained health professionals directing their Departments of Health and Temperance. Their counterparts in the Conferences of many Unions were also professionally trained men and women. Our hospitals had health educators reaching out into the communities around them.

And then a paper, emanating from one of our medical institutions, purported to show that health education was not cost effective. What a demonstration of ignorance; it showed a complete failure to understand the real purpose of our health message!

Within a year or two, the hospitals had reduced their staff of health educators or eliminated them altogether. The Conferences and Unions followed suit.

Ellen White makes it crystal clear that the promotion of our health message is to "prepare the soil for the reception of the gospel seed." Prejudices are broken down, minds are opened, and the once hard soil is now ready to receive the words of life. This is what health evangelism is all about. Health is not the gospel message; it is like John the Baptist's cry, "Prepare ye the way of the Lord." The expectation of baptisms after a few months of health lectures is missing the whole point of our health message. Evangelism today is virtually at a stand still in the most developed countries. Could one of the reasons be that we as a people are poor farmers? Are we scattering precious seed on ground ill-prepared to receive the life giving truths?

Let me give you an example that will help to demonstrate what I mean.

Lifestyle Change and Evangelism

Sabbath was approaching rapidly, when my wife and I arrived in Melrose, a city in the suburbs of Boston, Massachusetts. We had driven across the continent and were weary and worn. Automobiles in those days had no air conditioners! I went into the bathroom of the apartment we had rented to have a shower. A brochure, with the picture of a young couple on the cover, was advertising a series of health lectures. I later said to my wife, "Margaret, we should get acquainted with these people."

Sunday morning, before we had even gotten out of bed, there was a knock at our door. Opening it, I recognized the couple standing in front of me, as the couple whose picture was on the brochure. "Come in, come in," as I welcomed them (our apartment consisted of a room with kitchen privileges). Harold Brendel and his wife Norma were the Pastor and his wife of a small church in the city of Stoneham, adjoining Melrose.

Earlier that summer, Harold and Norma had become convicted regarding reforming their way of life, both in eating and in living. They were enthusiastic about what they were learning and were anxious to share their newfound beliefs with everyone they met! They had literally been thrown "out of the synagogue" (Melrose Sanitarium and Hospital) for some of their teachings. The long and the short of it, we became good friends.

Sometime before Christmas, Harold asked if I might be interested in giving a series of health lectures in the church school gym, beginning the first Sunday in January. I debated whether I should take on any more than the heavy school program I was already on. But after meditation and prayer I agreed. He had three small churches in his district, the largest being the Stoneham Church. We visited all three, encouraging all to come to the meetings. But their coming was based on two stipulations, that no two Adventist families sat together, and that no Adventist was to ask any questions.

The opening night the auditorium was standing room only. The mix was encouraging, approximately 60 per cent were non-members and 40 per cent were Adventists. This ratio remained constant throughout the series and the attendance was steady with never a vacant seat. On the opening night, after I had been introduced, I looked over the audience and said, "It is my custom, at the beginning of my first lecture of the day, to read a verse from the Scriptures, bring out an inspirational thought, and have a short prayer. I hope none of you object for this what I am going to do." With that I did what I said I would do. To my recollection no one has ever objected. To the contrary, many have expressed their appreciation for the thoughts and prayer.

From my years of experience, praying before a lecture has proved to be a wondrous experience, as it brings into the room an atmosphere of quiet reverence. And what is more, the audience at once realizes that spiritual thoughts and comments will not be out of place. There are so many who hesitate to do this, planning sometime down the way to introduce the spiritual, using some mythical bridge to pass from the health to the religious. No such bridge exists. Once the secular approach has been established, interjecting the spiritual causes resentment on the part of a large segment of the audience. There develops a feeling that they have been led along for something other than their perceived goal.

The preacher or evangelist who is planning to continue the meetings must identify with the program from the beginning to the end. He must be the one to first introduce the speaker. He must greet the people as they come to the lectures and must wish them well as they leave telling them, "I will see you here at the next meeting." He should be active in passing out any literature and carry the roving microphone for the question and answer section. On occasion, he should ask a question himself. The idea must be conveyed to the attendees that the preacher and the speaker are a single unit.

Health Evangelism

The meetings, once a week on Sunday evenings, went well and Harold did a masterful job of identifying with both the speaker and the audience. The topics went from the physical, nutritional, mental, emotional, to the spiritual. In the final talks the need for God's help to make the needed changes in one's lifestyle were pointed out to be imperative. The end of the school year was fast approaching, which meant I would soon be leaving. My final comments expressed the belief that "if they, the listeners, were to follow and do the things I had presented they would live longer, happier lives. But if they would do what my friend Harold would present, they would live forever."

I had spoken every Sunday evening through January, February, March, April and May. Harold continued the meetings into November when he welcomed into the church, by baptism, 90 per cent of those who had been non-church members. May God be praised. In the following years, as I attended camp meetings in this area, it was not uncommon for someone to approach me and say: "Dr. Hardinge, do you remember those health meetings that you gave? It was then that I joined the church."

Each in His Own Armor

The method I have outlined above is not the only way in which to do health evangelism. Each individual must fight according to his own ability and interest, and in his own armor. Some examples of programs that can be used: a cooking school, a demonstration of bread making methods, an anti-obesity program, a vegetarian banquet given on occasion. Some are more closely related to medical problems: diabetes or high blood pressure screening to find those who need help, anti-smoking and anti-alcohol clinics, and others according to the background and talents of the individuals. Each and every approach will be successful when carried forward humbly and with God's help. But remember, the spiritual must be introduced at the beginning in some simple way, even though it be a short prayer, thus to openly invite into the sessions the presence and power of God.

Lifestyle change is not made over night. As I have observed through the years, it takes time, weeks, months, and often years. But the well-prepared soil will accept the seed when planted, and, watered by the Holy Spirit, will bring in a rich harvest. Unfortunately, we live at a time when things must happen now. We have gone from months, to weeks, to days, to hours, to minutes, to milliseconds, and now to nanoseconds! And this is not the end. The slightest hesitation is considered a waste of time! In the spiritual realm it is no different. A few concentrated lectures today, and baptisms tomorrow! And if this does not happen, it is dubbed as being "non cost effective."

My term of service at the General Conference ended in August 1985 at which time we packed up and returned to Loma Linda.

Chapter 12

RETIREMENT AT LAST!

Soon after I returned to Loma Linda the Pacific Press Publishing Association asked if I would revise their colporteur book, *You and Your Health*, authored by Dr. Harold Shryock. To this I agreed and after about two years it was published under a new name, **Family Medical Guide**.

After moving to Brewster, Washington, I began a task that I had long been interested in—namely, to thoroughly research the statements by Ellen White, principally on drugs, but also on simple and natural remedies. The preparation of a compact disc containing all of Ellen White's statements on these subjects was of untold assistance in the project. After some three years of work, the results were published by the Review and Herald Publishing Association, under the title "*A Physician Explains Ellen White's Counsel on* **Drugs, Herbs, and Natural Remedies**."

Total Health Lifestyle Center

While Fred, my son, was the Pastor of the church in Albany, Oregon, he received a request from the President of the Upper Columbia Conference in the State of Washington. He was asked to consider filling a desperate need, that is, to take charge of a small institution in his conference, called Total Health Lifestyle Center. Finally, after much prayer, he agreed to undertake the task.

The institution had a number of serious problems, the chief of which was a large debt towards which payments had to be made. There were also a number of creditors in the community who were anxious to receive remuneration for services they had rendered and for which they had not received payment. The Board Chairman assured Fred that within the year all the debts would be paid and that he should not worry over the finances! The problem of debt never was handled and five years later the program closed.

The programs offered were directed towards patients who were at high risk for coronary heart disease, those suffering from high blood pressure, diabetes, over weight, and smokers attempting to give up the tobacco habit. The goal was to modify lifestyles in order to decrease the risks inherent in unhealthful living habits. Programs were scheduled four to five weeks apart, and would last for three weeks. It was a live-in program where the guests were housed, fed a nutritious diet, exercised, and instructed by a series of lectures given by members of the staff.

Much of the time Fred was short-handed so my wife and I would drive up from Loma Linda, and I would give the lecture series to relieve some of the pressures of operating the facility. Margaret and I were returning to Loma Linda from one of these trips. The sun had set and it was getting dark, and we were on the lookout for a motel in which to spend the night. We were passing through a rural area with only an occasional farmhouse off to one side of the road. Suddenly the car slowed, and then stopped. We were able, fortunately, to get over to the shoulder of the road.

I attempted to hail a passing car or two without success. It was my hope that someone would convey a message to AAA to send us help. The day of cellular phones had not as yet arrived but we did send a wireless message to the highest heavens, asking that God would send the help we needed. And this is just what He did, but He did it in a way we would never have dream of.

The Kind-hearted Patrolman

A few minutes later a highway patrol car pulled up behind us. The officer came over and asked about our problem. I told him what had happened and to my surprise he asked me to pull the hood lever so he could take a look at the engine. I had expected he would call AAA for a tow truck or some other garage for help. However, he examined the engine and asked me to try starting it. The engine remained unresponsive. He then went over to his car and from the trunk took out a box of tools which he brought over.

I held his flashlight as he took some part of the engine apart. In a few minutes he exclaimed, "I think I've found the problem!" Then he went to his phone and talked with someone. On his return, he made, I thought, a most unusual suggestion. "I have just called an auto-parts dealer in a little town about four miles away. He is going to remain open till we come. If your wife will accompany me, we'll go and buy a replacement for this part, and I believe we'll have your problem solved." With that, he and Margaret got into his patrol car and disappeared down the freeway. In about twenty-five minutes they returned with the new part for which my wife had paid. Within a few minutes the officer had it installed.

"See if it will start," he suggested to me. I turned the ignition key and the engine came to life!

"Thank you, thank you so much. We surely appreciate what you have done for us. Let me give you something for all your trouble," and I reached for my wallet in my hip pocket.

"No, sir. Thank you all the same but I am on duty and this is part of my work. I would not think of accepting anything except a word of thanks. I'm just so glad the problem was something I could fix. I enjoy helping people in need." With that he picked up his tools and walked over to the trunk of his car. From its depths he got out some soap and water which he carried with him and washed the oil and grease off his hands.

"May I have your name and address, and also the name and address of your supervisor? I don't know how to express our appreciation for your kindness, but I want to write to your chief and report to him what you have done for us." I wrote down his name and address and that of his boss. We started down the freeway and had not gone far when he passed us with a wave of his hand. "Thank you Lord for answering our pray for help in such a wonderful way. God bless this man for his going the second mile."

A few days after arriving in Loma Linda I wrote two letters, one to the patrolman and another to his chief. I again thanked the patrolman for his wonderful help and let him know that I wished there were many more like him. To his supervisor I described the help he gave us, and congratulated him for permitting an officer to do what this man had done. I urged him to promote this patrolman at the earliest possible date, and place him in a more influential position in his department.

It was about three weeks later when the mail brought a letter from the supervisor. He thanked me for my letter and indicated that he had already received several similar letters from other grateful travelers to whom this man had been of help, all recommending that he be promoted. Then as I read on I couldn't believe what it said. "A few days after he helped you, as he was aiding another traveler in distress, a drunk driver sideswiped the car he was working on, and the officer was killed!"

I have pondered this experience many times, and believe that if Christ were here today He would use this story to teach us "Who is our neighbor?"

Another Trip to Total Health

My wife and I were on the way back to Loma Linda from the Total Health Lifestyle Center. It was our plan to spend the night with Margaret's youngest sister, Bette, whose home is in Sacramento. But about an hour's drive from their home two things happened, we were running out of gas and I was getting desperately sleepy! Just then the signs told us we were approaching an off ramp that would take us to a gasoline station. As I was paying the attendant for the gas with which we had filled our tank, I asked him if there were any motels in town.

"Oh, yes," he promptly replied and pointed to two signs, one of which was Motel 6 just a block away.

Mosquitoes!

We called Bette to tell her that we would see them in the morning and headed to the office of the motel. As I entered the office there was a single attendant wishing a client goodbye. She then turned her attention to a young woman. As the arrangements for her room were completed she cautioned the lady, "When you drive to the door with your number on it get together all the belongings you plan to take inside. You should have the key for your room ready, get out, shut your car door, open your room door, take your things in as fast as you can and slam the door shut!"

The clerk then turned to a gentleman whose turn was next. When all his arrangements were complete for a room, she gave him the same advice she had given the young lady. I was getting uneasy.

Was this motel in a tough area of town? Why was she giving such instructions to these people? As she was assigning me a room I asked if this neighborhood was unsafe.

"No," was her surprised reply, "why do you ask?"

I then reminded her of what she had told the last two guests; that they should get out of their cars and into their rooms as fast a possible.

She burst into laughter. "No, no, it's perfectly safe around here. It's just to keep the mosquitoes out of you room!"

At that particular time of year there *were* mosquitoes in the area all right. On both sides of the freeway (I-5) there were miles and miles of fields where rice was being gown. Rice requires the plants to be grown in water. And the water bred mosquitoes. Driving the freeway requires one to stop periodically and clean the windshield because of the accumulation of dead insects!

We did as the clerk had advised. We drove as close to our motel room door as we could, got together all our possessions we felt we would need for the night, jumped out key in hand, and as fast as we possibly could, entered our room. Fortunately we had a magazine with us. Folding it we killed mosquitoes for the next hour, 105 to be exact! We slept well but in the morning we discovered two that had escaped the slaughter of the night before. They were filled with our precious blood!

What an experience!

Wood for the Winter

Almost behind our house was a small planting of eucalyptus trees. They had been grown to provide wood for the orange growers to heat their homes during the winter months. For many years, to save heating costs, we had a wood stove that provided a lovely form of heat for our home.

It was in the fall of the year and late one afternoon I was cutting a few of the trees to provide wood for the coming winter. A ten acre orange grove to our east had been sold to a developer, and woodsmen had been hired to cut the orange trees into firewood. There were four cutters including the "boss." I had become casually acquainted with the men, especially the "boss."

The Woodcutter

As I was in the process of cutting one of the eucalyptus trees, about 6 to 8 inches in diameter, I noticed a shadow on the ground before me. Turning I recognized the "boss" of the woodcutters who was now standing just behind me. Much to my surprise he suggested, "If you bring me a file I'll sharpen that saw for you, and show you how to do it for yourself." Happily I walked to our garage, got a file, and handed it to him.

He knew what he was doing. He showed me how to recognize when the teeth were dull and just how much to file away. It wasn't long before he started the motor and began cutting. The saw made a purring sound and moved through the wood as if one was cutting cottage cheese! "No need to exert yourself, let the saw do the work," he remarked, as he turned and started back towards where his men were working.

I appreciated what he had taught me and thanked him for his kindness. Then for no reason I could figure out, he stopped and said, "By the way, no one ever does me dirty but I get even with him. Don't worry, I always do."

By the end of the week all the trees had been cut, the brush moved away, and all that remained to be done was to haul away the firewood. It was Sunday morning and we had just finished breakfast. I strolled out into our yard and noticed a pickup truck backing out from the grove beyond the one that was being prepared for subdividing. The truck could have come up by way of the land already cleared, but to back out from among the neighboring orange trees looked strange. So I ambled over and discovered that the owner of the truck was one of the three wood-cutters. He had two friends with him.

They hurriedly loaded the pickup with firewood and drove off the way they had come. While I was watching them I memorized the number on their license plate. I walked back to our yard and wrote down the numbers on the ground. About ten minutes later, who should drive up our driveway but the "boss?" He greeted me warmly.

"Seen anyone around here?" he asked as he pointed towards the piles of firewood.

"It so happens I did. A pickup truck backed out of those orange trees, loaded up with firewood, and drove away less than fifteen minutes ago. And by the way, I got their license plate number."

"You did! Can I have it?

"You sure can," and I led him to where I had scratched the numbers on the ground.

"Don't know how I can thank you, but I sure appreciate it. Don't worry, I'll get even with the guy. I always do. No one does me dirty but I get even."

About a week later the "boss" drove up our driveway again. He was chuckling to himself, and I knew he could hardly wait to tell me something. "You know that guy who robbed me of that wood. Well, I found out who he was. He was one of my cutters. And think of it, that guy, the day after I paid him up, robs me! But don't worry. When any one treats me dirty, I always get even. I found out that the three of them got hired to cut wood in the mountains, and I found out where. I know what woodcutters do. At the end of the day, they don't carry their saws back down the mountain from where they are cutting. Too much work to lug them up the next morning. So they hide them! I know, for I've done it myself for years. Well, I went up the other evening and I got me his saw. It's a beauty! It's worth $350! The wood he got from me would only get him about $30. I told you, when anyone ever does me dirty, I always get even. Don't worry!"

He then wanted to give me a cord of wood for my helping him find out who had stolen his wood. I thanked him but declined the offer as I already had all the wood I could use. As he drove away he called back, "Don't worry, nobody does me dirty but I get even!"

As I have thought of this experience off and on through the years, I have realized that his philosophy was certainly contrary to that of our Lord's.

Fixing Up Our Place

I had looked forward to the day when I would be retired to do some much-needed things in our yard. High on the priority list was to install a fence to keep out some unwanted dogs, and to build some block walls so as to terrace our sloping back yard to make gardening a bit easier.

The Miracle Cement Mixer

And here I must relate an experience I will never forget. I needed a small cement mixer with which to make the concrete to fill the blocks. And it so happened that a few days later I was at Home Base, a chain of large stores that provide most everything one needs to build and maintain a home, where I spotted a Taiwan-built cement mixer. It was just the size I needed.

After I assembled it I discovered a number of things about it that gave me some concern. When I turned the mixer on, the drum wobbled. There was no bearing in the yoke, just a hole in the cast iron in which the shaft turned! Also the shaft did not fit tightly into the bottom of the barrel, allowing fine sand to travel down the shaft into the "bearing." I realized that sooner or later the "bearing" would wear and the drum would cease to turn. But for the present it worked and I was satisfied.

But the day finally arrived. The "bearing" had become so worn and the wobble had become so great that the drum stopped turning. I took the barrel and the yoke to a machine shop in a neighboring town. The owner and his foreman assessed the situation. What I wanted was a new shaft that fitted snugly into the barrel bottom and a bronze bearing in the yoke in which the shaft would turn. The price they asked was the same as the original price of the mixer. Should I just buy a new mixer or have mine repaired? I decided to have it fixed.

About a week later the shop called to say it was fixed. I picked it up and reassembled the mixer. When I turned it on to my horror the hole they had drilled in the yoke to insert the new bronze bearing had followed the line of least resistance. The result was that the wobble was just as great as it had been before it was repaired. It would only rotate three quarters of a turn and then it would stop. I was disappointed. Now what was I to do?

A few days later I got an idea. With a piece of chalk I drew an arrow on the drum to indicate the direction in which I should bend the shaft so as to correct the wobble. I would heat the base of the shaft and hammer it in the right direction. It was a formidable task, to bend a one-inch steel shaft. But it was useless as it was. Why not give it a try? So I borrowed an acetylene torch from a friend and propped the barrel of the mixer in the proper position. My son, Fred, happened to be visiting so I asked him to give me a hand. I had hoped to heat the base of the shaft till it was red hot and then, with a heavy blow, strike the end of the shaft. Just how much I should bend it I had no idea.

Fred blasted away with the torch but the heat dissipated into the drum. The shaft would barely glow. So I gave the shaft the hardest blow I could muster. When it cooled we reassembled it and turned the motor on. The shaft hadn't bent an iota!

"I don't think you're going to bend it, Dad. The heat is lost in the barrel, and what is more, if you do bend it, how far should it be bent?" Fred's tone of voice showed no hope for a successful outcome of my idea. I was disappointed too.

"Let's give it one more try. But before we do, let's have a drink of water." It was a hot day and we were both sweating.

Fred finished his drink first and went back to heat the shaft. As I walked to where he was working I paused in the shade of a bottle-brush tree. And then I wondered to myself, "Would it be presumptuous to ask the Lord, the Creator and Upholder of the Universe, to help me bend the shaft of a cheap Taiwan-built cement mixer? But why not ask His help?" I closed my eyes and sent up a petition that He might help me bend the shaft and just the right amount.

I walked to where Fred was heating the shaft. "Dad," he said, "I don't think it is going to get any hotter. Why not give it a try." So I gave the end of the shaft a terrific blow, and as I did Fred shouted, "Give it another!" And I did. When the shaft had cooled enough for us to reassemble the mixer, we turned the motor on. The drum rotated smoothly and without the slightest wobble! I then told Fred of my prayer under the bottlebrush tree. We both knelt down and thanked the mighty God who hears and answers the prayer to fix a Taiwan-made cement mixer!

"Praise the Lord, oh my soul, and with all that is within me, praise His Holy Name."

As I write this little saga the cement mixer is parked some thirty feet away. Fifteen years have passed since that wondrous event. The mixer has been used by me and by many of my friends, and it still runs as smoothly as it did the day God helped me to bend that shaft. What a miracle and what a testimony to God's love!

In 1994 we moved from Loma Linda to be near our daughter, Jeanne Ekvall, and family. Merlin Ekvall had purchased a practice in Orthodontics near Brewster, Washington and we have lived there ever since.

Chapter 13

IN SICKNESS AND IN HEALTH

I have already described how I grew up in rural India. The medical facilities were few and far between. A hospital assistant and a missionary doctor were the only ones available for acute and chronic illnesses, and an itinerant Irish dentist who came to town once every three years! So we, as children, were diagnosed and treated by my Mother using a family medical guide.

I had most if not all the so called "childhood diseases," German measles, regular measles, chicken pox, pneumonia, mumps, whooping cough, and as a teenager, malaria. Vaccines that have now been available for decades for infants and children against most of these scourges did not then exist. We were vaccinated against small pox, supposedly once every seven years, unless there was an epidemic. But epidemics occurred annually! On occasion we were also vaccinated against typhoid fever and cholera.

Despite these illnesses which came and went, we enjoyed good health. In high school I developed a sore throat that persisted week in and week out. A physician who came to town was visited. He felt that my long uvula was irritating my throat so chopped off about half of it. That procedure did no good. Finally the hospital assistant decided that my tonsils needed removing, although I had had them removed when I was five! Who was to do the surgery? The missionary doctor was away on furlough and there was no local physician. After much persuasion on my Dad's part an army physician agreed to do the operation. The month was late September. Instead of returning home the same day, I was hospitalized for six weeks because of continual hemorrhaging. My final high school exams came at the end of

November for which I was ill-prepared. Much to my relief I passed and received my Senior Cambridge Certificate, but did not do as well as I had hoped.

But I'll jump ahead to finish this sad saga. My sore throats continued unabated all through my college years and until I was a junior medical student. I was on the Ear, Nose, and Throat rotation. One afternoon I had the last patient of the day. The Chief that day was Dr. Leland House. "Well," he mused, "I guess that ends the day."

"No, Doctor House, there is one more."

"One more? I thought that was the last one. Where is he anyway?"

"I'm the patient." I told him the background of my sore throats.

"Let's take a look." He carefully examined my throat and then said, "You need your tonsils out!"

"Again?" and I could hardly believe my ears. "That will make the third time!"

"Whoever took your tonsils out the last time removed everything in the back of your throat but missed the tonsils. They are infected and are embedded in scar tissue. He must have used a knife and fork to do the surgery!"

So at the close of my junior year he removed my tonsils. Losing that infected tissue gave me a feeling of well-being that is hard to describe. I felt like a different person even though I had remained physically active since completing high school.

Medical Problems

On the way to England in 1932, a five weeks voyage, I developed an extremely severe sore throat while passage through the Red Sea. By the time we arrived in Suez I had a rash, but told no one for fear I would be taken off board. I was sick for the next two weeks and could hardly drag myself around when I disembarked in South Hampton harbor, England. It was a Tuesday evening and my brother Les and Phyllis my sister, met me. Next day I stayed in bed till evening, and Thursday did the same. Friday I somehow made it to Young Peoples Meeting but Sabbath morning I told Phyl that I was sick, and could not go to church.

She called a physician who diagnosed me as having scarlet fever and typhoid fever! I was whisked off to an isolation hospital where I spent the next forty-two days. For the first week I thought I was going to die, as did the doctors and nurses. I passed not a drop of urine for seven consecutive days. I had developed acute glomerulonephritis, a complication of scarlet fever where the kidney stops producing urine. I then began to pass urine, first a few drops and finally normal flow. I'm grateful to the Lord that it did not turn into chronic glomerulonephritis, and that I did not have typhoid fever as at first thought.

I will not weary you, the reader, with all my subsequent illnesses except to say that after World War II I founded the CME (College of Medical Evangelists) Hiking Club and was considered, on the campus, as "Mr. Health." I was also known to teach "Health Principles" or "Personal Health" to the medical and other students on the campus. It was a rare day when I missed a class appointment because of sickness.

And then it happened! The unbelievable! It shook the campus, and it shook me. I had none of the risk factors for coronary heart disease; in fact, I used to give a lecture on how never to get one! My bad cholesterol has always been very low and my good cholesterol remarkably high. I've had no high blood pressure, had been on a low fat diet since 1949, and exercised fairly vigorously on a daily basis. In fact, I never had and still do not have any of the known risk factors for coronary heart disease. A couple of years ago I was seeing a neurologist, who asked me to list my risk factors. With a smile I replied, "I don't have any risk factors, I just have the diseases!"

My son and I had just climbed, without the trace of a problem, the highest peak in Yosemite National Park, Mt. Lyle (13,000+ ft.). Five days later my heart was bouncing about in my chest cavity. I knew there was something dreadfully wrong. The cardiologist looked at the EKG which he had taken and exclaimed, "Mervyn, we are going to have to act vigorously."

"You mean I should eat differently and exercise more?" My voice showed complete unbelief.

"No, no, you've done all that. You don't have time. You must come into the hospital immediately and have an angiogram as soon as possible."

So I was admitted into the Loma Linda Medical Center and had an angiogram first thing next morning. It showed a 99 per cent occlusion at the base of a large artery of the heart (the anterior descending branch of the left coronary artery). "You must have bypass surgery today," was his conclusion.

The surgery was scheduled at four o'clock that afternoon. I was lying in bed and happened to glance at the clock in my room. It was exactly one o'clock. And into the room walked my cardiologist, the ward cardiologist, the angiographer, a nurse, my wife, and my son Fred. Ray, my cardiologist came over to me and placed his hand on my arm. "Mervyn," he said, "everything is in order, and you don't have a thing to worry about."

And then it happened. "Ray, I have pain under my breast bone, now it's in my epigastrium (pit of my stomach), now in my back," and I remember no more.

They rushed me to surgery, did an open heart bypass procedure, and despite the fact that I suffered a massive coronary with a residual infarct (scar), with the blessing of God, I am alive today, twenty-eight years later! Three months after the attack, I was walking, in the hills south of Loma Linda, at the rate of four miles in 54 minutes and 8 miles in two hours!. This was in 1976 and things were going very well. Then in 1979, one year before I was to retire, I suddenly developed another problem.

We lived only a mile and one-half from the school and I had gone home for lunch as was my custom. I returned to the office at one. An hour later I could hardly walk. I called my cardiologist who suggested I come over immediately. He checked my circulation and found nothing wrong.

"You should see a neurologist right away," was his advice. "He will require a myogram so I will order one. This will save you time." The next day I had a myogram only to discover that the nerves to my muscles were only firing 30 to 40 percent of what they normally should. I was later diagnosed as having developed an autoimmune neuritis, where my immune system was attacking the nerves that stimulate my muscles. And this has plagued me ever since as it has made walking increasingly difficult. While the problem has affected my voluntary muscles in general, the neuritis has specifically targeted the muscles of my calves, and more recently my lower thigh muscles as well.

And sad to say, the scar formed 27 years ago on my heart, has stretched forming an aneurysm as large as a tangerine at the apex of my ventricle. This has reduced my ejection fraction to 30 per cent (lower limit of normal is 50 per cent). The cardiologist recommends surgery but no cardiac surgeon will touch me. They say the risk is too high!

A few of my readers may have experienced sitting before a physician and being informed that you have advanced metastatic cancer. Mine was of the prostate (PSA 534, normal 0-4). This was six years ago and I was devastated. How could it be? I have tried to live healthfully and have been a vegetarian all my life. But as I had done so many times in the past, I committed my life into the Lord's hands. My prayer was and has continued to be: "You are the Great Physician, take care of me the way you think best." I am taking an anti-testosterone agent, and my daughter Jeanne (a nutritionist) has placed me on a diet high in soy and anti-cancer vegetables, and the Lord has blessed. The urologist says "He's the one to thank," and I agree. My PSA has remained between 0.02 to 0.05 for the past five years.

A year after I was diagnosed with prostate cancer I developed a lump in my lower left neck. Radical surgery removed a malignancy (adenocarcinoma). No primary source was found.

Thank You Lord

But I praise the Lord, for most of the time I feel good, I can still drive locally, and my surroundings are most pleasant. Our daughter Jeanne lives next door and my son lives three hours driving time from here. Margaret's memory is steadily declining but otherwise she is doing very well. I have just completed my second book in the last four years, and look forward to celebrating my 90th birthday in a few more short months! Thank you, Lord.

Final Comment

With the blessings of the Lord Margaret and I have worked officially for the Seventh-day Adventist Church for more than 45 years, at Loma Linda University and at the General Conference.

And here I wish to thank the Lord for a wonderful family, first for a godly wife who has stuck by me for more than 66 years. After we were married I said, "Margaret, if we have any children and you give them your looks and your brains, I'll be completely satisfied." And she did just that! Second, with the Lord's help and blessing, we raised two godly children who have each married a dedicated spouse: Fred to April, a nurse, and Jeanne to an orthodontist, Merlin Ekvall. Fred is an ordained minister and Jeanne is a nurse. Both are registered dieticians and Preventive Care Specialists, and with their families have spent years in the mission fields of the Far East. As I write these last words, they and their children are all serving the Lord. To God be the glory.

POSTSCRIPT

Life is a journey that starts at birth. Each life varies in length, some short and others long. The end or stopping point is unknown. The path is seldom straight. For some the changes in direction are almost imperceptible, deviating slightly sometimes to the right and at other times to the left. Few are strewn with roses. Most paths are uphill, all too often hampered with ruts and boulders, landslides and washouts bringing progress to a crawl. Some appear blessed without measure, while others struggle against overwhelming odds.

Once I was young and now I am old. My journey is almost done. The road I have traveled was not chosen by me but by the Master Guide. Looking back from the heights of age I can see clearly the footsteps I have taken. The difficulties here, road blocks there, and at times, insurmountable barriers. But my Traveling Companion knew what lay ahead, and under His guiding hand progress continued. On occasion, I grumbled at the conditions I faced, but now I see they were the easiest of the ways for me to journey onward.

Friend, life without the Guide is like hiking Mount Whitney, or Mount McKinley, or Mount Everest without a map or compass. The hazards are too great. The Guide provides all the tools essential for the climb, the Bible and His providences. And what is more, He is waiting to be asked for His services.

APPENDIX 1

The experiences that I have recounted in my major narrative are all true. The following two stories come from an Urdu Reader which I used during my Sixth Standard when a modern language was introduced into the curriculum. One of the two could be true, the other is typical of village stories. My children and grandchildren have enjoyed them both!

Tit for Tat

As the tailor sat cross-legged in his tiny shop, he watched the activities of the village. The women left early in the morning to gather firewood, and would return in the late afternoon with huge loads of wood that they carried on their heads. They would then prepare the evening meal. At the same time, the men went out to cultivate the rice paddies, often with the help of a water buffalo. The merchants in the bazaar were each opening up his shop. There were the potter with clay pots for carrying water or cooking rice; the iron monger with his nails and screws; and the chemist (pharmacy) at the corner with large bottles of colored water to awe the children and advertise his presence.

Each morning a man with his elephant made his way through the village on his way to work. The tailor was a kindly man and had made friends with the elephant. As the animal passed his stall the elephant would amble over and place the end of his trunk in the lap of the tailor. The tailor, on his part, kept a bag of sugar cubes just for the purpose of giving the elephant one cube in the morning and another in the evening. He would place it in the end of the expectant trunk. The elephant, to show his appreciation, would rub his trunk against the tailor's leg.

The tailor had been doing this for several years and the elephant had learned to trust him as his friend. But this particular morning the tailor had no sugar cubes; the sack was empty. He had forgotten to buy some at the grocer's store. He saw the elephant coming down the road and knew that it would come over for the sugar cube he expected. What was he to do? It was too late to get any sugar cubes right then. And you won't believe what an evil thought came into his mind. The elephant came over, as he always did, and placed his trunk in the tailor's lap. But instead of giving him a sugar cube, he took his needle with which he was sewing, and jabbed it into the poor animal's trunk!

The startled elephant withdrew his trunk with a jerk and made a low moan. The tip of the trunk is very sensitive and that needle jab had really hurt the animal and his feelings too. The elephant moved back and looked at the tailor who was no longer his friend. Then he turned and walked away to where he worked all day.

As the elephant and his keeper were returning in the evening they had to cross a little stream just as they were entering the village. The animal often stopped to get a drink. This evening he stayed a little longer. After he had drunk all he wanted, he filled his trunk with water. He walked more carefully than usual for he did not want to spill any of the water he held in his trunk. As he always did he walked over to where the tailor was seated and laid his trunk in the tailor's lap. And then he took a deep breath and blew the water right into the face of the tailor!

Elephant's have long memories. They seldom forget. I never learned whether the tailor and the elephant made up, but one thing I am sure of, the tailor never, never stuck his needle into an elephant's trunk again!

And now another story from the Urdu reader.

The Tailor and his Caps

Although this tailor also lived in a small village, he always kept busy. When he wasn't making someone a shirt or trousers, or a lady a dress, he made caps. In fact he loved to make caps and made them better than anyone in the area. He would make khaki caps, and red caps, and yellow caps, and blue caps, and sometimes he would make a cap of two colors or even more. When he finished making a cap he would put it in a cloth bag he kept just for that purpose. Gradually the bag would get filled up, so instead of being flat and empty, it was full and round.

When he had made enough caps to fill his sack he would throw it over his shoulder and walk to another village so he could sell them. Boys and girls, and even men would come to see if he had just the cap that would fit their heads, and whether it was the right color or not.

One day he decided to go to a village that was quite a long way away. It turned out to be much farther than he had thought. The sun was beating down on him, and he was hot and tired. And then to his joy he saw, in the distance, a mango tree. "Aha," he said, "a mango tree gives the very best shade of any tree." When he finally reached the tree he was exhausted. He threw his sack to the ground, sat down beside it, and leaned back against the trunk, and closed his eyes. And what do you think happened? Before you could say snakes and elephants, he was fast asleep!

Now what he hadn't noticed was that up among the branches of the tree was a troop of monkeys. They were quiet and were sitting absolutely still. When they looked down at the tailor they noticed the sack and wondered what was inside it. Now monkeys are very curious animals, they want to find out about everything they see. They looked at one another and then looked at the sack. The longer they thought about the sack the more curious they became.

Then two of the braver monkeys decided to go down and find out. Quietly, without making a sound, they climbed down and stood by the sack. First one touched the sack and then the other. It did not hurt them. They became braver. One reached up and carefully put his hand into the sack. What he pulled out was a cap. They looked at the cap and then at the sleeping tailor who had a cap on his head! So the monkey took the cap he had in his hand and put it on his own head.

Now monkeys are not only curious but they are copycats. They like to do what other monkeys do. So the second monkey reached into the sack and pulled out a cap and slapped it on his head! Then they looked at each other and bounded up the tree. All the monkeys were watching and when they saw what the two monkeys had done, they began, one by one, scampering down the tree to get a cap of their own. Soon every cap was gone and the sack lay flat and empty on the ground!

But up in the branches of the tree was the funniest sight you have every seen. Monkeys, with caps on their heads! As they looked at each other they realized how funny they looked. Now monkeys don't laugh like we do, they chatter. And they began to chatter, and then jump up and down on the branches. The noise they were making got louder and louder until it woke up the sleeping tailor.

As he opened his eyes he saw something he had never seen in his life. Monkeys, of all things, with caps on their heads! "Where would monkeys find caps?" he thought to himself. And then he looked at his sack. It lay flat and empty on the ground! The monkeys had taken all his caps! Now what was he to do?

He jumped to his feet and shouted at the monkeys. He told them to give him back his caps, but they just sat there quietly looking at him. He became more and more angry. He shook his fist at them. He yelled and then began to scream. But the monkeys never moved. They stopped chattering, and just sat quietly and never uttered a sound. Then the tailor, angry and disgusted, grabbed the cap on his own head, and pulling it off, threw it to the ground. "You've taken all my caps," he shouted, "so you might as well have this one too!"

As soon as the monkeys saw him pull his cap off his head, they grabbed the caps on their own heads and pulling them off threw them towards the ground! And down from the branches dropped caps, khaki caps, and red caps, and blue caps, green and yellow caps! The tailor quickly picked them up, stuffed them into his empty sack, which soon got fuller and fuller, and then throwing it over his shoulder, set off towards the next village.

Now remember, it's not always wise to be a copycat, is it?

APPENDIX 2

The selection of the project for my doctoral research was indeed directed and blessed by the Lord. Vegetarianism was a quirky idea and only selected by a few odd balls. The main members of my research committee ridiculed the nutritional basis for such diets. Yet this is the topic I was impressed to study, and this is the topic for which I obtained the approval of the committee!

The findings of the study were unexpected but highly significant. Here is a summary of some of the results:

1. The nutritional adequacy of a vegetarian diet for adults—men and women, pregnant mothers, and adolescents—boys and girls, was, for the first time established on a scientific basis.

2. The relationship between the intake of animal fat, not total fat, and blood cholesterol was first reported. This led to the finding that saturated animal fats raised cholesterol levels, and that plant-based diets with low levels of saturated fats, but high levels of unsaturated fats tended to lower cholesterol levels.

3. We found for the first time that dietary fiber influenced the blood cholesterol levels. High intakes of dietary fiber found in vegetarian diets are conducive to lower blood cholesterol levels. Animal foods contain no dietary fiber.

4. The focus of nutritional research was shifted from protein requirements to dietary fat and fiber. Increasing numbers of research papers on various aspects of vegetarian diets led, in subsequent years, to changed attitudes towards a plant-based diet. Once ridiculed, they were then tolerated, later accepted, and finally eulogized.

The recent findings that phytochemicals and antioxidants found entirely in plant foods play an important role in the prevention of such problems as coronary heart disease, cancer and other degenerative diseases.

God's selection of my research project has indeed brought honor to his cause.

—*"I have put my trust in the Lord."* Ps. 73:28 (KJ)

PHOTO GALLERY

Left: Mervyn at age 5.

Top: Dad, Mervyn, Alan, and Mother.

Bottom: My Dad's office and workers. Mervyn, front row, first on left.

Top: Kitchen duties at Newbold College, England.

Middle: Meryvn, right, studying at Newbold College, England, 1934.

Bottom: Cycling in Scotland, 1934.

PHOTO GALLERY

Left: Newbold College, England.

Right: The Vegetarian Cookbook that changed our lives.

Bottom: My mother's signature on the inside cover of the cookbook with the date she bought the book.

Above Left: Margaret at Pacific Union College, California

Above Right: My graduation from medicine, 1941.

Lower Left: Margaret and me by campfire.

Clockwise from Top: Hiking with students; In office, Dean School of Public Health, 1970; With Fred; Top of Mt. Whitney (14,396 ft.), With Fred (10), and Jeanne (8); With our cat; Meryvn, Jeanne, Fred, and Pokey.

Right: With my young family.

Bottom: Jeanne, Margaret, Mervyn, Fred.

PHOTO GALLERY

Top: Anatomy Department cartoon by student Kenneth Wong, 1945.

Middle: Retired at last!

Bottom Left: portrait, 1945.

Bottom Right: Margaret and Mervyn.

We'd love to have you download our catalog of titles we publish or even hear your thoughts, reactions, or criticism about this or any other book we publish at:

www.TEACHServices.com
or
info@TEACHServices.com

Or call us at:

518/358-3494